Partners in Public Service

Partners in
Public Service

Government-Nonprofit
Relations in the
Modern Welfare State

Lester M. Salamon

The Johns Hopkins University Press
Baltimore and London

© 1995 The Johns Hopkins University Press
All rights reserved. Published 1995
Printed in the United States of America on acid-free paper

04 03 02 01 00 99 98 97 96 95   5 4 3 2 1

The Johns Hopkins University Press
2715 North Charles Street
Baltimore, Maryland 21218–4319
The Johns Hopkins Press Ltd., London

Library of Congress Cataloging-in-Publication Data

Salamon, Lester M.
    Partners in public service : government-nonprofit relations in the
modern welfare state / Lester M. Salamon.
        p.   cm.
    Includes bibliographical references and index.
    ISBN 0–8018–4962–4 (alk. paper).—ISBN 0–8018–4963–2 (pbk. : alk.
paper)
    1. Nonprofit organizations—United States.   2. Social service—Gov-
ernment policy—United States.   3. United States—Social policy—
1980–1993.   I. Title.
    HD62.6.S34   1995
    361.7′63′0973—dc20   94-31040

A catalog record for this book is available from the British Library.

For Lynda,
who has been with me
through it all

Contents

List of Figures and Tables

Figures

Tables

Acknowledgments

This book pulls together over a dozen years of work on the scope and structure of the American nonprofit sector and the relationships between nonprofit organizations and government. The work was carried out in the midst of a raging national debate over the relative roles of public and private institutions in coping with national problems and against a backdrop of widespread ignorance about the actual roles that government and nonprofit organizations were playing, separately or in tandem, in the American version of the modern welfare state.

I am indebted to Jackie Wehmueller and Henry Tom of the Johns Hopkins University Press for initiating the idea to publish my work in this form. I am also indebted to the organizations that supported this work and to the incredibly skillful and devoted colleagues without whose help it would not have been possible. Foremost among the former are the Rockefeller Brothers Fund, the Carnegie Corporation of New York, the Rockefeller Foundation, the Ford Foundation, the Equitable Life Assurance Society, Shell Companies Foundation, Amoco Foundation, Atlantic Richfield Foundation, the Alcoa Foundation, the General Electric Foundation, AT&T Foundation, the Prudential Foundation, the Chicago Community Trust, the San Francisco Foundation, the Pittsburgh Foundation, and the Joseph B. Whitehead Foundation. Foremost among the latter were Alan J. Abramson, Michael Gutowski, James C. Musselwhite, Jr., Carol J. DeVita, David Altschuler, and the Local Associates of the Urban Institute Nonprofit Sector Project. I also owe a deep debt of gratitude to Jacquelyn Perry, whose production assistance and general administrative support have played a crucial role in the preparation of this manuscript as well as in most of my other work.

    Chapter 1 of this volume was originally published under the title "Rethinking Public Management: Third-Party Government and the Changing Forms of Government Action" in the Summer 1981 edition of *Public Policy* (29, no. 3: 255–57). Chapter 2 is a slightly shortened version of an article that appeared in the January-June 1987 edition of the *Journal of Voluntary Action Research* (16, nos. 1–2: 29–49). Chapters 3 and 5 are drawn from chapters 2 and 4, respectively, of *The Federal Budget and the Nonprofit Sector* (Washington: Urban Institute Press, 1982), coauthored with Alan J. Abramson. Chapters 4 and 6 draw heavily on a paper I prepared with the assistance of James C. Musselwhite, Jr., and Carol J. DeVita entitled "Partners in Public Service: Government and the Nonprofit Sector in the American Welfare State." This paper was delivered at the 1986 Independent Sector Research Forum but has not been previously published. Chapter 7 draws on material originally published in an article entitled "The Scope and Theory of Government-Nonprofit Relations" in W. Powell, ed., *The Nonprofit Sector: A Research Handbook* (New Haven: Yale University Press, 1987, pp. 99–117). Chapter 8 pulls together material originally published in this same *Research Handbook* article with material originally included in my January-June 1987 *Journal of Voluntary Action Research* article (16, nos. 1–2: 29–49). Chapter 9 is a slightly shortened version of an article that appeared under the title "Social Services" in Charles Clotfelter, ed., *Who Benefits from the Nonprofit Sector?* (Chicago: University of Chicago Press, 1992, pp. 134–73). Chapter 10 was originally published as "Nonprofit Organizations: The Lost Opportunity" in John L. Palmer and Isabel Sawhill, eds., *The Reagan Record* (Cambridge: Ballinger Publishing Co., 1984, pp. 261–85). Chapter 11 is a shortened version of an article coauthored with Charles Clotfelter that appeared in the June 1982 issue of *National Tax Journal* (35: 171–87). Chapter 12 originally appeared in 1986 as "Government and the Voluntary Sector in an Era of Retrenchment: The American Experience," in the *Journal of Public Policy* (6, no. 1: 1–20). Chapter 13 reprints my article of the same title from the Spring 1989 edition of *Nonprofit and Voluntary Sector Quarterly* (18, no. 1: 11–24). Chapter 14 appeared in the March 1993 issue of *Social Service Review* (67, no. 1: 16–39) and draws on material originally presented in my book *America's Nonprofit Sector: A Primer* (New York: Foundation Center, 1992). Finally, an abbreviated version of chapter 15 appeared in the July/August 1994 edition of *Foreign Affairs* (73, no. 3: 111–24). I am indebted to all of these publishers for permission to draw on these materials for this book.
    I also want to express my thanks to Brian O'Connell and Robert Smucker of Independent Sector, to Gabriel Rudney of the Treasury

Department and Jack Schwartz of the American Association of Fund-Raising Counsel, and to Ben Shute of the Rockefeller Brothers Fund for interesting me in the nonprofit sector and stimulating my first research forays into this forgotten continent. Last, but certainly not least, I want to acknowledge my deep debt to my family, particularly to my wife, Lynda, for the support and peace of mind that have made it possible for me to devote the time and mental energy necessary to develop the work that is partially reflected here.

While the organizations and individuals noted here deserve a considerable portion of the credit for whatever merits the work reported here may enjoy, responsibility for any shortcomings is mine alone.

Introduction

One of the great ironies of modern American life is the fact that the set of social institutions that most vividly embodies the distinctive American penchant for private solutions to public problems has experienced its most dramatic growth during precisely the period of most rapid expansion of the state. Worse than that, there is overwhelming evidence that these two developments were not only temporally but also causally related. Between 1950 and 1980, a massive increase took place in the size and scope of America's private nonprofit sector. But this growth seems to have been fueled less by an expansion of private charitable support than by the accelerated extension of the American welfare state. By the late 1970s, in fact, the private nonprofit sector had become the principal vehicle for the delivery of government-financed human services, and government had, correspondingly, become the principal source of nonprofit human service agency finance.

Despite their scale and significance, however, these developments were largely ignored in both policy discussions and academic research. For most of the fifty years prior to 1980, the nonprofit sector essentially disappeared from public discourse in the United States as attention focused instead on the dramatic growth of the state. To read analyses of American social policy during this period, one could easily conclude that the nonprofit sector had ceased to exist sometime during the New Deal era of the 1930s, when federal involvement in social welfare began to grow. Both those on the political Left and those on the political Right seemed to join in this conspiracy of silence: the former out of concern that acknowledging the continued presence of a vital voluntary sector might weaken the case for an expanded governmental role, and the latter out of fear that the continued presence of a sizable nonprofit sector might throw into question long-standing conservative claims about the threat that expanded state activity supposedly posed for such private groups. Although taking quite different positions about the relative merits of government and the nonprofit sector, in other words, both liberals and conservatives viewed these sectors through a paradigm that emphasized the inherent conflict between the two. Since government was clearly growing, it therefore followed, given this paradigm, that the nonprofit sector must be withering away. Under the circumstances there was little reason to go looking for it.

Not surprisingly, therefore, little was known well into the 1970s about the scope and structure of the nonprofit sector, let alone about the nature and scale of its interactions with the state.[1] To the extent that attention focused on the realities of growing government-nonprofit interaction, moreover, the attitude was generally one of dismay. Government support, it was felt, threatened to lead the nonprofit sector astray, undermining its independence and distorting its basic goals. Rather than an opportunity to be grasped and shaped, government support was a danger to be shunned, even scorned, by those with integrity in the nonprofit field.[2]

It was against this backdrop of denial and dismay that the essays assembled in this book took shape. At a time when the role of the private nonprofit sector and the interactions between nonprofit organizations and the state were barely acknowledged either in policy circles or in the academic world, I undertook a series of preliminary explorations of this largely unexamined terrain. The initial motivation for this work was theoretical. For some time it had become clear that prevailing conceptions of the American welfare state, with their emphasis on the ever expanding role of a hierarchic state administration, were increasingly out of touch with the actual realities of government operation. Where prevailing concepts emphasized a clearly demarcated federal government gobbling up social functions and displacing other institutions, what existed instead was an expanding network of alliances between the national government and a host of public and private bodies—other levels of government, private businesses, banks, insurance companies, and, increasingly, private nonprofit agencies. In a sense, the public administration problem had spread well beyond the borders of the government agency, enveloping a wide variety of third parties that came to share with government a considerable portion of the discretionary authority for the delivery of publicly financed services. Neither students of public policy and public administration, nor policymakers and commentators, however, had yet to acknowledge this new system of "third-party government," let alone to examine it with any care.

Because they shared many of the same basic objectives as public agencies and operated in fields where the expansion of the state was especially concentrated, nonprofit organizations seemed likely candidates for this escalating pattern of third-party action, and therefore a likely arena in which to examine its contours and operations. It quickly became apparent, however, that the scale of interaction between the nonprofit sector and government was far more extensive than anyone truly appreciated. What began as a preliminary exploration of a neglected backwater thus became a major journey of discovery, which revealed a hidden subcontinent of enormous size and complexity, a luxuriant undergrowth of government-nonprofit relationships that challenged prevailing conceptions both about the scope and nature of America's nonprofit sector and about the character of the American welfare state.

With the launching of the Reagan administration's program of domestic budget cuts and program reforms in the early 1980s, this journey of discovery was transformed into a central issue of policy debate. Arguing that "we have let government take away many of the things that were once ours to do voluntarily," the Reagan administration elevated the presumed conflict between government and the voluntary sector into a central feature of its domestic program and set out to help the nonprofit sector by getting government out of its way. Overlooked in the process, however, was precisely the rich interplay of cooperative relationships between the voluntary sector and the state that was the subject of my research. Under the circumstances, a clearer understanding of the scope and character of these relationships became a matter not simply of theoretical interest but of urgent policy concern.

The importance of the issues examined here has hardly diminished with the passage of time, moreover. To the contrary, it has grown considerably. Despite the budget cuts of the Reagan-Bush years, the partnership between government and the nonprofit sector that is the principal focus of this book remains as much a cornerstone of American domestic policy today as it was when Ronald Reagan assumed the presidency in the early 1980s, especially in the human service field. Now, however, growing demands for improved governmental performance have made the smooth functioning of this partnership all the more critical. Under these circumstances, the need to understand this partnership and the special challenges it entails has grown apace. Yet there is mounting evidence that this relationship remains as poorly appreciated today as it was when Ronald Reagan set out to assist the nonprofit sector by cutting back on its government support. In its much-heralded report on "reinventing government" in 1993, for example, the Clinton administration displayed as much innocence of the central role of the voluntary sector in the implementation of domestic government in the United States as Ronald Reagan had done more than a decade earlier. While devoting an entire chapter to the empowerment of the local governmental authorities that administer many federal domestic programs, the Clinton-Gore National Performance Review Report never so much as mentions the private, nonprofit organizations that actually deliver the lion's share of the services these programs support (U.S. National Performance Review 1993). Nor does the "Contract with America" that helped fuel the Republican Congressional victories of 1994 come any closer to the mark. Making policymakers, policy analysts, and the public at large more aware of the close interrelations between government and the nonprofit sector thus remains as critical to the policy agenda of the present as it was to that of the 1980s.

The need for better understanding of the interaction between government and the voluntary sector is particularly important given the severe budgetary constraint that the Reagan and Bush administrations managed to fasten on national policy for the foreseeable future. Far from encouraging nonprofit activity, this constraint has exposed nonprofit organizations to tremendous financial strains, reducing, or severely limiting, the major source of their earlier growth. In the process, it has helped to set in motion important changes in the operation of these organizations and in the structure of our social welfare system. Understanding the connection between government budget decisions and the fiscal health of the nonprofit sector is thus important not only for historical reasons but for assessing the future evolution of the nonprofit sector and its role in American society more generally.

Finally, quite apart from these domestic considerations, the issue of government-nonprofit cooperation has also grown increasingly important at the international level. Ironically, at the very time that America seemed to be dismantling, or at least significantly reducing, its existing system of government-nonprofit cooperation, other countries began to turn to the American model to replace the government-dominated welfare state systems of the past. Contracting with nonprofit organizations expanded dramatically under the conservative regime of Margaret Thatcher in the United Kingdom (Taylor 1992). On the other end of the political spectrum, the Socialist government of François Mitterand in France launched an ambitious program of decentralization and program reform in the early 1980s that featured heavy reliance on nonprofit organizations to deliver publicly financed services (Tchernonog 1992), and similar developments are under way, or under consideration, elsewhere as well, most noticeably in the newly independent countries of central and eastern Europe (OECD 1992). Under these circumstances, the long-standing American model of government-nonprofit partnership has become a topic of growing interest abroad, creating additional incentives to understand this model better at home.

Structure of the Presentation

To help meet this need and bring the government-nonprofit relationship as it has operated in the American setting into better focus, this book assembles many of the major pieces I have written over the past dozen years exploring the concept of "third-party government" and the scope and character of government-nonprofit relations. These materials focus in particular on five major topics, which define the basic structure of the book: first, the theoretical basis of government-nonprofit ties; second, the prevailing realities of nonprofit size and of government-nonprofit relationships; third, the consequences of this cooperative pattern of service delivery for both the nonprofit sector and those it serves; fourth, the impact on this partnership of the retrenchment policies of the 1980s; and fifth, the prospects for the future, both in this country and abroad.

Theoretical Background

The book begins, naturally enough, with the theoretical issues that gave rise to my work on government-nonprofit cooperation. Chapter 1 presents the 1981 article in which I first called attention to the fundamental, but largely overlooked, transformation that took place in the nature of the state in the United States during the thirty or so years between the Second World War and the late 1970s. This transformation involved not simply an expansion in the scale of government activity, but more fundamentally a change in its basic form resulting from the proliferation of a host of new "tools" of government action, new instruments or technologies through which government pursued its objectives—loans, loan guarantees, tax subsidies, grants-in-aid, social regulation, purchase-of-service contracts, government corporations, and many more. Unlike much previous governmental activity, one of the distinguishing features of many of these new tools of government action is that they involve the pervasive sharing of responsibility for the delivery of publicly financed services and the exercise of governmental authority with a host of "third parties"—states, cities, counties, commercial banks, industrial corporations, savings and loan associations, builders, and many others. The result was the rise of a new form of government action, which I termed "third-party government" and which makes federal agencies increasingly dependent on a host of third-party institutions to carry out their public missions. The upshot was to alter rather fundamentally the practice of public management and render the traditional preoccupations of public administration, if not obsolete, then at least far less germane.

Chapter 2 applies this basic framework to the relationships between government and the nonprofit sector. The central argument of this chapter is that the widespread neglect of the massive growth of government-nonprofit relationships that characterized the 1960s and 1970s was a product not simply of a lack of research but, more fundamentally, of a weakness of theory. Both the theory of the welfare state and the theory of the voluntary sector were deficient, moreover— the former because of its failure to acknowledge the reality of "third-party government" and the latter because of a view of the voluntary sector that emphasized its role as a substitute for the state. Neither perspective left much room for a flourishing government-nonprofit partnership. To come to terms with the reality of widespread government-nonprofit cooperation, therefore, it is necessary to re-shape the conceptual lenses through which this reality is perceived, to replace traditional theories of the welfare state with the concept of "third-party government," and to replace prevailing "market failure/ government failure" theories of the nonprofit sector with a theory that acknowledges the possibility of "voluntary failure" as well, of inherent limitations of the voluntary sector. Equipped with this alternative set of theoretical lenses, the widespread partnership between government and the nonprofit sector comes into focus not as an aberration, but as a reasonable adaptation to the respective strengths and weaknesses of the voluntary sector and the state. Rather than a phenomenon to be shunned or discouraged, cooperation between government and the voluntary sector emerges from this analysis as a reasonable model to be promoted and improved.

Prevailing Realities

Against the backdrop of these theoretical perspectives, the chapters in part 2 report on my efforts to document the realities of nonprofit operations and government-nonprofit ties in the United States. The first chapter in this section (chap. 3) defines more precisely what is included within the "nonprofit sector" for the purposes of this book and then reviews the results of an early attempt to gauge the scope of this sector. What this analysis shows is that the nonprofit sector, even as defined here, is quite a bit larger than was commonly thought. At the same time, the chapter makes clear that private charity, long regarded as virtually the only source of nonprofit revenue, turns out to be a relatively modest source instead.

Chapter 4 examines the same reality from the local perspective through the prism of a major survey a team of colleagues and I conducted in the early 1980s of nonprofit public-benefit service organizations (exclusive of hospitals and universities) in twelve metropolitan areas and four rural counties throughout the country. Viewed in its local setting, the nonprofit sector appears even larger than it does nationally, with expenditures that typically equal or exceed those of local government, often by two or three times. In the process, these data reveal how substantial a role government funding played in allowing nonprofits to attain this substantial scale. As it turns out, such funding constituted the major source of nonprofit human service agency support as of the early 1980s, outdistancing both private charity and fee income.

Chapters 5, 6, and 7 zero in on the scope and structure of these nonprofit ties with government. Chapter 5 focuses on the national level and documents the early history of government support to the nonprofit sector and the tremendous scope that federal support alone had attained as of the early 1980s. Chapter 6 carries the analysis down to the local level in the same sixteen sites that were the focus of chapter 4. Drawing on an elaborate tracing of federal, state, and local spending in fields where nonprofit organizations are active, and of government contracting with nonprofit and for-profit organizations, this chapter documents the wide variety of different "welfare regimes" operating locally in the United States and the widespread reliance of government at all levels on private, nonprofit organizations to deliver publicly financed human services. Finally, chapter 7 draws these various threads together and demonstrates the deep historical roots of government-nonprofit cooperation in the United States and the extent to which the resulting partnership had become, by the late 1970s, the defining characteristic of the American welfare state.

The Consequences of Government-Nonprofit Cooperation

Part 3 takes up the important question of the consequences of this government-nonprofit partnership, both for the nonprofit sector and for those it serves. As noted earlier, even among those who acknowledged the tremendous growth of government support to the voluntary sector in the 1960s and 1970s, the attitude was generally one of deep despair because of the presumed danger to the independence and distinctive missions of nonprofit groups.[3] The chapters in part 3 seek to assess the extent to which these dangers have actually materialized.

In particular, chapter 8 reviews the evidence that is available concerning the overall impact of cooperation between government and nonprofit organizations on both the nonprofit sector and the state. The central conclusion that emerges from this review is that experience has generally not borne out the fears surrounding the government-nonprofit relationship. Although threats to agency independence, objectives, and preferred operating styles certainly exist, they are far less serious than many assume. Indeed, the more serious risks may be to the goals and objectives of the public agencies, which are often forced to rely on nonprofit agencies that do not fully share the objectives of the public programs or that otherwise have their own agendas. Nonprofit organizations, it turns out, bring their own resources to the bargaining table with the state, not the least of which is the fact that they are often the only mechanism available to deliver the services that government agencies have been authorized to provide but for which they often lack the experience and staff. The real relationship between these two sets of institutions may consequently not be one of superior and dependent, but one of interdependence.

Chapter 9 pursues this point further by looking in detail at one particular facet of the impact that government might have on nonprofit organizations: the impact on the agencies' choice of clientele, particularly their attention to the poor. Historically, service to the poor has been one of the principal rationales for the tax deductions and tax exemptions that nonprofit organizations enjoy. As chapter 9 shows, however, less than 30 percent of all human service agencies focus primarily on poor clients. Does this mean that government has distorted the focus of the nonprofit sector, as some have claimed? The answer, it seems, is a fairly strong no. At the very least, government does not seem to have reduced agency focus on the poor. To the contrary, it seems to have increased it. In particular, based on a statistical analysis of clientele patterns of nonprofit human service agencies, chapter 9 shows that, other things being equal, the greater the government support the more likely an agency is to focus primarily on the poor. Far from distorting agency missions, government support thus seems to have enabled nonprofit agencies to carry out their charitable responsibilities more fully.

The Impact of Retrenchment

In part 4, attention turns to the significant challenge that was posed to this widespread pattern of government-nonprofit cooperation by the "Reagan Revolution" of the early 1980s. As chapter 10 notes, the Reagan administration had an extraordinary opportunity to make a positive impact on the relationship between government and the non-profit sector in the early 1980s. Despite its scale and importance, this relationship had evolved in a rather ad hoc fashion over the previous two decades. As a consequence, considerable strains and ambiguities existed, if only because the sheer number of programs was so great and the mechanisms for coordinating them and integrating their impacts were so limited. Because its political outlook inclined it to look much more favorably, and much more seriously, than its predecessors on the role that private nonprofit organizations play, the administration might have taken advantage of this opportunity to rationalize the prevailing pattern of government-nonprofit interaction and convert it into a true partnership for social improvement.

Instead, the Reagan administration retreated to the older paradigm of conflict and set out to help the nonprofit sector chiefly by getting government out of its way. In the process, however, as chapter 10 details, it dealt a serious blow to the substantial cooperative relationship that had formed over the previous four decades between the nonprofit sector and the state. Under the circumstances, the administration's rhetorical championing of "private-sector initiatives" came to have an increasingly hollow ring.

Although the administration hoped that its tax policies would offset some of the effects of its budget cuts by reducing tax rates, boosting after-tax income, and thus making more money available for private charitable giving, this hope overlooked the real relationship between taxes and private giving. While boosting after-tax income, lower tax rates also reduce the financial incentives for charitable contributions. Using a simulation analysis, chapter 11 shows that the expected increase in giving that could be expected from higher after-tax income would be more than offset by the reduced giving that would result from lowering the financial incentives to give. As a result, the administration's tax policies seemed likely to intensify the resource problems created for nonprofit organizations by its budget policies, and the evidence to date suggests that something very close to this did in fact occur (Clotfelter 1990, 203–35).

Chapter 12, finally, sets these policy changes explicitly against the backdrop of the themes developed earlier in this book. What it reveals is that the Reagan administration approached the nonprofit sector through a conceptual lens that failed to take account of the realities of government-nonprofit relations documented here. As a result, in an effort to make the nonprofit sector more "charitable" it dismantled, or significantly weakened, important components of the existing government-nonprofit partnership and set in motion forces likely to make the sector more commercial instead.

Future Trends

Part 5 looks beyond the policies of the Reagan-Bush years at the broader social, economic, political, and demographic developments that are helping to shape the future of the nonprofit sector and the relationship between nonprofit organizations and the state. Chapter 13 identifies four such developments in addition to the Reagan administration's legacy of fiscal constraint. These include shifts in the basic form, as opposed to the level, of government assistance; major social and demographic changes, such as the graying of the population and the growing labor force participation of women; and a subtle reconceptualization of the causes of some of our most critical social ills. Given these trends, chapter 13 argues that the nonprofit sector is likely to confront an increased demand for its services but also a very significant shift in the fiscal base of its operations—away from government and toward commercial sources of income instead.

Chapter 14 reviews the evidence that has accumulated about the impact these developments are already having. In particular, it argues that a pervasive "marketization" of welfare seems to be under way in the wake of the partial dismantling of the earlier system of government-nonprofit partnership, and that this is changing the basic character of our social welfare system. One facet of this change is the emergence of fees and service charges as the principal engine of nonprofit growth in the 1980s, not only among hospitals and universities, but also among social service and civic organizations. Equally important, however, has been a massive expansion of for-profit involvement in many of the traditional fields of nonprofit activity, such as hospital care, home health, and social services more generally. Although not without their positive consequences, these trends raise serious questions about the future of the nonprofit sector and about access to care by the disadvantaged.

Finally, chapter 15 places U.S. developments in the context of the even more dramatic developments affecting the nonprofit sector internationally. The increased attention being showered on nonprofit organizations in the United States turns out to be part of a broader "associational revolution" that seems to be under way at the global level. In the developed countries of North America, Europe, and Asia, in the developing countries of Asia, Africa, and Latin America, and in the former Soviet bloc, people are forming private nonprofit organizations at an astounding rate. Underlying this upsurge, chapter 15 argues, is an interrelated set of historical developments that has undermined the credibility of the state in a variety of disparate settings and opened new opportunities for a rich array of private, voluntary groups. While these developments reflect a weakening of confidence in government, however, they hardly suggest its total replacement by private, nonprofit organizations. To the contrary, the same kind of government-nonprofit partnership that fueled the expansion of the nonprofit sector in the United States in the 1960s and 1970s seems likely to characterize its evolution in other countries in the 1990s and beyond. Understanding the scope and character of this partnership in the American setting can thus make an important contribution to understanding its evolution abroad.

Conclusion

For the better part of a century, political rhetoric in the United States has emphasized the existence of a deep-seated conflict between the public and private sectors, between private institutions and the instrumentalities of the state. While the principal focus of this presumed conflict has been on the relationships between government and private business enterprises, the same language was used to depict the relationships between government and private voluntary or nonprofit organizations.

This rhetoric of conflict has served the useful purpose of preserving an arena of organized private action outside the official confines of the state. In the process, it has helped to protect a sense of private initiative in the pursuit of public purposes and hence of the right, and capacity, of people to take the initiative to improve their own lives. It has accomplished this by establishing the principle that nonprofit organizations deserve a measure of autonomy in the conduct of their affairs and require a meaningful level of private support for their activities.

At the same time, however, this rhetoric has obscured a development of signal importance to the contemporary position of the private nonprofit sector—namely, the growth of vitally important supportive relationships between nonprofit organizations and the state. As the chapters in this book thoroughly document, these relationships have a long history in America, but they have blossomed profusely over the past forty years, creating a vast network of partnership arrangements between nonprofit organizations and government agencies at all levels and in all fields—health care, education, research, day care, care for the aged, adoption assistance, housing, community development, environmental protection, and many more.

To say that these relationships constitute a "partnership" is not, of course, to suggest that they are wholly harmonious. Government-nonprofit cooperation took shape in this country not according to any grand design or basic philosophical decision. Rather it evolved, as most such things do in America, in pragmatic fashion in response to immediate problems—the presence of nonprofit providers in fields that government was entering, the absence of sufficient governmental personnel or expertise to deliver various services, popular resistance to the expansion of governmental bureaucracy, a desire for flexibility, or the need to test a particular idea. As a consequence, what has emerged is less a smoothly operating, integrated system than a strange congeries of disparate parts that, while gigantic in aggregate scale, hardly fit together in any coherent sense.

Not surprisingly, this "partnership" suffers from serious problems as a consequence. Programs are carved into narrow pieces that make it exceedingly difficult to mount integrated approaches to complex societal problems. Cumbersome and repetitive reporting and application procedures drain precious time away from agency programs. The task of keeping up with government programs distracts agency personnel from the task of keeping up with their own volunteer boards. And the maintenance needs of private agencies sometimes get in the way of the program goals of government officials.

To say that this arrangement has problems, however, is not to say that the basic concept is faulty or the alternatives to it superior. As I have shown, cooperation between government and the nonprofit sector makes a great deal of sense both conceptually and practically. These two massive sets of institutions share many of the same basic objectives and have strengths and weaknesses that are mirror images of each other. Under the circumstances, the recent efforts to dismantle, or significantly curtail, this partnership seem singularly ill advised, even if they were largely unintended. A more sensible approach would be to find ways to make this partnership truly work, not only for the "partners" but also for those being served. To do so, however, it will first be necessary to make clear how extensive the partnership is and what a substantial stake we all have in its effective operation.

The chapters presented in this book were originally written with this end in view. They were designed to lift the topic of government-nonprofit relations out of the obscurity to which it had long been consigned and provide a basis for bringing it to national attention. From the evidence at hand, it seems clear that this task is not yet complete, although an important start has been made. Now the challenge is to build on that start and set in motion a more basic effort to make government and the nonprofit sector not merely interconnected sets of institutions but true "partners in public service." If this book contributes to this process, it will have served its purpose well.

Theoretical Perspectives

Despite the fact that government in the United States relies more heavily on nonprofit organizations than on its own instrumentalities to deliver government-funded human services, and that human service nonprofits receive more of their income from government than from any other single source, the phenomenon of government-nonprofit collaboration has been largely overlooked until quite recently in both analyses of the welfare state and treatments of the voluntary sector.

The chapters in part 1 argue that this neglect of government-nonprofit ties has resulted not simply from a lack of research but more fundamentally from a weakness of theory. Both the theory of the welfare state and the theory of the voluntary sector have been deficient, moreover, the former because of its failure to acknowledge the significant transformation that has occurred in the operation of the public sector in the past fifty years, and the latter because of its failure to acknowledge the inherent limitations of the voluntary sector, not just the market and the state, in providing collective goods.

Chapter 1 takes up the first of these issues. It argues that the widespread adoption over the past fifty years of a host of new tools of government action—loans, loan guarantees, social regulation, purchase-of-service contracts, tax subsidies, grants-in-aid, and others—has fundamentally reshaped the nature of the public sector in the United States in ways that have rendered the traditional preoccupations of public administration, if not obsolete, then at least far less germane. Most important, many of these new tools involve the widespread sharing of governmental authority with a host of third-party institutions—other levels of government, banks, industrial corporations, hospitals, research institutes, and nonprofit organizations—that actually deliver the goods and services that government authorizes or finances. The result is an elaborate pattern of "third-party government" that calls into question traditional hierarchical conceptions of the modern state.

Chapter 2 links this concept of "third-party government" to the theory of the nonprofit sector. The prevailing theories in this field, by explaining the existence of the nonprofit sector as a solution to the problems of "market failure" and "government failure," suggest quite strongly that the nonprofit sector is most likely to operate where the state does not. In the process, they overlook the phenomenon of "voluntary failure," of inherent limitations of the voluntary sector as the primary provider of collective goods. Once traditional notions of the welfare state are adjusted to take account of the phenomenon of "third-party government," and traditional theories of the voluntary sector are adjusted to take account of the phenomenon of "voluntary failure," the partnership that has emerged in recent years between the nonprofit sector and the state comes into focus as a theoretically justified and clearly understandable development.

CHAPTER 1

Rethinking Public Management

Third-Party Government and the Changing Forms of Government Action

Government-nonprofit relations are part of a broader area of concern dealing with the implementation of government programs, and this field has long been stuck in a rut. Like Antimachus's hedgehog, which knew only one big thing, both students and practitioners of implementation have taken to discovering repeatedly a single, simple truth; programs do not work if they are poorly managed. "The Federal manager holds the key to successful agency performance" is how the *Manager's Handbook* issued by the U.S. Office of Personnel Management (1979, i) states the case, and few implementation studies would suggest any reason for doubt. If only more attention were given to implementation and management, goes the now standard refrain, government effectiveness would surge and critics would be forced to turn tail.

Without doubting the crucial importance of good management, it seems clear that "public management" is fast becoming for students of policy implementation what "political culture" became for students of political development: a kind of universal solvent expected to unravel all mysteries and explain all problems. What this rare substance really looks like, whether its needed properties differ systematically from program to program, and whether it can really be weighed and assessed are all questions that have rarely been raised, let alone examined in depth. Most important, perhaps, while demonstrating that poor management is associated with poor performance, no one seems able to show that the converse is true, giving rise in some quarters to the conclusion that it is not the absence of management, but the presence of government, that is the real explanation of public-program failure (Drucker 1969).

In this chapter I argue that implementation research is fast heading for a dead end not because of any failings in research, but because of a weakness in theory. The function of theory, it is well to remember, is not simply to provide "explanations"; it is also to raise useful questions and, perhaps most important, to identify the most fruitful unit of analysis for coming to grips with the central problems in a field.

It is the argument here that the major shortcoming of current implementation research is that it focuses on the wrong unit of analysis, and that the most important theoretical breakthrough would be to identify a more fruitful unit on which to focus analysis and research. In particular, rather than focusing on individual programs, as is now done, or even collections of programs grouped according to major "purpose," as is frequently proposed, the suggestion here is that we should concentrate instead on the generic tools of government action, on the "techniques" of social intervention that come to be used, in varying combinations, in particular public programs.

To demonstrate this point, I first examine the dramatic transformation of the public sector that makes greater attention to the tools of government action so important, then outline briefly some of the major analytical issues this approach would entail, and finally comment on the contribution it could make to our understanding of public policy and policy implementation. The purpose in this preliminary account is not to develop a full-blown new theory of public management, but to point the way toward which such theory might fruitfully evolve.

The Rise of Third-Party Government and the Changing Forms of Public Action

The Problem

The need for greater attention to the tools and techniques of public action should be apparent to anyone who has looked closely at recent trends in federal government activity and operations. While political rhetoric and a considerable body of academic research continue to picture the federal government as a rapidly expanding behemoth growing disproportionally in both scope and size relative to the rest of the society in order to handle a steadily growing range of responsibilities, in fact something considerably more complex has been underway. For, while the range of federal responsibilities has indeed increased dramatically, the relative size of the federal enterprise, in terms of both budget and employment, has paradoxically remained relatively stable. Between 1954 and 1979, for example, the rate of growth of the federal budget just barely exceeded that of the Gross National Product (GNP), so that the budget's share of the GNP increased only from 19.4 to 20.9 percent. Even more important, the rate of growth of federal civilian employment lagged far behind the real growth of the budget, so that the number of federal employees per 1,000 people in the population registered a decline during this twenty-five-year period of more than 10 percent.

What accounts for this paradox of relatively stable budgets and declining employment despite substantial growth in responsibilities is the dramatic change that has occurred in the forms of federal action. For one thing, a major proliferation has taken place in the tools of government action, as the federal government has turned increasingly to a wide range of new, or newly expanded, devices, for example, loans, loan guarantees, insurance, social regulation, and government corporations, many of which do not appear in the budget. In the process, moreover, a significant transformation has taken place in the way the federal government goes about its business—a shift from direct to indirect or "third-party" government, from a situation in which the federal government ran its own programs to one in which it increasingly relies on a wide variety of "third parties"—states, cities, special districts, banks, hospitals, manufacturers, and others—to carry out its purposes.[1]

In both respects recent developments have clear historical antecedents. Yet the recent developments have been so substantial as to constitute a qualitative, and not just a quantitative, change.

Illustrative of this has been the transformation that has occurred in the *grant-in-aid* system, perhaps the classic instrument of what is here termed "third-party government." From its meager beginnings in the nineteenth century, the grant-in-aid device has mushroomed into a massive system of interorganizational action. More than five hundred grant-in-aid programs are now on the books, making federal resources available to state and local governments for everything from emergency medical services to the construction of the interstate highway system. Since 1955 alone, grant-in-aid funding has grown 26-fold, three times faster than the budget as a whole. By 1979, therefore, grants-in-aid accounted for about 17 percent of all federal budget outlays, and over 40 percent of all domestic expenditures aside from direct income transfers like Social Security. What is more, the basic structure of the grant-in-aid system also changed markedly, with the introduction of new forms of grants (project grants, block grants, general revenue sharing) and a substantial proliferation in the numbers and types of entities—cities, counties, special districts, nonprofit corporations, and others—that, along with the states, are now eligible for direct grant assistance.[2]

But the recent changes in the forms of federal government action extend far beyond the transformation of the grant-in-aid system. Indeed, the grant-in-aid is now overshadowed by a host of other ingenious tools for carrying out the public's business—loans, loan guarantees, new forms of regulation, tax subsidies, government corporations, interest subsidies, insurance, and numerous others.

Since many of these latter tools are not reflected in federal budget totals, they have attracted far less attention. Yet their scope and scale are massive and growing. In fiscal year 1979, for example, the federal government made more than $130 billion in new *loan or loan guarantee* commitments for purposes as diverse as college education and crop supports. Federal *regulatory activities,* once primarily economic in focus, have now become major vehicles for the promotion of a wide array of health, safety, environmental, and social goals. Between 1970 and 1975 alone, seven new regulatory agencies were created, thirty major regulatory laws were enacted, and the number of pages published annually in the *Federal Register* tripled (Lilley and Miller 1977). Various estimates place the cost of these regulatory activities at anywhere from $40 billion to $120 billion annually. Increased use has also been made of the tax code as an instrument of policy, as *tax deductions* have been provided to encourage the hiring of the unemployed, to stimulate energy conservation, and for a host of other reasons. By 1979 the estimated total value of these "tax subsidies" stood close to $150 billion, up from $40 billion a decade earlier.[3] Beyond this, a number of *government-sponsored enterprises* have been created—Conrail, Amtrak, the U.S. Railway Association, Comsat, the Government National Mortgage Association—and various policy goals are also pursued through federal underwriting of *insurance.* This last activity alone now involves some $2 trillion in contingent liabilities for the federal government.

The proliferation, expansion, and extension of these and other tools of federal policy have substantially reshaped the landscape of federal operations. In almost every policy sphere, federal operations now involve a complex collage of widely assorted tools mobilizing a diverse collection of different types of actors to perform a host of different roles in frequently confusing combinations.

What is involved here, moreover, is not simply the contracting out of well-defined functions or the purchase of specified goods and services from outside suppliers. The characteristic feature of many of these new, or newly expanded, tools of action is that they involve the sharing of a far more basic governmental function: the exercise of discretion over the spending of federal funds and the use of federal authority. They thus continually place federal officials in the uncomfortable position of being held responsible for programs they do not really control.

The $6–$8 billion that Congress annually appropriates for employment and training assistance, for example, goes not to the Department of Labor, which is regularly held accountable for its wise use, but automatically to more than 450 locally organized "prime sponsors," which enjoy substantial discretion in selecting both the training and the trainees, and over which the Labor Department has only limited control. In the loan guarantee programs, many of the key decisions are left to private bankers, who process the applications and extend the credit that the Federal government then guarantees. Even in the procurement area important changes of the same sort have taken place, as the government has been forced to rely on outside suppliers not only to provide products and services that the government has conceived and designed, but, at least in the acquisition of major systems, to do much of the conception and design work as well (U.S. Commission on Government Procurement 1972).

What makes this situation especially problematic, moreover, is that those who exercise authority on the federal government's behalf in these programs frequently enjoy a substantial degree of autonomy from federal control. State and local government agencies, for example, have their own source of independent political support, while many of the federal government's private partners frequently find themselves in the fortuitous position of needing the federal government less than the federal government needs them. Instead of a hierarchical relationship between the federal government and its agents, therefore, what frequently exists in practice is a far more complex bargaining relationship in which the federal agency often has the weaker hand.

The Implications

This set of changes has profound implications for the character of democratic government and the management of public programs. In the first place, it raises serious questions of accountability because those who exercise public authority in these programs are only tangentially accountable to the elected officials who enact and oversee the programs. This is all the more troublesome, moreover, because many of the "third-party" implementers are especially touchy about the exercise of federal oversight, creating pressures to restrict accountability to narrow, technical questions of fiscal control and administrative procedure and to sidestep more value-laden issues of program results.

Closely related to these questions of accountability, moreover, are serious issues of management. In a word, many of these new forms of action render the traditional concerns of public administration and the traditional techniques of public management if not irrelevant, then at least far less germane. The "street-level bureaucrats"[4] in these forms of action are frequently not public employees at all, but bankers and businessmen, hospital administrators, and corporate tax accountants. Under these circumstances, a body of knowledge that focuses on how to organize and operate a public agency, how to motivate and supervise public employees, has far less to say. What is needed instead is a far more complicated political economy of the tools of public action that clarifies the incentives of the non-federal actors, helps inform choices about the appropriateness of different tools for different purposes, and provides guidance about how federal managers can bargain more successfully to shape the behavior of the erstwhile allies on whom they are forced to depend. Under these circumstances, public management takes on a whole new dimension that the implementation literature has yet to acknowledge.

Finally, these changes in the forms of government action have important implications for the coordination of government activities. The problems the federal government has recently been called upon to resolve—poverty, urban distress, environmental degradation—can rarely be solved through individual programs. To address them meaningfully requires the successful orchestration of a number of different activities. Yet the program structure that has evolved, by parceling varied chunks of authority among a number of different actors in ways that are barely visible, let alone subject to control, complicates the task of coordination and taxes the integrative institutions of government.

New Focus for Public Management Research

What these comments suggest is that the failures of public action about which so much has been written may result less from the incompetence or malfeasance of government managers than from the tools we have required them to use and the curious ways we have required them to act. Under these circumstances, the improvement of government performance requires not simply better management, but a clearer understanding of the tools through which the government's business is performed.

It is my argument here that the development of such a systematic body of knowledge about the alternative tools of public action is the real "missing link" (Hargrove 1975) in the theory and practice of public management. Filling in this missing link, however, will require a basic reorientation of existing research and the acceptance of a new unit of analysis that focuses on alternative tools of intervention rather than on individual programs or policies.

The Existing State of Knowledge

This is not the first time that attention has been called to the importance of examining the tools of government action. As early as the 1950s Dahl and Lindblom (1953) observed that the proliferation of new techniques of social action had displaced the competition of ideologies in the Western world and represented "perhaps the greatest political revolution of our times."

If so, however, it has also been the least well examined such revolution. For, despite the impressive endorsement, the systematic study of the techniques of government action has hardly gotten off the ground. To be sure, some impressive work has been done in identifying federal "subsidy" programs and calculating their costs and distributive effects.[5] What is more, some individual tools, like grants-in-aid, have been examined in depth (see, e.g., Elazar 1962; Grodzins 1966; Ingram 1977; Monypenny 1960; Nathan et al. 1975; Sanford 1967; U.S. Advisory Commission on Intergovernmental Relations 1977a, b, 1978, 1979). But most tools have hardly been scrutinized at all, and there has been a virtual absence of systematic comparative work analyzing different tools or examining the changing forms of action as a whole.[6]

As late as 1977, for example, the Congressional Budget Office found that no comparative data existed on default rates, risk factors, or other key features of Federal loan guarantee programs, even though these programs involved outstanding liabilities in excess of $300 billion (Peat, Marwick, and Mitchell 1979). A special Interagency Council on Accident Compensation and Insurance reported in 1979 that it could not only not provide an accurate estimate of the contingent liabilities the Federal government has incurred through its various insurance programs; but also that it was not sure how many such programs exist.[7] Although regulatory programs have been examined more closely, much of this work has focused on the more traditional economic regulation rather than the newer "social" regulation. Moreover, some of the key operational features of regulatory programs, such as the relationships between federal and state authorities, have been "little explored" (U.S. General Accounting Office 1980). Indeed, it was not until 1978 that the first list of Federal regulatory programs was even compiled (U.S. General Accounting Office 1978).

In short, whatever value there is in developing a systematic body of knowledge about the tools of public action—and the argument here is that it is great—that body of knowledge is still far from complete. As the U.S. Office of Management and Budget (1980a) concluded after an intensive two-year study: "the relative effectiveness of different forms of assistance such as grants, loans, and risk assumption for meeting different types of program objectives has not been systematically reviewed in the public literature. In light of the scope, magnitude, and importance of assistance as a tool of national leadership, much more needs to be known." Lest the present call for more attention to the tools of government action go the way of the earlier one, therefore, it may be well to explore, at least in a preliminary way, how such an approach might be structured and what it would entail.

Central Premise

The central premise of the reorientation of implementation analysis that is suggested here is that different tools of government action have their own distinctive dynamics, their own "political economies," that affect the content of government action. This is so for much the same reasons that particular agencies and bureaus are now considered to have their own personalities and styles—because each instrument carries with it a substantial amount of "baggage" in the form of its own characteristic implementing institutions, standard operating procedures, types of expertise and professional cadre, products, degree of visibility, enactment and review processes, and relationships with other societal forces.

A loan guarantee program, for example, will typically involve reliance on local bankers, who tend to approach their responsibilities with a "risk minimization" perspective, who tend to resist nonfinancial criteria for program operation or evaluation, and who traditionally utilize conservative tests of soundness. In addition, such programs regularly escape review by executive branch or Congressional budget agencies, are most closely scrutinized, if at all, by the Treasury Department, are the province of the Banking Committees, not the Appropriations Committees, in the Congress, and are of special concern to the Federal Reserve and the financial community generally because of their potential implications for the allocation of credit in the economy.

It is reasonable to assume that these features systematically affect the operation of this type of program and that they are quite different from the comparable features affecting a grant-in-aid or tax incentive program. When Congress decided in the early 1930s to shift from a direct loan to a loan guarantee form of program to cope with the urban housing problem, for example, it wittingly or unwittingly built into the nation's housing policy the prevailing perspectives of the bankers and realtors who help to operate the program locally. The result, as the Douglas Commission reported in 1968, was to confine benefits "almost exclusively to the middle class, and primarily only to the middle section of the middle class," while "the poor and those on the fringes of poverty have been almost completely excluded" on grounds that they were "bad credit risks and that the presence of Negroes tended to lower real estate values" (U.S. National Commission on Urban Problems 1968).

In short, each tool involves a finely balanced complex of institutional, procedural, political, and economic relationships that substantially shape the character of the government action that results. By the same token, however, these features affect the likelihood that different tools will be enacted. In other words, the choice of program tool is a political, and not just an economic, issue: it involves important questions of power and purpose as well as of equity and efficiency.

Two questions thus form the core of the analysis of tools of government action that is suggested here:

1. What consequences does the choice of tool of government action have for the effectiveness and operation of a government program?

2. What factors influence the choice of program tools? In particular, to what extent are political or other administrative or symbolic reasons involved? Why are some tools chosen over others for particular purposes?

Basic Analytics

To answer these questions, it is necessary to begin with a clearer understanding of the major types of program tools, and the central differences among them. At a minimum, this requires a basic descriptive typology of program tools. Under current circumstances, however, even such a basic descriptive framework is unavailable. The *Catalog of Federal Domestic Assistance,* for example, lists fifteen types of federal assistance ranging from "Formula Grants" through "Dissemination of Technical Information." The catalog, however, ignores many critical program tools, for example, tax incentives, regulations, government-sponsored corporations. In addition, the catalog's groupings obscure many important distinctions (e.g., it groups "interest subsidies" under the general category of "Direct Payments for Specified Use" and fails to distinguish between price supports and Social Security payments).

Even more important than a descriptive framework, however, is the formulation of a more cross-cutting set of analytical categories in terms of which the various tools can be measured and assessed, and on the basis of which reasonable hypotheses, geared to the two questions above, can be generated and tested. Since this is the more difficult task, it may be useful to sketch out here in a purely suggestive way some of the major dimensions such an analytical framework might entail and some of the hypotheses it might support. Although the discussion here draws on literature where available, it should be clear that the intent is to stimulate further thinking rather than advance a definitive framework for the field. In this spirit, five dimensions of the tools of government action seem worthy of attention.

1. The Directness/Indirectness Dimension. The first such dimension concerns the extent of reliance on nonfederal actors that a particular tool entails. Direct federal activities have long been suspect in American government, as much out of a philosophical hostility to concentrated governmental power as out of a concern about the rigidity and unresponsiveness supposed to accompany centralized operations. Recent research on the implementation of public programs suggests, however, that indirect forms of action have their own substantial drawbacks. Pressman and Wildavsky (1973) demonstrate convincingly, for example, that federal efforts to encourage economic development and employment in Oakland were frustrated by a form of action that vested critical responsibilities in a large number of federal and nonfederal actors, each of which had its own priorities and perspectives that had to be reconciled anew at each of several dozen decision points that stood between program conception and completion. Similarly, Chase (1979) found that the most serious problems in implementing three social service programs in New York City all involved "some player or players in the implementation process whom the program manager does not control but whose cooperation or assistance is required." And Berman (1978) differentiates between the "macro-implementation" of a program and its "micro-implementation" to emphasize the looseness of the tie between the adoption of a policy and its actual operation by a largely autonomous local agent.

What is important about the use of indirect forms of action is not simply the administrative complexity of the resulting program structure, however. Of equal or greater importance is the incongruence that can arise between the goals of the federal government—as articulated, however imperfectly, in legislation, report language, or regulations—and the goals of the nonfederal implementing agents. This is clearly the case when the agent is a for-profit corporation. But it is equally true of state and local governments since different interests, different priorities, and different concerns find effective expression at different levels of government. Proposals to turn more decision-making power over to the states and localities thus involve more than questions of administrative efficiency; they also involve questions of program purpose and substance.

Taken together, these considerations suggest the following tentative hypothesis:

Hypothesis 1: The more indirect the form of government action—that is, the more it places important discretionary authority in the hands of nonfederal actors, and the more the interests and goals of these actors diverge from those of the federal government—the more difficult will be the implementation of the resulting program and the less likely will the program be to achieve its goals.

To the extent that this hypothesis is true, it raises significant questions about why so much of federal action now relies upon basically indirect devices. The answer, it appears, is that the dictates of implementation frequently diverge from the imperatives of enactment. In the first place, the success of federal programs frequently depends on access to a resource under some third party's control. Delivering a degree of authority to this third party is often the only way to get the program the resources it needs. This is especially true in view of a second factor, the hostility of key producer and provider groups (including state and local governments) to federal competition in their fields. The price of political acquiescence in the establishment of a federal role, therefore, is frequently the acceptance by the federal government of a tool of action that cuts these third parties into a meaningful piece of the federal action. Finally, as already noted, the use of indirect devices has strong philosophical and ideological roots because the protection of the private sector from governmental intervention and the preservation of state and local autonomy are viewed as political values in their own right, worth protecting even at the cost of some sacrifice of administrative efficiency or national purpose. What this suggests is a companion hypothesis:

Hypothesis 2: The more direct the form of government action, the more likely it is to encounter political opposition.

2. *The Automatic/Administered Dimension.* A second key dimension of different instruments of government action concerns the extent to which they rely on automatic, as opposed to administered, processes. An automatic process is one that utilizes existing structures and relationships (e.g., the tax structure or the price system) and requires a minimum of administrative decision making. A tax credit automatically available to all firms investing in new plant or equipment, for example, would represent a largely automatic tool. A similar sum made available through grants on the basis of separately reviewed applications would represent a more highly administered tool.

Generally speaking, automatic tools are operationally more efficient since they involve less administrative oversight and transaction cost. They are also less disruptive of ongoing social processes, such as the price system and the market. This suggests the following hypothesis:

Hypothesis 3: The more automatic the tool of government action, the easier to manage, the fairer the operation, and the less disruptive the side effects.

Despite these hypothesized advantages, however, instruments that rely upon essentially automatic processes have significant drawbacks. For one thing, there is far less certainty that they will have the results intended, especially when they are attached to processes with far different purposes. A program that seeks to promote worker safety by levying higher disability insurance charges on companies with poor safety records rather than by imposing detailed safety regulations, for example, may continuously be in the position of doing too little too late. In addition, while promoting administrative efficiency, such tools sacrifice "target efficiency," the effective targeting of program benefits. A tax credit program aimed at encouraging additional productive investment in plant and equipment, for example, may end up delivering substantial benefits to firms that would have made these investments anyway, or freeing resources for forms of investment that are nonproductive and speculative. Those most concerned about the achievement of program objectives and the targeting of program resources may consequently be wary of tools that lack sufficient controls. These considerations thus suggest the following additional hypothesis:

Hypothesis 4: The more automatic the tool of government action, the less certain the achievement of program purposes, the greater the leakage of program benefits, and the more problematic the generation of needed political support.

3. The Cash versus In-Kind Dimension. In assistance-type programs in particular, important differences exist between programs that deliver their benefits in the form of cash and those that deliver them in kind. Cash-type programs reserve far more flexibility to recipients and are typically easier to administer. In-kind programs (e.g., food stamps, housing assistance), by tying benefits to a particular service or good, constrain recipient choices, often providing more of a particular good than a recipient would freely choose and thereby reducing the marginal value of the benefit to the recipient. This suggests the following hypothesis:

Hypothesis 5: Programs that utilize cash assistance are easier to manage and more highly valued by recipients than programs that provide assistance in kind.

While cash forms of assistance have attractions from the point of view of recipients, however, they have drawbacks from the point of view of building political support. In the first place, in-kind programs, by committing resources to the purchase of a particular good or service, can stimulate support from the producers of that good or service that would otherwise not exist. The food stamp program, for example, enjoys support from agricultural and farm interests that would not be forthcoming for a general, cash income-assistance program. Similarly, builder support for aid to the poor is much stronger for programs that tie such aid to the production of housing than for programs that make such assistance available in the form of cash. In the second place, in-kind assistance is more likely to go for the purpose intended than is outright cash. Those who make a case for assistance in terms of a particular need may therefore feel obliged to champion the delivery mechanism most certain to apply that assistance to that particular need. What these considerations suggest, therefore, is the following companion hypothesis:

Hypothesis 6: The greater the reliance on in-kind tools of action, the greater the prospects for political support.

4. The Visibility-Invisibility Dimension. Because of the structure of the budget and legislative processes, certain tools of government action are far less visible than others. Tax incentives, for example, are far less open to regular scrutiny than outright grants. "Entitlement" programs, which establish legal rights to program benefits independent of the budget, are far less closely scrutinized than programs that are subject to yearly control. In some cases, the costs of federal action are not even known. This is the case, for example, with regulatory actions, the true impact of which appears not in the federal budget, but in the balance sheets of the regulated industries. What this suggests is the following hypothesis:

Hypothesis 7: The less visible a tool of government action is in the regular budget process, the less subject it will be to overall management and control.

To the extent this hypothesis is correct, it follows that invisibility is a politically attractive attribute of a tool. Indeed, research by Boulding and Pfaff (1972) found that the less visible federal subsidies delivered most of their benefits to the better-off while assistance to the poor came in far more visible forms. What this suggests is the following hypothesis:

Hypothesis 8: The less visible the costs of a tool, the more attractive the tool will be to those who will benefit from it. The more powerful the beneficiaries, therefore, the more likely they will be to receive whatever benefits they secure through less visible tools.

5. Design Standards versus Performance Standards for Program Control. Attention to the instruments of government action has implications not only for basic choices among different tools, but also for decisions about how different tools, once chosen, are managed. One of the central issues in this regard is the extent to which reliance is placed on performance standards as opposed to design standards in program operations. Design standards involve controls over detailed aspects of program operations: accounting procedures, fund transfers among different program accounts, personnel recruitment procedures, specific technological processes to adopt to reduce air pollution at particular types of sites. Performance standards, by contrast, specify desired outputs but leave to the discretion of program managers or their third-party agents the decisions about how to design activities to achieve these outputs. Students of social regulation have faulted much of the federal government's recent regulatory effort in precisely these terms, arguing that by placing too much stress on design specifications (e.g., the location and numbers of fire extinguishers in industrial plants) rather than on performance standards (the days lost through fires), these activities end up being far less efficient economically and far more cumbersome administratively than is necessary (Schultze 1977). Similar observations have been made about other programs where detailed restrictions are imposed on the mix of inputs (e.g., the ratio of welfare case workers to recipients) rather than focusing attention on outputs (e.g., the reduction of dependency) (Levine 1972). What these findings suggest is the following hypothesis:

Hypothesis 9: The more a form of government action uses performance standards instead of design regulations, the less cumbersome it is administratively and the more efficient is its use of resources.

Attractive as performance standards are, however, they are not without their problems. For one thing, program purposes are frequently kept deliberately vague in order to hold together the political coalition often required for passage. Moreover, programs often serve multiple purposes, and opinions can differ over the priorities to attach to each. In addition, the measurement of success and failure in terms of particular performance criteria can often be quite subjective, creating added possibilities for conflict and confusion, especially where responsibility for program decisions is split between federal authorities and their "third-party" agents. Finally, the use of performance standards involves greater uncertainty since results are not apparent for a considerable time and great opportunity exists for mistakes along the way. Those responsible for program oversight can therefore be expected to find such uncertainty exceedingly unattractive. Based on these considerations, therefore, the following hypothesis seems plausible:

Hypothesis 10: The more a tool involves reliance on federally determined performance standards, the more likely it is to encounter political opposition and resistance from its administrators.

6. Summary—The Public Management Paradox. Taken together, the hypotheses identified above suggest an important paradox that may lie at the heart of much of the recent disappointment with federal program performance. *Simply put, this paradox is that the types of instruments that are the easiest to implement may be the hardest to enact; conversely, the forms that are most likely to be enacted are also the most difficult to carry out.*

Conclusions and Implications

Whether the hypotheses outlined here are accepted or rejected, the discussion should demonstrate the character and range of issues that open up when the unit of analysis in implementation research is changed from the individual program to the generic tools of government action. These are not, moreover, simply theoretical issues. They are tangible questions that face decision-makers day-to-day as they decide whether to use a regulation, a tax credit, a grant, or a loan guarantee to encourage electric utilities to switch from oil- to coal-powered generators; or whether to build an economic development strategy on the basis of grants to local governments, loan guarantees through private banks, employment tax credits to business, or equity assistance to community development corporations.

Up to this point, these decisions have not been informed by any systematic understanding of the consequences that the choices of tools of government action have for the operations of public programs. As a result, the political pressures have not encountered any analytical counterpoise and have typically prevailed, often trapping program managers in no-win situations that are doomed from the start. For implementation researchers then to come along and declare programs a failure because of "poor management" or inattention to implementation is to add insult to injury and invite justifiable scorn.

What is needed instead is a usable body of knowledge about how different tools of government action work and how they can be adapted to different purposes. It is this body of knowledge that is the appropriate domain of implementation study. And it is this range of issues on which implementation research can finally cut its theoretical teeth.

CHAPTER 2

Of Market Failure, Voluntary Failure, and Third-Party Government:

Toward a Theory of Government-Nonprofit Relations in the Modern Welfare State

Few facets of the American welfare state have been so thoroughly overlooked or so commonly misunderstood as the role of the nonprofit sector and the relationships between nonprofit organizations and government. Yet few facets also are as important.

According to widespread beliefs, the social welfare programs of the New Deal and Great Society effectively displaced voluntary agencies in the United States and led inevitably to their decline. In fact, however, the voluntary sector has retained a vital, indeed growing, role in the American welfare state. It has done so, moreover, not in spite of government but, to an important degree, because of it. This is so because government has turned extensively to private, nonprofit organizations to deliver publicly financed services. In some cases, government has even created new nonprofit organizations where none existed. In others, nonprofit organizations have benefited from government payments to individuals for the purchase of services that nonprofits provide (e.g., higher education, hospital care).

Through these and other channels an elaborate network of partnership arrangements has come into existence linking government and the nonprofit sector. So extensive are these arrangements, in fact, that in a number of human service fields—such as health and social services—nonprofit organizations actually deliver a larger share of the services government finances than do government agencies themselves (Salamon 1987a; see also chap. 7). Not only is the resulting partnership important for government, however. It is also important for the nonprofit sector. In fact, government has emerged as the single most important source of nonprofit human service agency income, outdistancing private giving and service charges as sources of support. In short, cooperation between government and the voluntary sector has become the backbone of this country's human service delivery system, and the central financial fact of life of the country's private nonprofit sector.[1]

Despite its scale and importance, however, this partnership between government and the voluntary sector has attracted surprisingly little attention, and what attention it has attracted has generally been hostile. In fact, after a flurry of interest in the late nineteenth and early twentieth centuries (Warner 1894; Fetter 1901–2; Fleisher 1914; Dripps 1915), the subject of government-nonprofit relations largely disappeared from public debate and scholarly inquiry, as did the broader question of the role of voluntary organizations in the modern welfare state. More recently as well, a blind spot has persisted with respect to the relationships between the voluntary sector and government. A major three-year project on mediating structures conducted by the American Enterprise Institute in the mid-1970s, for example, advanced as its major conclusion the proposal that government should rely on voluntary organizations to deliver publicly funded services without ever acknowledging the extent to which current government operations already embody this approach (Berger and Neuhaus 1977). In his influential *Power and Community,* sociologist Robert Nisbet (1962) posits an inherent conflict between voluntary organizations and government, attributing to government much of the responsibility for the weakening of voluntary institutions and the resulting rise of alienation and anomie in the modern world. This theme finds expression as well in other treatments of the voluntary sector, which portray a mythical "golden age" of voluntary-sector purity that has been corrupted by receipt of government funds.[2] This is ironic not only because no such golden age existed but also because the early turn-of-the-century students of government-nonprofit cooperation objected to government support of nonprofits not because it would hurt nonprofits (the current concern) but because it might inhibit the development of the new welfare institutions of government, which were viewed as more comprehensive and fair.

The upshot, however, is that even the basic scope of the partnership between government and the nonprofit sector has been unknown until recently, while serious analyses of its strengths and weaknesses have been virtually nonexistent. Like the broader question of the scope and character of the voluntary sector, the phenomenon of government-nonprofit interaction has been largely ignored in both public debate and scholarly inquiry, as attention has focused instead on the expansion of the state.

That this is so is not due simply to the newness of the phenomenon or an oversight in research. As chapter 7 shows in more detail, government-nonprofit cooperation has substantial roots deep in American history. Long before the American Revolution, colonial governments had established a tradition of assistance to private educational institutions, and this tradition persisted into the nineteenth century and broadened considerably (Whitehead 1973, 3–16). A 1901 survey of government subsidization of private charities, for example, found that "Except possibly two territories and four western states, there is probably not a state in the union where some aid [to private charities] is not given either by the state or by counties and cities" (Fetter 1901–2, 360). Nor can the lack of attention to government-nonprofit relations be attributed simply to a lack of research. The reality of extensive government support of the voluntary sector has been too apparent for too long to accept this as an adequate explanation, especially since other aspects of voluntary-sector operations—such as board structures, staff-board relations, and professional-volunteer interaction—have come under closer scrutiny. Why, then, did this relationship fail to attract serious attention? Why has so important a feature of modern American social policy remained so obscure for so long?

The Need for Theory

It is the argument here that the real answer to these questions is more conceptual than empirical. The partnership between government and the nonprofit sector has been overlooked, in my view, not because of its novelty or a lack of research but because of a weakness in theory. Both students of the voluntary sector and students of the welfare state have failed to appreciate or come to terms with the reality of extensive government-nonprofit relationships until relatively recently because of faults in the conceptual lenses through which they have been examining this reality. It is the role of theory, after all, to direct attention to the facts that are most relevant to a particular process. As Thomas Kuhn put it in his classic book, *The Structure of Scientific Revolutions*, "In the absence of a paradigm [or theory] . . . all of the facts that could possibly pertain to the development of a given science are likely to seem equally relevant" (Kuhn 1962, 15). Lacking a valid theory, crucial facts can therefore be overlooked or misperceived. "Facts do not speak for themselves," Stephen Jay Gould has observed, "they are read in the light of theory" (Gould 1977). It is for this reason that Karl Deutsch has argued that "progress in the effectiveness of symbols and symbol systems [i.e., theory] is . . . basic progress in the technology of thinking and in the development of human powers of insight and action" (Deutsch 1963, 10).

It is the argument here that such "basic progress in the technology of thinking" is very much needed in the analysis of the voluntary sector and its relationships with government. Our failure to perceive the reality of extensive government-nonprofit ties is, I believe, a product in substantial part of the limitations of the conceptual equipment through which this reality is being perceived. Both the theory of the "welfare state" and the theory of the voluntary sector, moreover, have been at fault. Neither leaves much conceptual room for a flourishing government-nonprofit partnership. To the contrary, both suggest quite strongly that such cooperation could not, and should not, exist. Equipped with such theories, it is no wonder that observers have tended to overlook such cooperation or question it when it appears. To come to terms adequately with the facts, therefore, it is necessary to reconfigure the lenses, not simply to add more information.

It is the purpose of this chapter to undertake such a reconfiguration. To do so, we first examine where the existing lenses fall short and suggest an alternative set of concepts focusing particularly on the notions of "third-party government" and "voluntary failure" that do a far better job of coming to grips with the reality of government-nonprofit cooperation and therefore have a claim to greater "explanatory power."[3] A final section then uses these new concepts to help guide our thinking about how such cooperation should evolve in the future.

The Shortcomings of Prevailing Theories

Two sets of theories are largely responsible for the widespread neglect of government-nonprofit partnerships in the American version of the modern welfare state: first, the prevailing theories of the welfare state, and second, the prevailing theories of the voluntary sector.

The Theory of the Welfare State

At the core of the misperception of government's relationship with the nonprofit sector in the American context has been the prevailing conception of the welfare state. Focusing on the dramatic expansion of government social welfare expenditures that began in the Progressive Era and accelerated during the New Deal and the Great Society, most observers have jumped easily to the natural conclusion that what has been under way in the United States has been a gigantic enlargement of the apparatus of government—particularly the national government—at the expense of other social institutions, among them private nonprofit groups. The central image has been that of a large bureaucratic state, hierarchic in structure and monolithic in form, taking on social functions previously performed by other social institutions.

This image carries over into the American context a concept of the state that is essentially European in origin and that stresses the power of governmental institutions and their dominance over private, voluntary ones. Interestingly, moreover, both liberals and conservatives have had reason to embrace such an image. For liberals, faith in the capabilities of a professionalized public service and of an integrated state administrative apparatus has long been crucial in the battle to win political support for an expanded governmental role in social problem solving. Not surprisingly, therefore, when the practice of governmental subsidization of private charitable institutions expanded in the late nineteenth century it was the progressives who voiced the most concern, fearing that this practice would interfere with the development of a far more desirable system of professional public care (Warner 1894; Dripps 1915; Fetter 1901–2; Fleisher 1914).

If liberals have thus had reason to exaggerate the capabilities of the state in order to buttress their case about the need for governmental involvement in public problem solving, conservatives have had an even stronger incentive to exaggerate the power of the modern welfare state in order to emphasize the threat that the state poses to individual liberty and other important social values. This tendency is clearly evident in the work of sociologist Robert Nisbet, whose *Power and Community* has become a centerpiece of conservative ideology. For Nisbet, an inherent conflict exists between government and various "mediating institutions" such as voluntary organizations—a conflict that government has been winning. The result, Nisbet believes, is a serious deterioration in the sense of community in the modern world and a troubling rise in anomie. As Nisbet puts it (1962, 68, 109):

The conflict between the central power of the political state and the whole set of functions and authorities contained in church, family, gild, and local community has been, I believe, the main source of those dislocations of social structure and uprootings of status which lie behind the problem of community in our age.

The real conflict in modern political history has not been, as is so often stated, between state and individual, but between state and social group.

"The logical conclusion of our present course," two students of Nisbet thus conclude, "is that the state eventually becomes the sole provider of all social services" (Kerrine and Neuhaus 1979, 18).

This tendency to emphasize the monolithic character of the American welfare state and to deemphasize the continuing role of voluntary groups in public programs has also been encouraged by the focus of much of the national policy debate, and most academic policy analysis, on the formulation of policy, which has moved decisively into the governmental sphere, rather than on its implementation, which is where nonprofits have retained a substantial role (Hargrove 1975). Taken together, the overall result has been to stress the expansion of the state, to convey an impression of governmental dominance of societal problem solving and service provision, and to leave little conceptual room for a vibrant nonprofit sector.

The Prevailing Theories of the Voluntary Sector: Market Failure, Government Failure, and Contract Failure

While the prevailing conception of the modern welfare state has left little room for a vibrant, private, nonprofit sector or for a blossoming government-nonprofit partnership, the existing theories of the voluntary sector likewise leave little room to expect effective cooperation between nonprofit organizations and the state. In fact, it was to get away from such blurring of the boundaries between the public and private sectors that the concept of the private nonprofit sector was invented in the latter nineteenth century. Prior to this time, charitable organizations were considered part of the public sector because they served public objectives. As business interests sought to free themselves from government involvement in economic affairs in the latter 1800s, however, it became important to draw a sharper distinction between public and private action, and the notion of a separate private, nonprofit sector took shape as one of the consequences (Hartz 1948; Stevens 1982).

If the concept of the nonprofit sector thus had its origins in a broader effort to distinguish the private sector from government, this division has since been further elaborated in the more formal economic theories of the voluntary sector that have surfaced in recent years. Broadly speaking, two such theories have been advanced to explain the existence of the voluntary sector, and neither provides much reason to expect extensive government-nonprofit cooperation.

The Market Failure/Government Failure Theory. The first of these theories views the existence of the voluntary sector as the combined product of what economists term "market failure" and "government failure"; that is, of inherent limitations in both the private market and government as providers of "collective goods" (Weisbrod 1977). "Collective goods" are products or services like national defense or clean air that, once produced, are enjoyed by everyone whether or not they have paid for them. Providing such goods exclusively through the market will virtually ensure that they are in short supply since few consumers will volunteer to pay for products they could enjoy without having to pay. With market demand low, producers will produce less of these goods or services than the public really needs and wants. This phenomenon is commonly referred to as the "free rider" problem, and it serves in traditional economic theory as the major rationale for government. Since government can tax people to produce "collective goods" it can overcome this "market failure."

But government too has certain inherent limitations as a producer of collective goods. Most important, in a democratic society it will produce only that range and quantity of collective goods that can command majority support. Inevitably, this will leave some unsatisfied demand on the part of segments of the political community that feel a need for a range of collective goods but cannot convince a majority of the community to go along.

It is to meet such "unsatisfied demand" for collective goods, the argument goes, that a private, voluntary sector is needed. Private, nonprofit organizations thus exist, according to the market failure/government failure theory, to supply a range of "collective goods" desired by one segment of a community but not by a majority. From this it follows that the more diverse the community, the more extensive the nonprofit sector it is likely to have. Because the nonprofit sector is viewed as a substitute for government, providing goods and services that the full political community has not endorsed, however, government support to nonprofit organizations has little theoretical rationale. To the contrary, under this theory, to the extent that nonprofits deliver services that government underwrites, they violate their theoretical raison d'être, which is to supply the goods government is not providing. The market failure/government failure theory would thus predict that little government-nonprofit cooperation would occur, and that what little of it exists cannot be easily justified.[4]

The "Contract Failure" Theory. The second broad theory of the voluntary sector attributes the existence of voluntary organizations to a different kind of market failure, what one theorist terms "contract failure" (Hansmann 1981). The central notion here is that for some goods and services, such as care for the aged, the purchaser is not the same as the consumer. In these circumstances, the normal mechanisms of the market, which involve consumer choice on the basis of adequate information, do not obtain. Consequently, some proxy has to be created to offer the purchaser a degree of assurance that the goods or services being purchased meet adequate standards of quality and quantity. The nonprofit form, in this theory, provides that proxy. Unlike for-profit businesses, which are motivated by profit and therefore might be tempted to betray the trust of a purchaser who is not the recipient of what he buys, nonprofit firms are in business for more charitable purposes and may therefore be more worthy of trust.

Since most government programs involve a substantial amount of regulation, however, this theory provides little rationale for government reliance on nonprofits, or for government regulation of nonprofits (Rose-Ackerman 1985). In fact, since government agencies might be expected to have even less reason to betray trust than nonprofit ones, this theory might lead one to expect more reliance on government agencies than nonprofit ones.

Third-Party Government and Voluntary Failure: Toward a New Theory of Government-Nonprofit Relations

Given the prevailing perceptions of the American welfare state and the prevailing theories of the voluntary sector, it should thus come as no surprise to find little awareness of the continued vitality of the nonprofit sector or of the immense importance of government-nonprofit cooperation. In neither set of theories is there much of a hint that the nonprofit sector should play as substantial a role as it does in the provision of government-financed services. How, then, are we to account for this phenomenon? Are the continued vigor of the nonprofit sector and the extensive pattern of government-nonprofit cooperation accidents, or is there some theoretical rationale that can better help us come to terms with these phenomena?

It is the argument here that the answer to these questions lies in certain shortcomings in the prevailing theories. Both the theory of the welfare state and the theory of the voluntary sector, moreover, are deficient, though for different reasons. To bring the prevailing reality into better focus, therefore, both sets of theories need to be reworked.

Third-Party Government: A New Theory of the American Welfare State

The central problem with the theory of the welfare state as it has applied to the American context is its failure to differentiate between government's role as a provider of funds and direction, and government's role as a deliverer of services. In point of fact, it is largely in the former capacity that government—certainly the national government—has grown in the United States. When it comes to the actual delivery of services, by contrast, the national government has turned extensively to other institutions—states, cities, counties, universities, hospitals, banks, industrial corporations, and others. Far from the bureaucratic monolith pictured in conventional theories, the welfare state in the American context makes use of a wide variety of third parties to carry out governmental functions. The result is an elaborate system of "third-party government" (Salamon 1981), in which government shares a substantial degree of its discretion over the spending of public funds and the exercise of public authority with third-party implementers.

This pattern of government action is evident in a wide assortment of domestic program areas and involves a diverse array of actors. Under the more than nine hundred grant-in-aid programs, for example, the federal government makes financial assistance available to states and local governments for purposes ranging from aid to families with dependent children to the construction of interstate highways. Under the federal government's "loan guarantee" programs, close to $150 billion in loan money is lent by private banks to individuals and corporations, with federal backing, for everything from home mortgages to college education.

In each of these programs the federal government performs a managerial function but leaves a substantial degree of discretion to its nongovernmental, or nonfederal, partner. In the Aid to Families with Dependent Children program, for example, the federal government reimburses states for a portion of their payments to mothers with dependent children, but leaves to the states the decision about whether to have such a program, what the income eligibility cutoffs will be, and even what the benefits will be.

This form of government action reflects America's federal constitutional structure, with its sharing of governmental functions between federal and state governments (Grodzins 1966; Elazar 1972). But "third-party government" extends well beyond the domain of relations among the different levels of government. It also applies to relationships between government and a host of private institutions. As such, it reflects as well the conflict that has long existed in American political thinking between a desire for public services and hostility to the governmental apparatus that provides them. Third-party government has emerged as a way to reconcile these competing perspectives, to increase the role of government in promoting the general welfare without unduly enlarging the state's administrative apparatus. Where existing institutions are available to carry out a function—whether it be extending loans, providing health care, or delivering social services—they therefore have a presumptive claim on a meaningful role in whatever public program might be established.

This pattern of government action is also encouraged by the country's pluralistic political structure. To secure needed support for a program of government action, it is frequently necessary to ensure at least the acquiescence, if not the whole-hearted support, of key interests with a stake in the area. One way to do this is to give them a "piece of the action" by building them into the operation of the government program. Thus, private banks are involved in running the government's mortgage guarantee programs, private health insurers and hospitals in the operation of the Medicare and Medicaid programs, states and private social service agencies in the provision of federally funded social services.

Finally, this pattern of government action is motivated in part by concerns about flexibility and economy. Where existing institutions are already performing a function, government can frequently carry out its purposes more simply and with less cost by enlisting these other institutions in the government program, thereby avoiding the need to create wholly new organizational structures or specialized staffs. This is particularly true where programs are experimental. This way of organizing government services also makes it easier to adapt program operations to local circumstances or individual needs and thus to avoid some of the drawbacks of large-scale governmental bureaucracy and some of the limitations of the civil service. Finally, some argue that the use of outside contractors lowers costs by stimulating competition and promoting economies of scale, though the evidence here is far from conclusive (Fitch 1974; Savas 1984).

Private, nonprofit organizations are among the most natural candidates to take part in this system of third-party government. Far more than private businesses, these organizations have objectives that are akin to those of government. Indeed, as noted earlier, they were regularly considered part of the "public sector" until the late nineteenth century because they served essentially "public" purposes. In addition, in a wide range of fields, nonprofit organizations were on the scene before government arrived. It was therefore frequently less costly in the short run to subsidize and upgrade the existing private agencies than to create wholly new governmental ones.

In short, the extensive pattern of government support of nonprofit institutions can be viewed as just one manifestation of a much broader pattern of third-party government that reflects deep-seated American traditions of governance as well as more recent concerns about service costs and quality. Instead of the hierarchic, bureaucratic apparatus pictured in conventional images, the concept of third-party government emphasizes the extensive sharing of responsibilities among public and private institutions and the pervasive blending of public and private roles that is characteristic of the American welfare state. Because a number of different institutions must act together to achieve a given program goal, this pattern of government action seriously complicates the task of public management and involves real problems of accountability and control (Salamon 1981; Smith 1975a; Staats 1975). But it also has much to recommend it. It makes it possible to set priorities for the expenditure of societal resources through a democratic political process while leaving the actual operation of the resulting public programs to smaller-scale organizations closer to the problems being addressed. It thus creates a public presence without creating a monstrous public bureaucracy. And it permits a degree of diversity and competition in the provision of publicly funded services that can improve efficiency and reduce costs.

So long as the image of the welfare state in America remains tied to its conventional European model, the phenomenon of extensive government support to voluntary organizations has no apparent place and therefore tends to be overlooked. But once we adjust our conceptual lenses to take account of the reality of third-party government, it becomes clear why nonprofits play so important a role. These organizations predated government in many fields and operate in ways that are congenial to public objectives. Given a welfare state that is characterized by an extensive pattern of third-party government, the persistence of a voluntary sector and widespread government-nonprofit cooperation are not anomalies at all: they are exactly what one would expect.

Voluntary Failure: A New Theory of the Voluntary Sector

If the failure to acknowledge the reality of third-party government in the conventional image of the American welfare state explains part of the neglect of government-nonprofit relationships in recent decades, shortcomings in the existing theories of the voluntary sector explain the rest. Essentially, as we have seen, those theories explain the existence of the voluntary sector in terms of failures of the market system and of government. The voluntary sector is thus seen as derivative and secondary, filling in where those other systems fall short.

It may be more meaningful, however, to turn this theory on its head, to reject the view that government is the typical response to market failure and to see voluntary organizations as the primary response mechanism instead. Rather than treating voluntary organizations as derivative institutions filling in for "government failure," for inherent limitations of government as a mechanism for providing collective goods, such a theory would turn the argument around and view government as the derivative institution responding to "voluntary failure," to inherent limitations of the voluntary or nonprofit sector.

The central argument for this reformulation is that the "transaction costs" involved in mobilizing governmental responses to shortages of collective goods tend to be much higher than the costs of mobilizing voluntary action. For government to act, substantial segments of the public must be aroused, public officials must be informed, laws must be written, majorities must be assembled, and programs must be put into operation. By contrast, to generate a voluntary-sector response, a handful of individuals acting on their own or with outside contributed support can suffice. It is reasonable to expect, therefore, that the private, nonprofit sector will typically provide the first line of response to perceived "market failures," and that government will be called on only as the voluntary response proves insufficient. So conceived, it becomes clear that government involvement is less a substitute for, than a supplement to, private nonprofit action. What is more, this reformulation of the market failure theory does a far better job of making sense of the fundamental reality of extensive government-nonprofit ties. And it suggests a theoretical rationale for these ties that fits into a broader, and more positive, conception of the voluntary sector, thus rescuing this fundamental fact of voluntary-sector life from the limbo to which it has been consigned by existing theories.[5]

But what are the "voluntary failures" that have necessitated government action and that justify government support to the voluntary sector? Broadly speaking, there are four: first, philanthropic insufficiency; second, philanthropic particularism; third, philanthropic paternalism; and fourth, philanthropic amateurism.

Philanthropic Insufficiency. The central failing of the voluntary system as a provider of collective goods has been its inability to generate resources on a scale that is both adequate enough and reliable enough to cope with the human service problems of an advanced industrial society. In part, this is a reflection of the "free rider" problem inherent in the production of collective goods. Since everybody benefits from a society in which those in need are cared for whether or not they have contributed to the cost of the care, there is an incentive for each person to let his neighbor bear most of the cost. So long as sole reliance is placed on a system of voluntary contributions, therefore, it is likely that the resources made available will be less than those society considers optimal. Only when contributions are made involuntary, as they are through taxation, are they therefore likely to be sufficient and consistent. As one early student of American charity put it: "The law is primarily an agency for bringing up the laggards in the march of progress, and when the community on the average wants benevolent work done, this is the method of pushing forward those who hang back. . . . The stingy man is not allowed to thrive at the expense of his benevolent neighbor" (Warner 1894, 306). Since the range of "benevolent work" that is thought necessary has expanded considerably over the years, moreover, this problem has grown increasingly important over time.

Beyond this "free rider" problem, however, philanthropic insufficiency also results from the twists and turns of economic fortune. The economic fluctuations that have accompanied the growing complexity of economic life mean that benevolent individuals may find themselves least able to help others when those others are most in need of help, as happened with disastrous results during the Great Depression. Similarly, the voluntary system often leaves serious gaps in geographic coverage, since the resources are frequently not available where the problems are most severe. In short, the voluntary system, despite its advantages in terms of reducing transaction costs and creating a meaningful sense of social obligation and legitimacy, nevertheless has serious drawbacks as a generator of a reliable stream of resources to respond adequately to community needs.

Philanthropic Particularism. If resource inadequacy is one source of voluntary-sector weakness, the "particularism" of the voluntary sector constitutes another. Particularism, the tendency of voluntary organizations and their benefactors to focus on particular subgroups of the population, is, of course, one of the purported strengths of the voluntary sector. Voluntary organizations provide the vehicle through which such subgroups—ethnic, religious, neighborhood, interest, or other—can join together for common purposes. Indeed, in some theories, as we have seen, it is precisely this particularism that provides the theoretical rationale for the existence of the nonprofit sector.

But particularism also has its drawbacks as the basis for organizing a community's response to human needs. For one thing, there is the possibility that some subgroups of the community may not be adequately represented in the structure of voluntary organizations. Even voluntary organizations require resources, after all, and it is quite possible that those in command of the needed resources—financial as well as organizational—may not favor all segments of the community equally. As a result, serious gaps can occur in the coverage of subgroups by the existing voluntary organizations. Close observers of the nonprofit scene in New York City, for example, have observed that up through the early 1960s, the lion's share of the child welfare services were provided through essentially Catholic and Jewish agencies. Since most of the poor blacks who migrated to the city in the post–World War II era were Protestants, they did not immediately find a "home" in the established agency structure (Beck 1971, 271). Other groups—gays, the disabled, Hispanics, women—have found similar difficulties establishing a niche in the voluntary system and locating a source of support for their activities. More generally, the private nonprofit sector has long had a tendency to treat the more "deserving" of the poor, leaving the most difficult cases to public institutions. Indeed, the survey we conducted of 3,400 human service organizations revealed that the poor comprised the majority of the clients of only about 30 percent of the agencies, and that for half of the agencies, the poor constituted less than 10 percent of the clientele (Salamon 1984b; see chap. 5).

Not only can particularism, and the favoritism that inevitably accompanies it, leave serious gaps in coverage, but it can also contribute to wasteful duplication of services. Voluntary organizations and charitable activity are motivated not alone by considerations of social need, but also by considerations of communal or individual pride. Each group wants its own agencies, and appeals to donors are frequently made along religious, ethnic, or sectarian lines. The upshot is that the number of agencies can increase well beyond what economies of scale might suggest, reducing the overall efficiency of the system and increasing its costs. This was a great concern of early students of American social welfare policy, who viewed the duplication of facilities and the resulting waste of resources as one of the great drawbacks of the private, voluntary system (Fetter 1901–2, 380; Fleisher 1914, 111). As Amos Warner (1894, 359) put it in his classic treatise on American charity in the 1890s: "The charities of a given locality, which should for useful result be systematically directed to the accomplishment of their common purposes, are usually a chaos, a patchwork of survivals, or products of contending political, religious, and medical factions, a curious compound, in which a strong ingredient is ignorance perpetuated by heedlessness." Left to their own devices, therefore, voluntary organizations may leave significant elements of the community without care and make wasteful use of what resources are available.

Philanthropic Paternalism. A third class of problems with the voluntary system of responding to community problems results from the fact that this approach inevitably vests most of the influence over the definition of community needs in the hands of those in command of the greatest resources. This is so despite the importance of volunteer effort in this sector. For one thing, voluntarism itself requires resources of time and knowledge. But in addition, the growing need for professional approaches to social problems has made it necessary to go beyond voluntary effort. So long as private charity is the only support for the voluntary sector, those in control of the charitable resources can determine what the sector does and whom it serves. The nature of the sector thus comes to be shaped by the preferences not of the community as a whole, but of its wealthy members. As a consequence, some services favored by the wealthy, such as the arts, may be promoted, while others desired by the poor are held back. Since these private contributions are tax-deductible, moreover, they have the effect not only of allocating private expenditures, but also of allocating foregone public revenues as well, though without the benefit of any public decision process.

Not only is this situation undemocratic, but also it can create a self-defeating sense of dependency on the part of the poor since it gives them no say over the resources that are spent on their behalf. Aid is provided as a matter of charity, not of right. And in the past it was often accompanied by various moral preachments of the sort that George Bernard Shaw immortalized in his play *Major Barbara*. A central premise of much early philanthropic activity, in fact, was that the poor were responsible for their own destitution and needed to be uplifted religiously and morally through the work of sectarian agencies. Even in more recent times, close students of social policy have criticized the funneling of funds "into the hands of upper-class and middle-class people to spend on behalf of the less privileged people" as "the most pernicious effect" of the private, charitable system because of the dependency relationship it creates (Beck 1971, 218). In short, for all its strengths and value, private, charitable support cannot easily escape its "Lady Bountiful" heritage and establish a claim to assistance as a right.

Philanthropic Amateurism. One final problem with the voluntary system has been its association with amateur approaches to coping with human problems. In part, this has been a reflection of the paternalism of the sector noted above: for a considerable period of time, the problems of poverty and want were attributed to the moral turpitude of the poor. Care of the poor, the insane, the unwed mothers was therefore appropriately entrusted to well-meaning amateurs and those whose principal calling was moral suasion and religious instruction, not medical aid or job training.

As sociological and psychological theory advanced, however, these approaches lost favor and emphasis turned to more professional treatment modes involving trained social workers and counselors. Agencies stressing volunteer effort and limited by dependence on contributions from providing adequate wages were in a poor position to attract such professional personnel. It was partly for this reason that social welfare advocates of the late nineteenth and early twentieth centuries opposed public support for private charitable institutions, fearing this would siphon off resources needed to build an adequate system of professional, public care. As one of these advocates put it in 1914: "No appropriations should be made to charities under private management until the reasonable needs of the charities managed and supported by the state have been fully met and an adequate system of state institutions developed" (Fleisher 1914, 112).

Summary: A Theory of Government-Nonprofit Partnership

In short, for all its strengths, the voluntary sector has a number of inherent weaknesses as a mechanism for responding to the human service needs of an advanced industrial society. It is limited in its ability to generate an adequate level of resources, is vulnerable to particularism and the favoritism of the wealthy, is prone to self-defeating paternalism, and has at times been associated with amateur, as opposed to professional, forms of care.

Significantly, however, the voluntary sector's weaknesses correspond well with government's strengths, and vice versa. Potentially, at least, government is in a position to generate a more reliable stream of resources, to set priorities on the basis of a democratic political process instead of the wishes of the wealthy, to offset part of the paternalism of the charitable system by making access to care a right instead of a privilege, and to improve the quality of care by instituting quality-control standards. By the same token, however, voluntary organizations are in a better position than government to personalize the provision of services, to operate on a smaller scale, to adjust care to the needs of clients rather than to the structure of government agencies, and to permit a degree of competition among service providers. Under these circumstances, neither the replacement of the voluntary sector by government, nor the replacement of government by the voluntary sector, makes as much sense as collaboration between the two. In short, viewed from a theoretical perspective that acknowledges the widespread pattern of third-party government in the American version of the modern welfare state, and that posits the voluntary sector as the principal mechanism for providing collective goods, but one that has certain inherent limitations or "failures," extensive collaboration between government and the nonprofit sector emerges not as an unwarranted aberration, but as a logical and theoretically sensible compromise. The "voluntary failure" theory of the voluntary sector and the "third-party government" theory of the American welfare state outlined here thus allow us to come to terms with the reality of government-nonprofit relationships far more effectively than the alternative concepts now in use. Given the fundamental importance of these relationships, this is reason enough to lend these theories some credence.

PART II

Prevailing Realities: The Nonprofit Sector and Government

Until very recently the nonprofit sector was largely overlooked both in policy discussions and academic research. As a consequence, neither the overall scope and character of this sector nor the true extent of its interactions with the state was known with any precision.

The chapters in part 2 report on my early attempts to fill these gross gaps in knowledge about the American nonprofit sector. The first chapter in this section (chap. 3) clarifies the definition of this set of institutions and then offers an overview of its scale and structure drawing on data generated from U.S. Internal Revenue Service data files. Chapter 4 explores the character of this sector in more detail through a survey of nonprofit human service organizations carried out in a cross section of sixteen local areas spread broadly across the country. Chapters 5, 6, and 7 concentrate on nonprofit involvement with government. In chapter 5 the focus is on the federal, or national, government, which as of 1980 was providing a larger share of the income of nonprofit organizations than all sources of private giving combined. In chapter 6 attention turns to the local level through a detailed tracing of federal, state, and local government spending, and overall government contracting with nonprofit and for-profit service providers. Finally, chapter 7 summarizes the pattern of interactions between the non-profit sector and the state.

What emerges quite clearly from these chapters is the conclusion that the nonprofit sector has hardly withered away with the expansion of the modern American welfare state. On the contrary, it has grown apace, and it has done so not in spite of, but to an important extent because of, the growth of the state. The result is a diverse and varied set of institutions connected to government at all levels through a rich network of interactions that differ markedly from place to place in response to local circumstances, traditions, and needs.

CHAPTER 3

What Is the Nonprofit Sector?

An Overview

In order to make sense of the relationship between government and the private, nonprofit sector, it is necessary to begin with a clear understanding of what this sector is. This is particularly important in view of the general lack of attention that has been paid to this set of institutions in both public policy debates and academic research over the past several decades, and the considerable confusion that surrounds it as a consequence. Contributing to the confusion as well is the wide assortment of entities that qualify for tax-exempt or nonprofit status under U.S. tax laws. In fact, the Internal Revenue Code makes provision for over twenty different types of tax-exempt organizations, ranging from chambers of commerce to burial societies, from mutual insurance companies to community-based development organizations. Sorting out these organizations is therefore a major undertaking.

Types of Nonprofit Organizations

For our purposes here, three crucial dimensions of this range of organizations can usefully guide such a sorting-out process: first, whether the organization is essentially member-serving (i.e., focused on providing services to the organization's own members) or public-serving (i.e., focused on providing services to a broader public); second, whether the organization actually provides services or merely distributes funds to other service providers; and third, whether the services the organization provides are secular or sacramental and religious.

Based on these dimensions, it is possible to group most nonprofit organizations into four more or less distinct classes. The first are *funding agencies,* or fund-raising intermediaries, which exist not so much to deliver services as to channel resources to those who do. Included here are private foundations, United Way organizations, Blue Cross and Blue Shield, religious fund-raising federations, and the like. The second group of nonprofits are *member-serving organizations* that exist primarily to provide goods or services to their immediate members, rather than to society or the community at large. Included here are professional organizations (e.g., the bar associations), labor unions, cooperatives, trade associations, mutual insurance companies, and the like. The third are *public-benefit organizations* that exist primarily to serve others, to provide goods or services (including information or advocacy) to those in need or otherwise to contribute to the general welfare. Included here are educational institutions, cultural institutions, social welfare agencies, day care centers, nursing homes, hospitals, and the like. The fourth category embraces religious congregations or other organizations pursuing essentially sacramental religious functions.

Of these four types of nonprofit organizations, the ones of greatest concern to us here are those in the third group. These are the organizations most directly involved in delivering services that promote community welfare or serve broad public or educational purposes.[1] We will refer to these organizations as "public-benefit service organizations."[2]

These public-benefit service organizations have long played a vital role in American life. They supply a considerable portion of the social services, health care, education, research, culture, community improvement, and public advocacy that occurs in this country. In the process they provide an important mechanism by which groups of citizens can band together in support of a wide variety of community purposes and a channel through which philanthropic impulses can be applied to worthwhile goals.

How Large Is the Nonprofit Service Sector?

Despite their importance, however, until recently we have known little about these organizations. To be sure, nonprofit organizations other than churches are required each year to file a special return (form 990) with the Internal Revenue Service listing all receipts as well as related financial data. Although portions of the resulting data are extracted from these forms by the Internal Revenue Service and converted into data files, this process has gross imperfections that have impeded serious analysis. For one thing, there is considerable double counting because service providers and funding agents are grouped together in the data. A United Way grant to a nonprofit organization thus shows up twice, once as revenue for United Way and once as revenue for the service organization. Although the Internal Revenue Service has an activity code system that could be used to reduce this double counting, in practice the coding system is very flawed, and many organizations are coded incorrectly.[3] Beyond this, compliance with the reporting requirements is extremely uneven. Numerous organizations apparently do not file their forms, and others do so incorrectly. Finally, the information extracted from the forms by the Internal Revenue Service is limited and does not include many data items needed to analyze agency finances with care.

Fortunately a much more rigorous body of statistical data on the nonprofit sector became available in 1981 when the Census Bureau published the results of a special survey it conducted of tax-exempt service providers in 1977. Drawing on IRS lists of nonprofit organizations and other sources,[4] the Census Bureau made a serious effort to exclude funding organizations and eliminate double counting in the data it collected.[5]

By "aging" the census data to 1980 and adjusting the IRS data to exclude funding organizations and to take account of the miscoding of entries, it was possible to develop a composite estimate of the size of the nonprofit sector as of 1980 by averaging these two.[6]

The results of this analysis, reported in figure 3.1, indicate that the public-benefit service portion of the American nonprofit sector had expenditures in 1980 of approximately $116 billion. This represented about 5 percent of the gross domestic product. Quite clearly, this set of organizations represents a major economic force.

These expenditures are not, of course, spread evenly among all types of nonprofit organizations. Rather, as figure 3.1 also shows, health organizations—mostly hospitals—accounted in 1980 for 60 percent of all nonprofit expenditures. Education organizations ac-

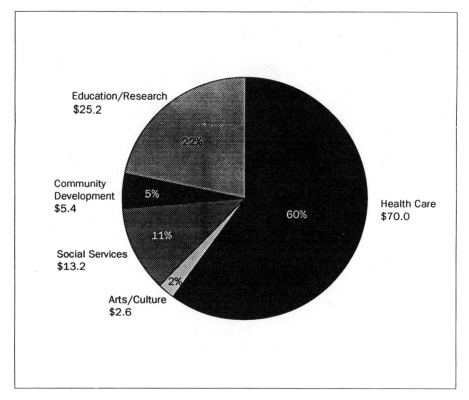

Figure 3.1 The nonprofit public-benefit service sector, 1980, in billions of dollars. Total expenditures: $116.4. *Source:* Author's estimates based on U.S. Census Bureau and Internal Revenue Service data.

counted for another 22 percent. This means that all the remaining types of nonprofit agencies—day care centers, family counseling programs, neighborhood groups, advocacy organizations, arts agencies, and others—accounted for less than 20 percent of the total expenditures. Yet these organizations still represent a major presence in communities throughout the country. Clearly, the nonprofit sector has not withered away with the growth of government over the past several decades. To the contrary, this set of organizations remains a very vital force.

The Private Philanthropic Base

While maintaining, and possibly expanding, its economic position, the nonprofit sector has experienced important changes in the compo-

TABLE 3.1

Private Charitable Giving as a Share of Nonprofit Revenues, 1980

($ Billions)

Type of Organization	Total Revenues	Private Giving	Private Giving as Percentage of Revenues
Religious congregations	$22.3	$22.3	100%
Service providers	116.4	26.8	23
Total	$138.7	$49.1	35%

SOURCES: Nonprofit revenues based on estimates developed from census and IRS data; data on private giving from AAFRC (1985).

sition of its revenues over the past several decades or longer. In particular, the sector has gone well beyond its roots in private charitable giving. As noted in table 3.1, private giving, which embraces contributions or grants to charitable organizations by individuals, foundations, and corporations, totaled $49.1 billion in 1980, of which $22.3 billion went to churches and other religious congregations and $26.8 billion went to the service organizations of primary interest to us here (AAFRC 1985, 4–5). In other words, of the $116 billion in revenues received by nonreligious, nonprofit service providers in 1980, only 23 percent came from private giving. Even if religious organizations were included, moreover, the private philanthropic share of total nonprofit revenues would still not exceed 35 percent. In fact, these data on private giving probably overstate the extent of private support in the annual operating budgets of nonprofit organizations because they include contributions to endowments and gifts of appreciated assets like art collections that are not available for annual operating support.[7]

This limited reliance on private giving as a source of revenues is evident, moreover, in virtually all the major segments of the nonprofit sector. Although the data on private giving are not grouped exactly the same way as the overall revenue data and are somewhat overstated (because multiyear bequests and endowment contributions are included as if they were available for spending in the year in which they are made), it is still possible to shed some light on the extent of reliance on private giving by different types of nonprofit organizations if we compare our estimates of overall nonprofit revenues with the available data on private giving to different types of recipients. What emerges from such an analysis, as reflected in table 3.2, is that private giving constitutes less than half of the revenues of all types of nonprofit organizations except cultural organizations. In the case of cultural organizations, the data on private giving are clearly inflated by the inclusion of multiyear bequests and endowments as well as gifts of paintings and

TABLE 3.2

Private Giving as a Share of Nonprofit Revenues, by Type of Organization, 1980

($ Billions)

Type of Organization	Total Nonprofit Annual Revenues	Private Giving	Private Giving as a Percentage of Total Nonprofit Revenues
Social service	$13.2	$5.0	38%
Community development, civic	5.4	1.5	28
Education/research	25.2	6.9	27
Health care	70.0	6.7	10
Arts/culture	2.6	3.2[a]	[a]
Other[b]		3.5	
Total	$116.4	$26.8	23%

SOURCE: See Table 3.1.

NOTES: [a]Excess of private giving over total annual revenues of arts organizations reflects the inclusion of endowment contributions and the value of contributed artwork in the private giving data.

[b]Other includes a mix of organizations involved with foreign aid and technical assistance, international activities and education, and foundation endowment.

other art recorded at market value but not readily available for organizational support.

Summary

The nonprofit sector thus remains a sizable and important component of American social and economic life. Embodying a distinctive national commitment to private action and voluntary association, nonprofit organizations have held their own in a shifting economic climate by taking full advantage of their distinctive base of private charitable support, but also by not being bound by it. In particular, nonprofit organizations have clearly developed other sources of financial support and formed supportive links with other sectors of American society. One of these routes of evolution has been in the direction of increased reliance on self-generated income from dues, fees, and sales. Equally important, however, have been the relationships nonprofit organizations have established with government—relationships that are now very much under challenge. Subsequent chapters will examine more closely the nature of these relationships between the nonprofit sector and government, and the impact on them of the major changes in federal policy that occurred in the 1980s and early 1990s. Before turning to these matters, however, it is useful to go beyond this national overview to examine the nonprofit sector in its local setting.

CHAPTER 4

The Nonprofit Sector at the Local Level

Although the nonprofit sector is an important national presence in the United States, its real roots lie at the local level, in the thousands of cities, towns, and communities scattered throughout the country. What is more, due to the gross imperfections of the existing national registers, the only way to get a reliable profile of even the national nonprofit sector is to focus on the local level and examine a reasonable cross section of local areas.[1]

To close the gross gaps in knowledge that have long existed about the American nonprofit sector, a group of colleagues and I launched a major survey in sixteen local field sites selected to provide a reasonable cross section of the nation in terms of region, size, socioeconomic condition, and philanthropic tradition.[2] These field sites included one large metropolitan area, one medium-sized metropolitan area, one small metropolitan area, and one rural county in each of the four major census regions of the country (see table 4.1).

This survey focused on the human services component of the nonprofit sector, namely, the organizations that actually provide services to a broad, general public, not just to their own membership. Included

TABLE 4.1
Field Sites for Local Survey Work

Northeast	South
New York	Dallas/Ft. Worth
Pittsburgh	Atlanta
Providence, R.I.	Jackson, Miss.
Fayette County, Pa.	Warren County, Miss.
Midwest	*West*
Chicago	San Francisco
Minneapolis/St. Paul	Phoenix
Flint, Mich.	Boise
Tuscola County, Mich.	Pinal County, Ariz.

in this definition are day care centers, programs for the elderly, museums, symphony orchestras, YMCAs, job training programs, advocacy groups, and many more. To learn about these agencies, we first developed a complete roster of them in our sixteen study sites drawing on IRS records as well as local directories and other information sources. We then distributed a mail survey to the entire population of such agencies in our medium- and smaller-sized sites, and to large samples of these agencies in the five largest sites. Only hospitals and higher education institutions were excluded from our study in order to make our survey more manageable and because good data on these two types of nonprofit organizations are already available (from the American Hospital Association in the case of hospitals and the National Center for Education Statistics in the case of higher education institutions). Altogether, 7,000 agencies were surveyed and more than 3,400 responded, yielding a response rate of 49.7 percent, which is quite good for research of this type.[3] Two years later, in the spring of 1984, we resurveyed the original respondents and received about 2,300 returns that could be linked to our Wave 1 data files. The result is an enormously rich body of data that challenges much of the conventional wisdom about this long-overlooked set of institutions. Five findings of this research in particular deserve mention here.[4]

Key Findings

Overall Scale

In the first place, the data resulting from our survey demonstrate even more forcefully than the national data presented in chapter 3 the tremendous role that the nonprofit sector plays in local communities throughout the United States. In fact, measured in economic terms

TABLE 4.2
*Distribution of Nonprofit Human Service Organizations
by Size of 1982 Expenditures*

	All Sites	
Agency Size	Percentage of Organizations	Percentage of Sector Expenditures
Less than $100,000	40%	2%
$100,000–$499,999	35	12
$500,000–$1 million	10	10
Over 1 million	15	76
Total	100%	100%
Expenditures		
Median	$150,000	
Mean	$758,058	

SOURCE: Salamon Nonprofit Sector Project Survey, rounds 1 and 2.

the nonprofit sector equals or surpasses the role played by local government. In the Pittsburgh metropolitan area, for example, the expenditures of private, nonprofit organizations exceed the total budget of the county government by a factor of six to one (Gutowski, Salamon, and Pittman 1984). In the Twin Cities area of Minnesota, the expenditures of the local nonprofit sector are as large as the combined budgets of the city of Minneapolis, the city of St. Paul, Hennepin County, and Ramsey County (Lukermann, Kimmich, and Salamon 1984). In the other local areas as well, the nonprofit sector turns out to be as significant an economic force as local government.

Concentration of Resources

These resources are not distributed evenly among nonprofit agencies, however. To the contrary, they are highly concentrated. While the largest proportion of nonprofit agencies are small, the vast majority of the resources are expended by a relative handful of large agencies. Thus, as table 4.2 shows, 40 percent of the nonprofit organizations in this study have expenditures of under $100,000, but these small agencies account for only 2 percent of the sector's resources. By contrast, the large agencies, those with budgets over $1 million, represent only 15 percent of the agencies yet account for three-quarters of the sector's expenditures. This picture of resource concentration is all the more striking, moreover, in view of the fact that it does not even include the largest institutions in the sector—hospitals and higher education institutions.

TABLE 4.3

Percentage of Agencies That Specialize in a Particular Service Area or Client Group

Service Category	Percentage of Agencies
Principal service area[a]	
Social services	24%
Culture/arts/recreation	18
Multiservices	16
Education/research	13
Health services	8
Institutional/residential care	6
Housing/community development	4
Employment/training/income support	4
Advocacy/legal services	4
Mental health	3
Total	100%
Client focus[b]	
Black	15%
Hispanic	4
Asian-American	3
Poor	29
Unemployed	19
Single parents	15
Disabled	13
Ex-offenders	2

SOURCE: Salamon Nonprofit Sector Project Survey, rounds 1 and 2.
NOTES: [a]Primary service area is defined as the area in which an agency spends 50 percent or more of its funds. If an agency does not meet this criterion, it was classified as a "multiservice" organization.
    [b]Agencies in which more than 50 percent of clients belong to a specified target group.

Sector Diversity and Client Focus

A third key finding of our survey is the tremendous diversity of the nonprofit sector, both in terms of activities and client focus. Although the popular image portrays nonprofits as principally focused on providing services to the poor, this stereotype does not reflect the realities of today's nonprofit world. Less than one-third of the agencies in our sample said that they focused primarily on serving a low-income or poor clientele. This finding in part reflects the broad range of the sector's activities. Nonprofits not only provide social services, they also offer culture/arts/recreational activities, education and research, health-related services, and a host of other activities that address broad community needs (see table 4.3). Furthermore, far fewer agencies focus on serving a particular ethnic, racial, or special need group than some theories of the nonprofit sector would suggest. Rather, most agencies serve a broad cross section of community members. Clearly,

TABLE 4.4
Revenue Sources of Nonprofit Human Service Organizations, 1982
(*n* = 2,304)

	Share of Total Nonprofit Revenue from Source	Percentage of Organizations with Any Support from Source
Government	38.4%	60.3%
Fees/dues/charges	29.6	68.9
Private giving		
Direct individual giving	6.4	58.2
United Way	5.4	23.4
Foundation grants	3.5	38.0
Corporate gifts	3.2	33.6
Other federated funders	1.5	6.9
Religious organizations	1.3	13.0
Subtotal, private giving	21.3%	N/A
Endowment/investments	4.6	32.7
Other[a]	5.7	23.6
Unspecified	0.4	N/A
Total	100.0%	N/A

SOURCE: Salamon Nonprofit Sector Survey, rounds 1 and 2.
NOTE: [a]Includes such sources of revenue as sales of products, special fund-raising events, and rental of facilities.

the nonprofit sector is not a homogenous entity with a common set of goals, purposes, or objectives.

Revenue Sources

Not only does the nonprofit sector serve a far more diverse clientele than is often assumed, but also it draws its resources from a far more varied array of sources. According to common stereotypes, American nonprofit organizations receive the lion's share of their resources from private charitable sources—from the donations of individuals, corporations, and foundations. In fact, however, the survey revealed that even excluding hospitals and universities, the largest single source of income for the nation's nonprofit human service organizations is not private giving at all, but government. In particular, as shown in table 4.4, 38 percent of the sector's 1982 income came from government, and 60 percent of the agencies received some portion of their funding from government sources. This was true, moreover, despite a significant budget cut pushed through by the Reagan administration in 1981. The second major source of funding is income from dues, fees, and service charges, accounting for 30 percent of the total. Fee income

TABLE 4.5

Nonprofit-Sector Income by Service Area and Funding Source, 1982

| | Percentage of Income from | | | | | |
	Government	Fees	Private Giving	Endowment Investments	Other	Total
Mental health	62%	28%	6%	3%	1%	100%
Social services	54	14	27	3	2	100
Legal services/advocacy	53	14	28	1	5	100
Housing/community development	52	27	18	3	1	100
Employment/training/income support	51	10	13	3	23	100
Institutional/residential care	50	32	12	4	2	100
Multiservices	44	24	26	3	3	100
Health	30	52	13	3	3	100
Education/research	26	32	30	9	6	100
Culture/arts/recreation	14	28	31	11	17	100
All agencies	**38%**	**30%**	**21%**	**5%**	**6%**	**100%**

SOURCE: Salamon Nonprofit Sector Project Survey.
NOTE: Numbers may not add to 100 percent because of rounding.

also is the most widely used source of agency support with nearly seven out of ten nonprofit agencies collecting this type of revenue. By contrast, private charitable giving ranks third among all major funding sources and accounted for only 21 percent of the sector's 1982 income. What is most surprising is the relatively small proportion of agencies that actually received private philanthropic support. Only 38 percent of the agencies in our study received foundation grants, 34 percent corporate gifts, and 23 percent United Way funding. Direct individual giving is more prevalent but still benefits a smaller proportion of agencies than do government and fee income. Although philanthropic giving may be a distinctive feature of the nonprofit sector, in other words, it is government that provides the major source of support.

Variations in Funding Patterns by Service Area and Community

Aggregate statistics, like those presented above, tend to mask differences among the various components of the sector. For example, as table 4.5 shows, while the organizations in six of the ten service areas in our study relied on government support for half or more of their funds, those in four others did not. Thus, fee income was the principal funding source for health services and education/research organizations, while private giving was the principal source of support in only one service area—culture/arts/recreation.

Similarly, in each of our study communities there was considerable

TABLE 4.6
Nonprofit Revenues, by Source, by Site, 1982

Site	Percentage of Organizations' Total Revenues Coming from		
	Government	Fees/Dues/ Charges	Private Giving
Jackson	66%	7%	25%
Pittsburgh	51	21	17
Providence	51	27	16
Boise	44	14	34
San Francisco	44	33	15
New York	43	17	20
Phoenix	41	28	23
Minneapolis/St. Paul	37	33	22
Atlanta	36	34	23
Dallas/Fort Worth	34	25	29
Flint	33	32	17
Chicago	32	29	29
All-site average[a]	**38%**	**30%**	**21%**

SOURCE: Salamon Nonprofit Sector Project Survey.
NOTE: [a]Includes data from the four nonmetropolitan study sites as well as from the twelve metropolitan sites listed.

variation in funding patterns (see table 4.6). Although government funding was the principal source of support for nonprofits in each local community, the extent of reliance on government ranged from 66 percent in Jackson, Mississippi, to 32 percent in Chicago. As in our national picture, fee income tended to be the second most important source of funding in seven of our twelve metropolitan sites. In only four communities—Jackson, Boise, New York, and Dallas/Fort Worth—did private giving rank as the number two source of income.

Conclusions

The data presented here hardly exhaust the insights available from this survey of nonprofit human service agencies. They should be sufficient, however, to demonstrate that this sector is far more complex, and plays a far more significant role in our national life, than is widely understood. Nonprofit organizations are engaged in a bewildering array of activities that reflect the diversity of human interests and the full scope of community life. Far from focusing exclusively on the poor or needy, they serve a broad cross section of the population and respond to a wide variety of needs. What is more, these organizations come in all shapes and sizes, with most of the agencies being small, but most of the expenditures made by a relative handful of large institutions. Finally, and perhaps most interestingly for the purposes of this book, these organizations have grown well beyond the private charitable base that once provided their primary source of income. In particular, government has emerged as a major source of income both overall and in most of the individual fields of activity.

The findings presented here have important implications not only for our understanding of the nonprofit sector, however. They also have important implications for our understanding of the modern American welfare state. Most strikingly, they challenge conventional images that depict government programs largely run by government bureaucrats. What the data here suggest, rather, is a reality of extensive cooperative relationships between government and nonprofit agencies. To make sense of the survey results, therefore, it is useful to turn our attention from the nonprofit sector itself to the interactions between this sector and the state.

CHAPTER 5

The Federal Budget and Nonprofit Revenues

As a first step toward understanding the relationship of government to the nonprofit sector in the American version of the modern welfare state, it is useful to focus on the federal, or national, government level. This is so, first of all, because much of the government human service spending originates at this level. Equally important, the significant retrenchment in social welfare spending that dominated the national policy process throughout the 1980s and into the 1990s was premised in important part on the contention that little relationship existed between the federal government and nonprofit organizations, that the growth of federal involvement had essentially displaced the nonprofit sector. Under these circumstances, it becomes crucial to examine this relationship with some care.

When this is done, it becomes clear that the relationship between government and nonprofit institutions in this country is far different, and far more complex, than prevailing theories acknowledge. While competing with nonprofit organizations in some areas, the federal government has also extensively underwritten their activities and stimulated the expansion and elaboration of their role.

TABLE 5.1
*Federal Subsidies to Nonprofit Organizations
through Deductibility of Charitable Contributions, FY 1985*
($ Billions)

Type of Organization	Amount	As a Percentage of Total
Education	$1.4	10%
Health	1.6	12
Other	10.4	78
Total	$13.4	100%

SOURCE: U.S. Office of Management and Budget (1988), G-30, G-40.

Federal tax policy, for example, by exempting individual and corporate charitable contributions from taxation, effectively delivers an implicit subsidy to the sector. According to U.S. Treasury data, this subsidy was estimated to be worth $13.4 billion in FY 1985. As table 5.1 shows, about 10 percent of this implicit subsidy flows to the education component of the sector, about 12 percent to the health care component, and the remaining 78 percent to all other nonprofit organizations including churches.

Even more important than these tax subsidies, however, are the direct programmatic resources that nonprofit organizations receive as a result of their participation in federal programs. The growth of federal activism, it turns out, has not involved simply an expansion of the federal bureaucracy and the displacement of nonprofit providers. Rather, the federal government has turned to a host of "third parties" to help it carry out its expanded responsibilities, and nonprofit organizations have figured prominently among them.[1] In the process, an elaborate pattern of "nonprofit federalism" has taken shape linking governments at all levels to nonprofit organizations across a broad front. Far from being an alternative to or a competitor of nonprofit organizations, the federal government has emerged as a partner of these organizations, financing nonprofit operations, encouraging nonprofit involvement in new fields, and often helping to create new types of nonprofit entities where none had existed.

To be sure, these arrangements are not without their strains. Nonprofit organizations complain about excessive paperwork, insufficient provision for overhead costs, and burdensome regulatory requirements. Yet few doubt that, on balance, these relationships have been quite productive, providing needed resources for nonprofit action and creating a useful amalgam of public and private capabilities.[2] What, then, is the nature and scale of this federal support to nonprofit organizations?

The Origins of Nonprofit Federalism

To answer this question effectively, it is important to recognize from the outset that government support for nonprofit organizations is not a recent development in this country. To the contrary, it is rooted deeply in American history. In fact, some of this country's premier private, nonprofit institutions—such as Harvard University, Massachusetts General Hospital, the Metropolitan Museum of Art, and Columbia University—owe their origins and early sustenance to public-sector support. "Through most of American history," one close observer thus has written, "government has been an active partner and financier of the Third Sector to a much greater extent than is commonly recognized" (Nielsen 1979, 14).

Although the partnership between government and the nonprofit sector has deep roots in American history, it has expanded in both scope and scale in recent decades. Moreover, it has taken new and more elaborate form with the emergence of the federal government as a key participant in the funding and support of nonprofit action.

Typical of these developments has been the evolution of the mixed economy of social services. Prior to the 1960s, the provision of social services was a shared responsibility of the voluntary sector and state or local governments. State government activities throughout much of the nineteenth century focused on the development of institutions for the care of deaf, blind, and mentally or physically disabled persons, while private agencies handled home care and various forms of direct assistance. As state and local government involvement in the social services field expanded during the Progressive Era at the turn of the century, however, it was accompanied by an increased flow of public funds to voluntary agencies to provide a broader range of services. In the process, a significant pattern of government-nonprofit partnership began to take shape to cope with the nation's social service needs. Thus by the 1890s half of government spending in support of the poor in New York City was channeled through private, voluntary agencies that delivered the services financed by public funds (Warner 1894, 336–37).

Although the federal government entered the social welfare field in the 1930s, in the three decades that followed, Washington concentrated almost exclusively on providing financial support to state and local governments to help them support their cash assistance programs for orphans, the disabled, and the needy elderly. Not until the early 1960s did the federal government become a significant provider of funds for social services. As it did so, however, it made specific provision, through the 1962 amendments to the Social Security Act and even more so in the 1967 amendments, for state agencies to enlist nonprofit organizations in the actual delivery of the services.[3] By 1971, in fact, purchases from nonprofit providers constituted about 25 percent of the expenditures under various social service programs that in 1972 were folded into the federal Title XX program, and that ultimately became part of the Social Services Block Grant program in 1981. This pattern of contracting out has, moreover, increased even further in recent years (Benton et al. 1978; U.S. Department of Health and Human Services 1981).

Federal support for nonprofit organizations has evolved similarly in other fields as well—in health care, education, research, neighborhood development, and the arts. In some areas, federal support has led to the creation of whole new classes of nonprofit organizations to provide a range of services that existing institutions were not equipped to handle and that the federal government did not want to handle on its own. In this way, the federal government has significantly extended the structure of the nonprofit sector. Typical of these developments was the stimulus the federal government gave to the creation of a network of community health clinics in poverty areas throughout the country. Funded originally out of resources provided under the Economic Opportunity Act of 1964, almost nine hundred such centers existed as of 1980. Other examples include the creation of a network of multicounty economic development districts to stimulate economic development in distressed areas, the formation of community action agencies and Head Start programs for disadvantaged children, and the organization of metropolitan councils of government (COGs) to encourage regional planning in metropolitan areas.

Scope of Government Support

Through these and other channels, an elaborate system of federal support for nonprofit organizations has taken shape. Broadly speaking, this support flows along three main routes, although it takes a variety of different forms. As illustrated in figure 5.1, one of these routes (depicted by a *solid line*) involves direct financial relationships between the federal government and nonprofit organizations. An ex-

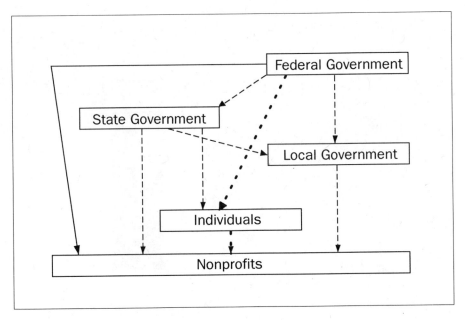

Figure 5.1. Channels of public funding of nonprofit organizations.

ample would be a federal research grant to a private medical school. The second route (depicted by a *broken line*) involves federal grants to state and local governments, which then contract out to nonprofit providers or others to deliver a particular service. A classic example here is the Social Service Block Grant program, which channels federal assistance to the states and leaves to the states the option of providing the services themselves, contracting with other levels of government, or contracting with for-profit or nonprofit providers. Finally, the third route (depicted by a *dotted line*) involves federal in-kind assistance to individuals, who then are free to purchase services from nonprofit institutions. This is the route followed in the college student assistance programs and Medicare.

Despite the scale and importance of this system of support, no comprehensive statistical data on it are assembled anywhere in the federal government. There is no data source on federal support to nonprofit organizations that is comparable, for example, to the special analysis prepared by the Office of Management and Budget each year on the extent of federal grant-in-aid support to state and local governments. Nor does reliable information exist on funds channeled to nonprofits by individual programs. As a consequence, policymakers and non-

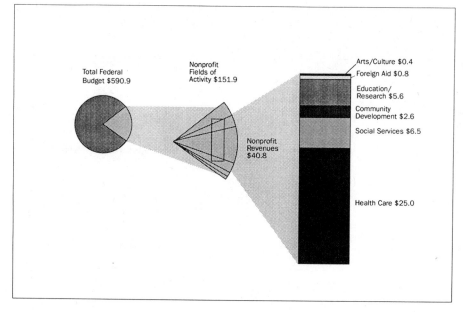

Figure 5.2. Nonprofit revenues from federal sources, FY 1980, in billions of dollars. *Source:* Based on the application of authors' nonprofit share estimates to actual FY 1980 outlay data in U.S. Office of Management and Budget, *Budget of the U.S. Government, FY 1982,* unpublished backup materials.

profit managers have had to operate very much in the dark with respect to the effects of budget decisions on this important sector of national life.

To remedy this situation, estimates were developed of the share of program resources flowing to nonprofit organizations under each of the federal programs identified as being relevant to the nonprofit sector. These estimates were based on detailed examination of programmatic data, scrutiny of existing program evaluations, and extensive discussions with program managers.[4]

Drawing on this analysis, we found that in FY 1980 federal support to the nonprofit sector, exclusive of tax subsidies, amounted to more than $40 billion, as noted in figure 5.2. Given the size of the sector discussed earlier, this means that the federal government accounted for about 35 percent of the sector's total revenues. By comparison, as we have seen (see chap. 4), private charitable contributions to nonprofit service providers from individuals, corporations, and foundations combined totaled $26.8 billion that same year. In other words,

TABLE 5.2

Nonprofit Revenues from Federal Sources Compared to Private Giving and Total
Nonprofit Revenues, by Type of Organization, FY 1980

($ Billions unless Otherwise Indicated)

Type of Organization	Total Revenue	Private Giving	Federal Programs	Federal Support as a Percentage of Total Revenue
Social service[a]	$13.2[a]	$5.0	$7.3[a]	55%
Community development, civic	5.4	1.5	2.6	48
Education/research	25.2	6.9	5.6	22
Health care	70.0	6.7	25.0	36
Arts/culture	2.6	3.2[b]	0.4	
Other		3.5		
Total	$116.4	$26.8	$40.8	35%

NOTE: Columns may not add to totals due to rounding.
[a]Includes social services and foreign aid.
[b]Includes endowment revenue and contributions of appreciated assets such as works of art.

nonprofit organizations other than churches derived a larger share of their revenues from the federal government than from all private giving combined.[5]

As figure 5.2 shows, more than 60 percent of this federal support to nonprofit organizations flowed to health care organizations, mostly hospitals. This reflects the tremendous scale of the federal Medicare program, which reimburses hospitals for medical care to the elderly, and the Medicaid program, which underwrites hospital and nursing home care for the poor. In addition, however, social service and education and research institutions also receive substantial amounts of federal support. In fact, as shown in table 5.2, nonprofit social service organizations received over half their total revenues from federal sources in FY 1980. Other types of nonprofit organizations were somewhat less dependent on federal sources of support, but for virtually all, this support is a significant component of overall revenues, typically outdistancing private giving by a substantial margin.[6] Under these circumstances, nonprofit organizations have a significant stake in federal budget decisions. These decisions are now one of the major determinants of the fiscal health of the sector, and of the viability of several of its components.

Conclusion

In short, an immense and complex set of partnership arrangements has developed between the federal government and nonprofit organizations. These arrangements have deep roots in American history. Most of them operate indirectly, through state and local governments and individual purchasers of services. Taken together, however, they account for a substantial share of nonprofit revenues, especially for social service and community development organizations. Indeed, in dollar terms, they represent a larger share of nonprofit revenues than all private giving combined. While the relationships that lie behind these figures have not been without their strains, they also have had much to recommend them. They have offered an innovative way to combine the revenue-raising advantages of the federal government with the service-providing advantages of private, voluntary agencies. As such, they represent an important adaptation in the design of the modern welfare state.

CHAPTER 6

The Government-Nonprofit Partnership in Local Welfare Regimes

Although the federal government has become the predominant source of government human service spending in the United States, it is by no means the only source. State and local governments also play significant roles, in both service delivery and finance. The general picture of government-nonprofit relationships portrayed in chapter 5 thus obscures as much as it reveals. Much of the federal activity, as we have seen, operates through state and local governments, which often add their own resources and, in turn, have wide discretion about whether to provide services themselves or subcontract with private nonprofit or for-profit providers. The result is not a single, nationwide welfare system, but a crazy-quilt pattern of different welfare "regimes" that reflect widely divergent local attitudes toward human service provision and varied traditions of reliance on nonprofit organizations. To understand the true character of government-nonprofit relations in this country, therefore, it is necessary to go beyond an exclusively federal focus and examine a cross section of state and local activity as well.

Unfortunately, however, the data needed to do this are even more inadequate than the data on the overall scope and structure of the nonprofit sector. While it is possible to collect the budgets of states and local governments, these documents typically cover different geographic areas, apply to different time periods, use different groupings of programs, and take very little account of the extensive flows of funds from one level of government to another. As a consequence, there is no single source to which one can turn to get a complete, unduplicated count of the extent of spending by all levels of government on a given range of services in a particular geographic area. Nor are data available on the extent of government contracting with nonprofit providers in these fields. As a consequence, leaders in both the public and private sectors, as well as the general public, are poorly equipped to set priorities, sort out public and private roles, or assess the implications of government policy changes on either the demand for nonprofit services or the revenues of nonprofit organizations.

To remedy this state of affairs, we systematically tracked federal, state, and local government spending, and overall government contracting with nonprofit and for-profit providers in six service fields (health, social services, employment and training, housing and community development, arts and recreation, and income assistance) in the same sixteen communities covered by the survey discussed in chapter 4. The result is the first comprehensive human services budget available in a comparable form across communities. The data were collected with the help of local associates living in the research sites. A standard research instrument was used, and considerable verification was carried out by a core national staff to ensure that the data collected were both accurate and comparable from community to community.[1] The resulting data shed important new light on the way our social welfare system operates. For our purposes here, four key findings are worth noting.

Key Findings

Multiple "Welfare States"

Our analysis of federal, state, and local social welfare spending in sixteen communities makes clear that, despite efforts to smooth out inequities among locales in the provision of social welfare services, immense variations remain. There is, in this sense, no single welfare state in America, but rather many distinct levels of government support and commitment to human services in different types of communities. In New York City, for example, per capita government spending in the

TABLE 6.1
Total Government Spending in Six Major Social Welfare Fields, 1982

Community	Per Capita Spending
New York City	$1,670
San Francisco, Calif.	1,633
Atlanta (Fulton County), Ga.	1,088
Chicago (Cook County), Ill.	1,076
Minneapolis (Hennepin County), Minn.	1,072
Pittsburgh (Allegheny County), Pa.	1,018
St. Paul (Ramsey County), Minn.	1,009
Providence, R.I.	996
Jackson (Hinds County), Miss.	911
Caro (Tuscola County), Mich.	821
Flint (Genesee County), Mich.	797
Casa Grande (Pinal County), Ariz.	701
Boise (Ada County), Idaho	595
Phoenix (Maricopa County), Ariz.	563
Vicksburg (Warren County), Miss.	562
Dallas (Dallas County), Tex.	506
Means	
Unweighted	$939
Weighted	$1,188

SOURCE: Compiled from federal, state, and local government sources.

six major social welfare fields we examined is more than three times the level in Dallas (see table 6.1). Although there are exceptions, government social welfare spending is generally greater in the Northeast and Midwest, and in larger communities, than elsewhere. These differences are accounted for by a combination of varying local political philosophies, financial capacities, and needs. It is interesting, however, that the areas where government spending is highest are also the areas where the nonprofit sector is most highly developed, and vice versa. This suggests that government spending and private, nonprofit activity are products of the same impulses, a finding that casts doubt on theories that posit a conflict between these two sectors.

The Dominant Fields: Health and Income Assistance

Reflecting, in part, the immense size of the federal Medicare program, spending for health care alone accounts for nearly 60 percent of government spending in the fields we examined, while income assistance accounts for an additional 25 percent. Therefore, these two program areas together account for about 85 percent of total spending.

This means that the four remaining program areas—social services, employment and training, housing and community development, and

TABLE 6.2
Federal Share of Total Government Spending for Social Welfare, 1982

Community	Federal Share
Jackson (Hinds County), Miss.	91%
Boise (Ada County), Idaho	85
Vicksburg (Warren County), Miss.	84
Dallas (Dallas County), Tex.	78
Phoenix (Maricopa County), Ariz.	77
Pittsburgh (Allegheny County), Pa.	77
Atlanta (Fulton County), Ga.	77
Providence, R.I.	73
Minneapolis (Hennepin County), Minn.	71
Flint (Genesee County), Mich.	70
Chicago (Cook County), Ill.	68
St. Paul (Ramsey County), Minn.	67
New York City	63
San Francisco, Calif.	62
Casa Grande (Pinal County), Ariz.	57
Caro (Tuscola County), Mich.	57
Means	
Unweighted	72%
Weighted	67%

SOURCE: Data compiled and estimated from federal, state, and local government sources.

arts and culture—together account for only about 15 percent of all government spending in the social welfare field. This suggests that there are real limits to the budget savings that are available in these four fields.

Federal Financing/State and Local Administration

The federal government is the dominant source of funding for government social welfare programs, as might be expected given the tremendous expansion of the federal government over the last several decades. In the six program areas of interest here the federal share of total spending in 1982 averaged approximately 70 percent (see table 6.2).

Although federal spending is prominent in all communities, however, its role varies considerably from community to community. This is likely due to differences in the socioeconomic characteristics of communities, different traditions of state and local involvement in the social welfare field, the presence of disproportionately large regional institutions in some communities, and differences in community aggressiveness in pursuing federal funds, including those that are channeled through state government. Among our sixteen study sites, the

federal share of spending ranged from 91 percent in Jackson, Mississippi, to 57 percent in Tuscola County, Michigan, and Pinal County,
Arizona. As a general rule, however, the federal government accounts
for a larger share of government human service spending in the more
conservative areas of the South and Southwest than in the larger urban
areas of the Northeast and North Central regions, where more extensive state and local government support is available.

While the federal government is the dominant source of funding
for government social welfare programs, however, state and local governments continue to play a crucial role. For one thing, state and local
governments provide about 30 percent of the funding overall and
more than 40 percent in some fields, such as social services, although
these figures vary widely among communities. Beyond their financial
role, however, state and local governments play an even more critical
role in administering social welfare programs. In fact, if Medicare is
excluded, state and local governments have administrative control
over two-thirds of the federal funds spent in these program areas in
addition to the control they have over their own programs. This is the
case because many of the federal programs channel their funds
through state and local governments. Taken together, therefore, about
80 percent of all government social welfare spending, excluding Medicare, is administered by state and local governments (see table 6.3).
These governments thus make most of the decisions about how these
services are delivered and by whom.

Nonprofit Delivery

While the federal government finances most government human
service programs, and state and local governments do most of the administration, it is nonprofit organizations that actually deliver the preponderance of the services. Despite the recent calls for "privatization"
of human services, in other words, it appears that privatization has
long been an established fact in the human service field.[2] In fact, exclusive of income assistance, governments at all levels actually deliver less
than half of the social welfare services they finance. In the typical community, government delivers directly just under two-fifths of the services it funds in these fields (see table 6.4). The remaining three-fifths
is contracted out to private nonprofit and for-profit organizations. Of
this, just over two-fifths of total government spending in social welfare
goes to nonprofits, and just under a fifth goes to for-profits. This high
level of contracting out was in place long before the Reagan adminis-

TABLE 6.3

State and Local Government Administration of Social
Welfare Programs, Exclusive of Medicare, 1982

Community	Percentage of Spending Administered by State and Local Government[a]
Caro (Tuscola County), Mich.	95%
Flint (Genesee County), Mich.	92
St. Paul (Ramsey County), Minn.	91
New York City	87
Chicago (Cook County), Ill.	86
Providence, R.I.	83
Pittsburgh (Allegheny County), Pa.	80
Atlanta (Fulton County), Ga.	80
Casa Grande (Pinal County), Ariz.	80
Minneapolis (Hennepin County), Minn.	79
San Francisco, Calif.	77
Vicksburg (Warren County), Miss.	75
Phoenix (Maricopa County), Ariz.	74
Dallas (Dallas County), Tex.	72
Boise (Ada County), Idaho	60
Jackson (Hinds County), Miss.	56
Means	
Unweighted	79%
Weighted	85%

SOURCE: Data compiled and estimated from federal, state, and local government sources.

[a]This figure excludes the large Medicare program, which is federally funded and administered. The Medicare program is a health care financing program for the elderly that makes direct payments to hospitals, doctors, and other providers of health services.

tration and was the mechanism of choice for many of the new programs of the 1960s and 1970s.

Government reliance on nonprofits to deliver publicly financed services is particularly extensive in the fields of day care, elderly services, legal services, and hospital services, in all of which nonprofits deliver over half of the publicly funded services. Nonprofits are also major providers of publicly funded services in the fields of family services, services for the disabled, child welfare services, mental health and drug abuse services, employment and training, and arts and culture.

Government's use of nonprofits also varies considerably among communities (see table 6.4). As a rule, governments in the Northeast and larger communities tend to use nonprofits more than governments in other parts of the country and smaller communities. For example, in the Pittsburgh area nonprofit organizations deliver fully half of all government-funded human services. By contrast, in Tuscola County, Michigan, they deliver only 12 percent of such government-

TABLE 6.4
Providers of Government-Funded Social Welfare Services, 1982

	Percentage of Total Spending Delivered by		
Community	Nonprofit Organizations	For-profit Enterprises	Government
Pittsburgh (Allegheny County), Pa.	50%	18%	32%
Chicago (Cook County), Ill.	48	18	35
New York City	43	18	39
Providence, R.I.	40	22	38
San Francisco, Calif.	40	19	41
St. Paul (Ramsey County), Minn.	40	24	36
Minneapolis (Hennepin County), Minn.	38	21	42
Phoenix (Maricopa County), Ariz.	37	27	36
Vicksburg (Warren County), Miss.	34	27	37
Boise (Ada County), Idaho	33	17	50
Flint (Genesee County), Mich.	28	31	41
Dallas (Dallas County), Tex.	27	24	49
Atlanta (Fulton County), Ga.	27	20	53
Jackson (Hinds County), Miss.	23	16	59
Casa Grande (Pinal County), Ariz.	16	18	66
Caro (Tuscola County), Mich.	12	18	71
Means			
Unweighted	34%	21%	45%
Weighted	42%	19%	39%

SOURCE: Data compiled and estimated from federal, state, and local government sources.

funded services. Generally speaking, government use of the nonprofit sector is greatest where the sector is strongest, and most limited where the sector is weakest.

What all this means is that, in the human service field at least, less attention needs to be given to building public-private partnerships from scratch than to improving those that already exist. At a minimum, in our zeal to encourage privatization, care must be taken to avoid damaging the extensive partnership arrangements that already exist between the public sector and the private nonprofit sector.

Implications

The data presented here on government spending and use of nonprofits make it clear that government budget cuts and program changes of the sort that were pursued throughout the 1980s and early 1990s can have very different impacts on different communities. Beyond this, these data demonstrate that it is not possible to understand the nonprofit sector by examining it in isolation. In practice, nonprofit organizations are tied closely to the public sector in the human service field in a complex network of relationships that vary markedly from place to place. Because of the complexities of our governmental system and the inadequacy of existing data sources, it has been difficult to see these relationships very clearly. Yet their importance cannot be denied. What is more, the country presents a crazy-quilt pattern of welfare regimes, each representing its own distinctive variation on the common theme of mixed federal, state, and local finance and administration, and public and private provision of human services. The particular mixture in any particular place reflects the specifics of local history and tradition, but the existence of mixed public and private roles and widespread public-private collaboration is a constant almost everywhere.

To date, this complex nonsystem has escaped serious scrutiny or widespread understanding. Yet, until its basic contours come into better view, our ability to manage it effectively will continue to lag.

CHAPTER 7

The Scope of Government-Nonprofit Relations

A Summary

When contributions are hard to get, when fairs and balls no longer net large sums, when endowments are slow to come, the managers of private charities frequently turn to the public authorities and ask them for a contribution from the public revenues. On the other hand, when local or State legislatures see the annual appropriations bills increasing too rapidly, and when they see existing public institutions made political spoils, and the administration wasteful and inefficient, they are apt to think of giving a subsidy to some private institution instead of providing for more public buildings and more public officials   (Warner 1894).

In recent years, government has emerged in the United States as . . . the major philanthropist in a number of the principal traditional areas of philanthropy. The nonprofit sector has become an increasingly mixed realm, part private, part public, in much the same sense that the profit-making sector has—and not unlike the nonprofit sector itself once was   (Commission on Private Philanthropy and Public Needs 1975).

When Alexander Fleisher pointed out in 1914 that no problem of social policy is "more harassing, more complex and perennial than that of determining the proper relation of the state to privately managed charities within its border" (110), he was calling attention to a point that, as previous chapters have made clear, is fundamental to an understanding of modern American social policy, but that recent observers of American society have tended to ignore: that the "welfare state" has taken a peculiar form in the American context, a form that involves not simply the expansion of the state but also an extensive pattern of government reliance on private nonprofit groups to carry out public purposes. In fact, in a number of fields, government has turned more of the responsibility for delivering publicly financed services over to nonprofit organizations than it has retained for itself. In the process, government has become the single most important source of income for most types of nonprofit agencies, outdistancing private charity by roughly two to one. What Fleisher (1914, 110) termed "the sore thumb of public administrative policy" has thus become the core of the nation's human service delivery system and the financial mainstay of the nation's private nonprofit sector.

In previous chapters I have sketched some of the dimensions of this extensive government-nonprofit partnership, identified some of the shortcomings in prevailing theories of the welfare state and of the nonprofit sector that explain why this partnership has failed to receive the attention it deserves, and outlined an alternative set of theories that brings these realities into far better theoretical focus. The purpose of this chapter is to outline somewhat more completely and systematically the dimensions and contours of the resulting government-nonprofit relationships that these new concepts help us to perceive. More specifically, I focus here on the history of government-nonprofit ties, their extent, both generally and in particular subsectors, the role they play in nonprofit finances, the forms that government assistance takes, and the variations that are evident among different types of communities. With this overview of the basic contours of this critical relationship as background, it will then be possible in the next part to examine some of the consequences of the relationship, both for the nonprofit sector and for the progress of U.S. social policy.

Background: The History of Government Support of Nonprofit Organizations

According to conventional wisdom, government support of the voluntary sector is a relatively recent development in this country, and one that runs counter to the historic independence of the voluntary sector. In point of fact, however, government support of voluntary organizations has roots deep in American history. Well before the American Revolution, for example, colonial governments had established a tradition of assistance to private educational institutions, and this tradition persisted into the nineteenth century. In colonial Massachusetts, for example, the commonwealth government not only enacted a special tax for support of Harvard College but also paid part of the salary of the president until 1781 and elected the college's Board of Overseers until after the Civil War. The state of Connecticut had an equally intimate relationship with Yale, and the state's governor, lieutenant governor, and six state senators sat on the Yale Corporation from the founding of the school until the late 1800s. The prevailing sentiment was that education served a public purpose and therefore deserved public support regardless of whether it was provided in publicly or privately run institutions (see Whitehead 1973, 3–16).

A similar pattern was also evident in the hospital field. A survey of seventeen major private hospitals in 1889, for example, revealed that 12 to 13 percent of their income came from government (Stevens 1982). A special 1904 Census Bureau survey of benevolent institutions estimated the government share of private hospital income at closer to 8 percent nationwide, but reported that it exceeded 20 percent in a number of states (Stevens 1982). So widespread was the appropriation of public funds for the support of private voluntary hospitals, in fact, that an American Hospital Association report referred to it in 1909 as "the distinctively American practice" (Stevens 1982; Rosner 1980).

If government support was important to the early history of private, nonprofit hospitals and education institutions, however, it was even more important to the early history of private social service agencies. Hospitals and higher education institutions, after all, had access to fees and charges. Agencies providing care for the poor usually did not. As the social problems that accompanied urbanization and industrialization increased in the late nineteenth century, therefore, governments were increasingly called on to respond. But in a substantial number of cases, public officials turned to private nonprofit agencies for help. In New York City, for example, the amount the city paid to private benevolent institutions for the care of prisoners and paupers grew even faster than total city expenditures for these purposes—from under $10,000 in 1850 to over $3 million in 1898, from 2 percent of total city expenditures on the poor to 57 percent (Fetter 1901–2, 376). Similarly, in the District of Columbia, about half of the public funds allocated for aid to the poor went to private charities as of 1892. What is more, private charitable institutions absorbed two-thirds of the funds the District granted between 1880 and 1892 for construction of charitable facilities (Warner 1894, 337). In other words, the Congress, which set the District budget, was willing not only to compensate private charities for services they were providing to the District poor but also to finance construction of the facilities these organizations needed.

Nor were these isolated instances. To the contrary, a 1901 survey of government subsidization of private charities found that "except possibly two territories and four western states, there is probably not a state in the union where some aid [to private charities] is not given either by the state or by counties and cities" (Fetter 1901–2, 360). In many places, moreover, this public support was extensive enough to replace private charity as the principal source of income for nonprofit organizations. A study of two hundred private organizations for orphan children and the friendless in New York State in the late 1880s showed, for example, that twice as much of their support came from the taxpayers as from legacies, donations, and private contributions. Similarly, private benevolence accounted for only 15 percent of the income of private charities in the District of Columbia as of 1899 (Warner 1894, 337; Fetter 1901–2, 376). In short, there is nothing novel about extensive interaction between government and the voluntary sector in this country. No wonder one close student could conclude that "collaboration, not separation or antagonism, between government and the Third Sector . . . has been the predominant characteristic" throughout most of our history (Nielsen 1979, 47).

Although government support of the voluntary sector has deep historical roots in this country, this support has grown considerably in scope and depth over the past thirty years. Unfortunately, the generation of data needed to chart this growth has not kept pace. Although the Office of Management and Budget prepares a yearly "special analysis" of federal support to state and local governments, for example, no government-wide overview of federal support to nonprofit institutions is available. We know that nonprofit organizations are eligible participants in 564 out of the 988 separate federal programs listed in the *Catalogue of Federal Domestic Assistance,* but few of these programs maintain data systems that make it possible to identify the scale of program resources flowing to nonprofit institutions. Similarly, few state or local governments collect data on this facet of program operations. As a consequence, to examine government support to the voluntary sector it is necessary to stitch together data from a variety of disparate sources.

One of the more recent efforts to do this was the research conducted for the Commission on Private Philanthropy and Public Needs (the Filer Commission) by Rudney in the early 1970s. Rudney (1977) estimated that government support to private tax-exempt organizations totaled $23.2 billion in 1974. By comparison, these same organizations received an estimated $13.6 billion in private philanthropic support that same year. In other words, by Rudney's reckoning, private nonprofit organizations (exclusive of churches, which are not eligible for government support) received a larger share of their income from government as of 1974 than they did from all sources of private giving combined—corporate, foundation, and individual.

More recent work in which I have been involved[1] makes it possible to bring the current status of government support to the nonprofit sector into clearer focus. In particular, on the basis of this work it is possible to identify five major characteristics of the existing pattern of government support to the nonprofit sector. Let us look at each of these characteristics in turn.

The Extent

The first notable dimension of government support to the voluntary sector is its considerable extent. According to our estimates, federal support to the nonprofit sector alone amounted to $40.4 billion in 1980, which represented about 36 percent of total federal spending in these fields (Salamon & Abramson 1982a, 37–42). State and local government own-source revenues would likely add another $8 billion to $10 billion to this total. By comparison, private contributions to these same kinds of organizations in 1980 totaled approximately $25.5 billion (American Association . . . 1981), or about 40 percent less than the federal contribution and about 50 percent less than the overall government contribution. These findings confirm the central conclusion of the Filer Commission that government is a more important source of revenue to nonprofit service providers (exclusive of churches) than all private giving combined.

As can be seen in table 7.1, the extent of reliance on nonprofit organizations to deliver federally funded services varies widely among service fields. In the fields of research, arts and humanities, social services, and health, close to half or more of all federal funding goes to support services provided by nonprofit organizations. In the fields of community development, higher education, and foreign aid, in contrast, the nonprofit share of total federal spending is less than 25 percent.

This pattern of government reliance on nonprofit organizations to deliver publicly funded services is even more clearly apparent in table 7.2, which is based on data assembled through analysis of contracting patterns in sixteen representative field sites of varying sizes throughout the country, and which covers state and local as well as federal spending in five human service fields.[2] These data show that, on average, over 40 percent of all government spending in the five fields goes

TABLE 7.1

Estimated Federal Support of Nonprofit Organizations, FY 1980

($ Billions)

Field	Federal Spending	Federal Support to Nonprofits	
		Amount	As Percentage of Total Federal Spending
Research	$4.7	$2.5	54%
Social services	7.7	4.0[a]	52
Arts, culture	0.6	0.3	50
Health	53.0	24.8	47
Employment and training	10.3	3.3	32
Elementary/secondary education	7.0	0.2	2
Higher education	10.3	2.6	25
Community development	11.5	1.8	16
Foreign aid	6.9	0.8	11
Total	$111.6	$40.4	36%

SOURCE: Data on federal spending from U.S. Office of Management and Budget, *Budget of the United States Government for Fiscal Year 1982*. Data on federal support to nonprofits from Salamon and Abramson (1982a).
NOTE: [a]Includes a limited amount of income assistance aid not covered in the total spending column.

TABLE 7.2

Share of Government-Funded Human Services Delivered by Nonprofit,
For-Profit, and Government Agencies in Sixteen Communities, 1982

(Weighted Average)[a]

Field	Proportion of Services Delivered by			
	Nonprofits	For-Profits	Government	Total
Social services	56%	4%	40%	100%
Employment/training	48	8	43	100
Housing/community development	5	7	88	100
Health	44	23	33	100
Arts/culture	51	[b]	49	100
All	42%	19%	39%	100%

SOURCE: Based on data collected from federal, state, and local government agencies.
NOTES: [a]Figures are weighted by the scale of government spending in the sites. Percentages shown represent the share of all spending in all sites taken together that fall in the respective categories.
[b]Less than 0.5 percent.

to support the provision of services by private nonprofit groups. In some fields, such as social services, the nonprofit share is even higher. In addition, another 19 percent of total government spending in these fields goes to for-profit businesses. By comparison, government agencies deliver about 39 percent of the services they fund in these fields. In other words, nonprofits deliver a larger share of publicly funded services in these fields than do government agencies. Although the inclusion of a number of very large sites that make extensive use of nonprofits (such as New York) inflate these figures somewhat, the picture does not change much when median values are used instead of weighted means. Nonprofits still emerge as major providers of publicly financed services.[3] (For additional details on local sites see, e.g., Musselwhite, Hawkins, and Salamon 1985; Grønbjerg, Musselwhite, and Salamon 1984; Harder, Musselwhite, and Salamon 1984.)

In addition to the direct government support to nonprofits identified above, nonprofits also receive indirect support in the form of the tax deductions provided to their contributors. These deductions represent revenue that would otherwise go to the U.S. Treasury but that the tax laws allow taxpayers to channel to nonprofit organizations instead as an incentive to private giving. According to U.S. Office of Management and Budget estimates, these "tax expenditures" provided an additional $8.4 billion in support to voluntary organizations in 1980, of which probably $5.5 billion went to nonreligious organizations (U.S. Office of Management and Budget 1981).[4]

Distribution among Types of Nonprofits

The extensive support that government provides to nonprofit organizations is not distributed evenly among all areas of nonprofit activity. Rather, nonprofits in some fields receive far more than do those in others. This is so because both the overall extent of government spending and the share of that spending that goes to nonprofits vary from field to field.

Reflecting this, health providers receive the lion's share of all federal support to nonprofit organizations. In particular, as noted in table 7.3, over 60 percent of all federal support to the nonprofit sector in 1980 went to hospitals and other health providers, and about 15 percent each went to social service organizations and educational or research institutions. The remaining 10 percent was split among community development, international assistance, and arts organizations.[5]

During the early 1980s, federal support to the nonprofit sector shifted even more heavily toward health care providers. This is a product of the continued rapid growth of federal health expenditures coupled with budget reductions in the nonhealth fields enacted during the early years of the Reagan administration. As a result, although the inflation-adjusted value of total federal support to nonprofit providers remained relatively constant between fiscal years 1980 and 1985, the

TABLE 7.3
Distribution of Federal Support among Types of Nonprofits, FY 1980
($ Billions)

	Revenues from Federal Sources	
Type of Organization	Amount	As Percentage of Total
Social service	$6.5[a]	16%
Community development	2.3	6
Education/research	5.6	14
Health	24.9	61
Foreign aid	0.8	2
Arts/culture	0.3	1
Total	$40.4[a]	100%

SOURCE: Salamon and Abramson (1982a, 43).
NOTE: [a]Includes a limited amount of income assistance aid.

share of that total absorbed by health care providers increased from about 60 percent to over 70 percent, and the share left for all other types of nonprofits shrank from 40 percent to under 30 percent.

Government Support as a Share of Total Nonprofit Income

Given the extent and distribution of government reliance on non-profit organizations charted above, it should come as no surprise to learn that government support constitutes a major share of total non-profit income. In fact, government has become the single largest source of support for the nonprofit sector, outdistancing the other major sources of support—fees and endowments as well as charitable contributions from corporations, foundations, and individuals.

This point is evident in table 7.4, which compares the extent of federal support for private nonprofit service organizations to the total revenues of these organizations, as estimated from U.S. Census and Internal Revenue Service data.[6] As the table shows, we estimate that federal support accounted for 35 percent of the total expenditures of non-profit service organizations (excluding religious congregations) in 1980.[7] For some types of organizations, however, the federal share is even higher than this—55 percent for social service organizations and over 40 percent for community development organizations. At the opposite end of the spectrum, arts organizations on average received only 12 percent of their revenues from federal program sources.

TABLE 7.4

*Nonprofit Revenues from Federal Sources as a Share of Total
Nonprofit Revenues, 1980*

Type of Organization	Total Revenue	Revenues from Federal Programs	Revenues from Federal Programs as Percentage of Total Revenue
Social service[a]	$13.2	$7.3	55%
Community development[b]	5.4	2.3	43
Education/research	25.2	5.6	22
Health	70.0	24.9	36
Arts/culture	2.6	0.3	12
Total	$116.4	$40.4	35%

SOURCES: Total revenues based on estimates developed from IRS and census data. Government support is based on estimates developed in Salamon and Abramson (1982a), 44.
NOTES: [a]Includes international assistance.
    [b]Includes civic associations and other.

An even clearer picture of the role of government support in the funding of nonprofit organizations is evident in table 7.5, which draws on the results of the survey I directed of some 3,400 nonprofit human service agencies—exclusive of hospitals and higher education institutions—in sixteen field sites across the country. (For further details, see Salamon 1984a, b; Gutowski, Salamon, and Pittman 1984; Lukermann, Kimmich, and Salamon 1984; Grønbjerg, Kimmich, and Salamon 1984.) According to this survey, federal, state, and local governments together accounted for 41 percent of the income of these agencies as of 1981. Service fees and charges provided the second largest source of income, accounting for 28 percent of the total, well behind the government share. Private giving—individual, corporate, and foundation—ranked third, with 20 percent. The results of this survey thus confirm the picture that emerged from the top-down estimates discussed above: that government is the largest single source of income for nonprofit service organizations, outdistancing private giving by a factor of two to one.

As table 7.5 also shows, however, there is some variation in the extent of reliance on government funding among different types of nonprofit agencies. In fact, it is possible to discern three more or less distinct types or "models" of nonprofit agencies in terms of their funding structures. The first, and most common, is the government-dominant model, which applies to those types of agencies for which government is the dominant funding source. As table 7.5 shows, seven of the ten major types of nonprofit agencies we identified fit this model. For each

TABLE 7.5

Sources of Support of Nonprofit Human Service Agencies, 1981

Funding Pattern Type of Agency (n)[a]	Percentage of Total Income from				
	Government	Private Giving[b]	Fees	Other	Total[c]
Government dominant					
Mental health (63)	67%	7%	23%	4%	100%
Housing/community development (91)	62	16	19	3	100
Legal services/advocacy (80)	62	23	10	5	100
Social services (538)	57	25	13	5	100
Employment/income assistance (103)	55	13	10	23	100
Institutional/residential (151)	51	11	32	5	100
Multiservice (314)	47	25	22	6	100
Fee dominant					
Health (196)	31	13	51	5	100
Education/research (278)	28	25	31	16	100
Private dominant					
Arts/culture/recreation (448)	15	30	27	27	100
All agencies (2,304)	41%	20%	28%	10%	100%

SOURCE: Round 1 Salamon Nonprofit Sector Project Survey.
NOTES: [a]Figures in parentheses represent the number of responding agencies in each category. Because some agencies failed to provide complete financial data and others neglected to provide information on their service focus, the number of respondents reflected in this table is smaller than the total respondents to the survey, and the number that provided both financial and service-area data is slightly smaller than the number that provided just financial data.
[b]Includes foundation, corporate, federated, and individual giving.
[c]Some rows may not add to 100 percent because of rounding.

of these types of agencies, government accounts for close to half or more of total income, and in three of the cases it accounts for more than 60 percent of the total. These types of agencies do vary in terms of where they get the remainder of their income, however. For legal services/advocacy and social services organizations, for example, the principal nongovernmental source of funds is private giving. For mental health and institutional/residential care organizations, in contrast, the principal nongovernmental source of funds is fee income. Nevertheless, for all these types of organizations the principal source of support, accounting for half or more of the total, is government.

The second nonprofit funding pattern is what might be called the fee-dominant model. The largest single source of income for agencies that follow this pattern is service fees and charges. As reflected in table 7.5, two types of agencies fit this model—health providers (exclusive of hospitals) and education and research institutions (exclusive of higher education institutions, which were not covered by our survey). In the case of health organizations, service fees constitute over half of total agency income. In the case of education/research organizations, fees exceed all other sources of income, but do not by themselves provide more than half of the total.

The final type of nonprofit funding pattern is the charity-dominant model, in which private giving—whether from individuals, corporations, or foundations—is the largest single source of income. This is the model that best fits the conventional image of the nonprofit sector, but as table 7.5 makes clear, only one set of agencies out of the ten examined—arts, culture, and recreation—fits this model. And even here the fit is far from perfect since arts and cultural organizations as a group received almost as large a share of their income from fees and charges as from private giving, and they might well have received more were we to take account of the sales of products, which are included in the "other" category.

To be sure, the groupings of agencies noted here obscure a considerable degree of diversity among individual agencies within each type. Whereas social service agencies as a group received 57 percent of their income from government, for example, many social service agencies doubtless received little or no income from government and many others received 90 to 100 percent. Nevertheless, these data serve to confirm again how faulty the conventional image of the funding structure of the voluntary sector really is. Although the sector is typically identified exclusively with its private philanthropic base, in fact government is its principal source of support.

This conclusion finds still further support, moreover, in a body of data assembled by United Way of America from information supplied to it by its local affiliates. According to these data, which are partially summarized in table 7.6, government support is strong among United Way member agencies in most of the mainline nonprofit fields of service, such as child welfare, aging, community development, and legal aid. This is particularly significant in view of the fact that United Way agencies not only have access to United Way support but also tend to be older and more established organizations with good access to other private sources of support as well.

The Forms of Government Assistance to Nonprofits

Not only is government support to the nonprofit sector extensive and therefore an important part of the sector's total income, but this support also reaches the sector in a variety of forms and through numerous routes. In some programs, assistance takes the form of outright cash grants. In others, purchase-of-service contracts are used,

TABLE 7.6

Government Revenue as a Share of Total Revenues for Selected United Way Agencies, 1980

Type of Agency	Percentage of Total Income from Government
Legal aid	84%
Community/neighborhood development	74
Aging	73
Child welfare	72
Planned parenthood	55
Catholic charities	46
Crippled children/adults	36
Cancer	29
YWCA	22
Salvation Army	17
Catholic youth organizations	13
Jewish community centers	7

SOURCE: United Way of America (1981).

and in still others government provides loans or loan guarantees. In the international assistance arena, government support to private voluntary organizations has taken even more varied forms, including ocean freight reimbursement, excess government property, surplus food, operational program grants, development program grants, institutional support grants, and several others as well (Bolling 1982).

Reflecting these different forms of assistance, federal aid reaches nonprofit organizations through a variety of routes. One such route involves direct financial dealings between nonprofit organizations and particular federal agencies, including such quasi-governmental or independent agencies as the National Science Foundation, the National Endowment for the Arts, and the National Endowment for the Humanities.

Federal assistance can also reach nonprofit organizations indirectly, through state and local governments that receive federal grants but retain substantial discretion in deciding whether to deliver the subsidized services themselves or to contract with nonprofit agencies or other public or private providers. The Social Services Block Grant (formerly the Title XX Social Services Block Grant program); the Administration on Aging grant programs; alcohol, drug abuse, and mental health programs; and the Community Development Block Grant program are all examples of federal assistance that reaches nonprofits through this route.

A third route for federal assistance to nonprofit organizations in-

TABLE 7.7

*Federal Government Support of Nonprofit Organizations by
Avenue of Assistance, FY 1980*

($ Billions)

	Nonprofit Revenue from Federal Sources	
Avenue of Federal Assistance	Amount	As Percentage of Total
Direct to nonprofits	$7.9	20%
Through state/local governments	10.9	27
Through individuals	21.6	53
Total	$40.4	100%

SOURCE: Salamon and Abramson (1982a).

volves payments to individuals or to financial agents acting on their behalf. Perhaps the classic example here is Medicare, which reimburses individuals for certain hospital-related expenses but leaves to the individual the choice of whether to utilize a private nonprofit, a public, or a for-profit institution. A similar pattern prevails with the college student assistance programs, which provide important financial aid to nonprofit colleges and universities, but channel this aid to the students, who retain the choice about which type of institution—public, private nonprofit, or private for-profit—to attend.

These differences in the mechanisms of assistance have important implications for the nature of the relationship between government agencies and nonprofit providers. Generally speaking, federal influence is greatest in those programs where the form of assistance is a direct contract or grant between a federal agency and a particular nonprofit organization. It is weakest where the assistance is provided to private citizens who are then free to purchase services from providers of their choice in the market. At the same time, however, the direct route is more certain, whereas nonprofits have no guarantee of aid when the assistance is channeled through the client.

In view of this, it is significant, as reported in table 7.7, that the direct route, involving contractual relationships between the federal government and nonprofit organizations, is the least heavily used of these three forms of federal assistance. Only 20 percent of all federal aid to nonprofits took this route in 1980. In contrast, 53 percent of the federal aid to the sector was channeled through individuals, and another 27 percent reached nonprofits through state and local governments. Clearly, if the federal government is affecting the nonprofit sector, it is doing so indirectly. What is more, because the budget cuts

TABLE 7.8

Extent of Government Reliance on Nonprofit Organizations
in Sixteen Sites, 1982

Site County (City)	Share of Total Public Spending Flowing to Nonprofits	
	All Fields[a]	All except Health
Allegheny (Pittsburgh)	50%	39%
Cook (Chicago)	48	26
New York City	43	46
Rhode Island	40	34
Ramsey (St. Paul)	40	26
San Francisco	40	39
Maricopa (Phoenix)	37	34
Hennepin (Minneapolis)	38	34
Warren (Vicksburg)	34	47
Ada (Boise)	33	18
Genesee (Flint)	28	15
Dallas	27	25
Fulton (Atlanta)	27	20
Hinds (Jackson)	23	23
Pinal, Ariz.	16	39
Tuscola, Mich.	12	25
All sites		
Average	34%	31%
Weighted average	42%	30%

SOURCE: Federal, state, and local government sources.
NOTE: [a]Covers the fields of social services, health, employment and training, housing and community development, and arts and recreation.

of the early 1980s hit harder at the direct federal aid programs and those involving grants to state and local governments than those involving payments to individuals, the trend is toward even greater use of this voucher-type mechanism.

Regional Variations

One final characteristic of the existing pattern of governmental support of nonprofit organizations worth noting is its variation among different parts of the country and among communities of different sizes. This is shown in table 7.8, which reports the extent of government reliance on nonprofit organizations to deliver publicly funded services in the sixteen local sites we examined. As this table shows, the proportion of total government spending that goes to support service delivery by nonprofit organizations in five major service fields ranges from a high of 50 percent in Allegheny County (Pittsburgh) to a low

TABLE 7.9
*Percentage of Social Service Agency Income Coming
from Government, by Site, 1981*

Site	Government Share of Income
Jackson	82%
San Francisco	74
Atlanta	70
Flint	65
Providence	65
Dallas/Forth Worth	59
Minneapolis/St. Paul	56
New York	54
Pittsburgh	53
Boise	42
Chicago	40
Phoenix	30
All sites	57%

SOURCE: Salamon Nonprofit Sector Project Survey, round 1.

of 12 percent in rural Tuscola County, Michigan. Although it is dangerous to draw conclusions on the basis of sixteen observations, the data in table 7.8 suggest two generalizations: first, government reliance on nonprofits to deliver publicly funded services tends to be less extensive in the South than in the Northeast and West; and second, such reliance also seems to be less extensive in small communities than in large ones. Thus of the eight sites reporting nonprofit shares of total government spending that are at or below the sixteen-site average, all either are in the South or are small sites, or both. In contrast, the sites at the high end of the scale are usually the large northern and western areas. What is more, with some notable exceptions (for example, Cook County, where the power of the city machine and its employees is unusually strong and contracting out is less extensive), this pattern holds even when health spending, which is quite large and somewhat unusual, is excluded.

Not only do regional variations exist in the extent of governmental reliance on nonprofits, but there are also regional variations in the share of nonprofit income that comes from government. This is apparent in table 7.9, which records the share of the income of nonprofit social service agencies that comes from government in the twelve metropolitan field sites we covered. As this table shows, the government share ranges from a high of 82 percent in Jackson, Mississippi, to a low of 30 percent in Phoenix. Although the patterns are less pro-

TABLE 7.10
Regional Variations in the Scope of the Nonprofit Sector

Region	Nonprofit Organizations per 100,000 Population	Nonprofit Expenditures per Capita
Northeast	58.2	$522
North Central	50.2	348
West	48.4	262
South	36.8	208
United States average	47.1	$323

SOURCE: Computed from U.S. Census Bureau, 1981.

nounced here, there is some tendency to find higher levels of reliance on government support in the smaller communities and those in the South than in the larger communities and those in the North and West.

What accounts for these variations in government reliance on nonprofits to deliver services, and in nonprofit reliance on government for income? One factor appears to be the availability of private charitable support and the extent of private nonprofit activity to start with. As it turns out, substantial differences exist among different sections of the country and different sizes of communities in the extent of nonprofit activity. As reflected in table 7.10, the regions in which government relies most heavily on nonprofits to deliver publicly funded services (the Northeast and North Central regions) also turn out to have the highest number of nonprofit organizations and the largest nonprofit expenditures per capita. In contrast, the region in which government makes the least use of nonprofits (the South) also has the least well-developed nonprofit sector. What this suggests is that where nonprofit organizations are a major presence government has turned to them extensively for help in delivering publicly funded services. Conversely, where the sector is less fully developed, government agencies have carried more of the human service delivery burden themselves, but nonprofits have had fewer private charitable resources to draw on, too. These data thus raise doubts about the conventional image of government and the nonprofit sector as competitors. The conclusion that emerges from the data, rather, is that both government and nonprofits are responses to the same desire for collective goods, and that where this desire is strong both government activity and nonprofit activity are extensive.

Summary

The data currently available thus make clear that government support of private nonprofit organizations is extensive, that it is particularly important to social service and community development organizations, that most of it reaches nonprofit organizations indirectly—through individuals or state and local governments—and that it varies markedly among different sections of the country. Taken together, these data suggest that, whatever else its impact, government has certainly not supplanted or displaced nonprofit organizations. Rather, it has become a major force underwriting nonprofit operations, providing, in this capacity, a larger portion of the revenues of nonprofit service providers (exclusive of churches) than does private giving.

The Consequences of Government Support

That government support of the nonprofit sector has a meaningful theoretical foundation and that such support has grown in both scale and scope are still not proof that the resulting partnership is good either for government or for the nonprofit sector. Indeed, there are those who question whether the resulting relationship is really a partnership at all. Turn-of-the-century social reformers, as we have seen, vehemently opposed the prevailing practice of government subsidies to private charities on grounds that it impeded progress in establishing a modern system of universal public protections by surrendering control over public resources to paternalistic, backward-looking organizations beholden to narrow ethnic and religious communities. More recent critics have been more preoccupied with the impact of government support on the nonprofit sector itself, charging that government support undermines the independence of these organizations, diverts them from their basic objectives, and leads to excessive professionalization that destroys the sector's voluntary roots (Butler 1985; Woodson 1977; Smith and Lipsky 1993). Other concerns focus on the difficult management challenges posed by the practice of "third-party government" and the potential loss of popular support for public social welfare activities that can result from the interposition of nonprofit agencies between the government and the recipients of its largesse.

How valid are these various concerns? To what extent has the cooperation between government and the nonprofit sector served the respective objectives of the two sides? At what cost? Have nonprofits been forced to alter their goals or their focus in significant ways? Have they truly lost their independence?

The two chapters in this section seek to answer these questions by drawing on the available empirical evidence. Chapter 8 first assesses the arguments that have been advanced about the impact of government contracting on the independence of the nonprofit sector. Based on the information available, it finds little foundation for the many fears that have been raised about the negative impact of government support on nonprofit organizations. While these organizations may be heavily dependent on government for financial support, they are not without resources of their own, not the least of which is government's need for them to carry out its own objectives. Instead of a situation of power and dependence, therefore, what has emerged is a pattern of interdependence in which both sides have significant bargaining advantages. At the same time, however, great care is needed to manage the resulting partnership effectively, and the chapter ends with a series of suggestions about how this can be done.

Chapter 9 goes beyond these administrative issues to evaluate the impact of government support on the purposes of nonprofit organizations, particularly as manifested in the choice of agency clientele. The central conclusion that emerges is that government support does not seem to have altered the basic purposes of nonprofit agencies, but it has induced them to broaden their client focus. Most important, it has encouraged them to focus more centrally on the poor. In fact, the single most significant factor explaining the extent to which nonprofit agencies focus on the poor is the extent of government support they receive. Generally speaking, the greater the government support, the more likely an agency is to focus its efforts on the disadvantaged. Government support thus does seem to have had an impact on agency operations, but largely in the direction of limiting the sector's elitist orientation and focusing its energies more extensively on those in greatest need.

CHAPTER 8

The Government-Nonprofit Partnership in Practice

To say that a strong theoretical rationale exists for government-nonprofit cooperation is not, of course, to say that this cooperation has worked out in practice the way the theory would suggest. To the contrary, any relationship as complex as this one is likely to encounter immense strains and difficulties, especially given the somewhat different perspectives of the two sides. Government officials, for example, must worry about the problems of exercising management supervision, ensuring a degree of accountability, and encouraging coordination when decision-making authority is widely dispersed and vested in institutions with their own independent sources of authority and support. Within the philanthropic community, the issues raised by the prevailing pattern of government support of nonprofit organizations are of a far different sort. Of central concern here are three other potential dangers: first, loss of autonomy or independence, particularly the dilution of the sector's advocacy role; second, "vendorism," or the distortion of agency missions in pursuit of available government funding; and third, bureaucratization or overprofessionalization and a resulting loss of the flexibility and local control that are considered the sector's greatest strengths.

In the absence of a firm theoretical basis for government-nonprofit relations, neither government officials nor nonprofits have managed to develop a meaningful and coherent set of standards in terms of which to guide their interactions. Rather, both sides have tended to view the relationship from their own perspective and to apply standards that are rigid and absolute.

The concepts developed above, however, suggest a more meaningful and balanced set of criteria by which the relationships between government and the nonprofit sector can be judged. To the extent that cooperation between government and the nonprofit sector reflects a fit between the respective strengths and weaknesses of the two, as is argued above, the appropriate standard is one that acknowledges the need to correct the shortcomings of the two sectors without doing unnecessary damage to their respective strengths. In practice, this means that government's need for economy, efficiency, and accountability must be tempered by the nonprofit sector's need for a degree of self-determination and independence of governmental control; but that the sector's desire for independence must in turn be tempered by government's need to achieve equity and to make sure that public resources are used to advance the purposes intended.

Regrettably, the empirical data needed to evaluate how successfully this partnership has met this test are sparse. As one student of the subject pointed out in 1975: "Although the potential hazards and benefits of government contracting for the purchase of service can be readily identified in the literature, little systematic research has been reported on failure or benefits that have actually come about. The concern is real, but the facts are not certain" (Wedel 1976, 102).

Although the situation has not changed much since Wedel wrote, it is possible to reach some tentative judgments about how this partnership has been working. In particular, the message that emerges from the limited analysis to date is that many of the concerns about the partnership have not materialized to anywhere near the extent feared. Let us look first at what is known about the impact of this partnership on the nonprofit world, and then examine how it has operated from the perspective of the public sector.

The View from the Nonprofit Sector

Agency Independence

Perhaps the central concern on the part of those worried about nonprofit involvement in government programs has been the fear that such involvement would rob nonprofits of their "independence." A fundamental feature of the nonprofit sector, in this view, is its availability as a reservoir of novel or unpopular ideas and its role as an agent of social and political change. To the extent that the sector becomes an "agent" of the state, the argument goes, it will lose this capability and be vulnerable to political retaliation. What is more, it will come to tailor its activities to the priorities of faraway political representatives rather than to those of the communities it serves. A more subtle version of this argument takes the form of a concern that undue stress on the service delivery function of the sector can "straitjacket" nonprofit organizations and dilute their advocacy role.

Although instances of governmental infringement on agency autonomy doubtless exist (most recently in the battle over Office of Management and Budget Circular A-102 designed to prevent the use of federal funds to promote advocacy activities), the preponderance of empirical evidence casts doubt on this line of argument. A recent study of private agencies serving the disabled by sociologist Ralph Kramer (1980, 292, 160), for example, concluded that "voluntary-agency autonomy is seldom compromised by the accountability requirements of governmental funding sources. More often, there is a low level of regulation and a closeness based on mutual dependency. . . . The impact of governmental funds in controlling voluntary social service organizations may be much less than is commonly believed."

The concern about the potential challenge to agency independence posed by government agencies must be evaluated, moreover, in light of the challenge that can be posed by private funding sources as well. The notion that the nonprofit sector is independent, after all, can be misleading. Financially, the sector is almost inevitably dependent—on private sources of funds if not public ones. And historically, private funds have often come with strings every bit as onerous and threatening to agency independence as any government has devised.[1] At the very least, the valid concerns about the potential loss of independence as a result of receipt of public funds need to be balanced by a recognition of the challenge to the independence of at least some kinds of organizations that can be posed by sole reliance on private funding as well.

Vendorism

An offshoot of the independence issue is the concern that government funding can distort agency missions by enticing agencies to concentrate their efforts in areas that may not coincide with what the nonprofit organization itself thinks is important or would like to do. Of particular concern here is the possibility that voluntary boards of directors can lose effective control of the agencies as a consequence, since the professional staff can develop funding sources outside of board influence or control.

Here, again, the empirical evidence is not supportive. A study of New York nonprofit agencies conducted by the New York United Way, for example, found little evidence that government funding had distorted agency missions (Hartogs and Weber 1978, 8–9). To the contrary, most agencies reported that government funding enabled them to carry out their existing missions better. Similarly, our survey of over 3,400 nonprofit agencies in sixteen local areas across the country turned up little evidence of agency concern that government had distorted agency missions. In only one significant respect did the agencies we surveyed report a change in their mission in response to receipt of government funds: they credited government with inducing them to focus more of their services on the poor. However, this fits well with the notion of philanthropic particularism cited above as one of the rationales for government involvement. Evidently, governmental support is having the effect that the theory developed here claimed for it—overcoming some of the favoritism of the nonprofit sector. Kramer's work on nonprofit agencies serving the disabled reached a similar conclusion. As he phrased it: "Generally, agencies did what they always wanted to do, but for which they previously lacked the resources" (1980, 163).

Here as well, moreover, pressures to alter agency purposes can also emanate from private nongovernmental funding sources. These sources frequently have their own priorities and concerns that may or may not accord with the priorities of voluntary agencies. Foundations, for example, have frequently been accused of preferring new experimental programs, making it difficult to find support for mainline services. Similarly, many advocacy groups feel that corporations and foundations tend to shy away from potential controversy. Over half of the respondents in our survey of nonprofit organizations, in fact, felt that corporations do not support their types of programs. This was particularly true of social service and advocacy organizations serving minorities and the poor. In the absence of government support, these agencies might be forced to alter their programs to fit the funding priorities of private funders.

Agency Management and Bureaucratization

A third major issue surrounding government support of nonprofit organizations has been a concern that involvement with government programs tends to produce an undesirable degree of bureaucratization and professionalization in the recipient agency. While relying on nonprofits to create a greater degree of heterogeneity and flexibility in service delivery than they can often provide themselves, government agencies must nevertheless guarantee that some features of program operations remain standard, even if carried out by nonprofits. These include effective financial management and accounting, maintenance of minimum quality standards, promotion of basic program objectives, and adherence to certain national policy goals such as equal opportunity, handicapped rights, and environmental protection. Government programs therefore often involve more red tape, cumbersome application requirements, and regulatory control than is common with other forms of financial support. In fact, over half (53%) of the respondents in our survey of nonprofit agencies agreed that "it is easier to deal with corporate and foundation funding sources than government funding sources," and less than a quarter disagreed. To cope with the financial accountability standards of government programs, the voluntary agency frequently has to develop internal management processes that reduce the agency's flexibility and often threaten its informal, voluntary character. In addition, government programs sometimes carry with them regulatory provisions that lead to greater reliance on professional staff and less on volunteers. Facilities sometimes must be certified and governmental guidelines on client/staff ratios, employment practices, provision for the disabled, and so on adhered to (see Berger and Neuhaus 1977; Rosenbaum 1981).

Of all the concerns raised about the impact of government funding on nonprofit organizations, this one probably is the most credible. But there is a tendency to ascribe more of the apparent bureaucratization and professionalization of nonprofit organizations to government support than is probably justifiable. The pressures for improved agency management, tighter financial control, and use of professionals in service delivery do not, after all, come solely from government. Increased professionalization has been a major trend for decades within the fields in which nonprofit organizations are active: social services, health, education, even arts and community organization. In fact, the push for professionalization came in part from the voluntary sector, and government has been used to spread the professional standards developed in individual fields. In addition, many private funders increasingly expect sound financial management on the part of the agencies to which they provide resources. This is particularly true, for example, of United Way.

In contrast to the perception that agencies may be overbureaucratized and preoccupied with internal management, moreover, a study of the impact of government funding carried out by the Greater New York Fund in the mid-1970s concluded that voluntary agencies may pay too little attention to this dimension of their operations: they often do not charge government enough to carry out publicly funded services and must dip into their own resources to help. As the authors of this study concluded: "The enemy to survival is not from without, i.e., the government, but from within the agency's own management practices" (Hartogs and Weber 1978, 10).

The View from Government

That the partnership between government and the nonprofit sector may not have worked out as badly for the voluntary sector as many have feared is due in part to the fact that the instruments for accountability and control available to government have often been far weaker than is assumed. For one thing, as we have seen, much government aid to the nonprofit sector takes the form of payments to individuals or reimbursements for services rendered to them. Under such arrangements, government's ability to hold the nonprofit institution to account for the cost and quality of service is limited. In fact, in the massive Medicare program, and to a lesser extent in Medicaid, government has been obliged to underwrite virtually any costs that private hospitals claim are needed, with little opportunity for effective cost control. The elaborate licensing and regulatory procedures put in place for new facilities and equipment purchase are merely efforts to come to terms with this fundamental fact of life, and they are imperfect efforts at that.[2]

Although more effective means of control are potentially available in the direct-grant and purchase-of-service arrangements, things have often not worked that way in practice because of the absence of some of the crucial prerequisites of cost-effective contracting—such as meaningful competition among providers, effective measures of performance, and government decision making geared to performance. Too often, decisions about whether to contract out services, and with whom, have been made under the pressures of unreasonable program deadlines, with too little information, and with little opportunity to search out potential contractors. As a consequence, governments have often had to accept the services the prevailing network of providers could supply rather than seek those the needs of the target population required. What is more, because performance criteria have been difficult to fashion and apply, government has often resorted to accounting controls and application and reporting procedures that increase the burdens on agencies without providing an effective means of oversight for government (DeHoog 1985).

Summary and Implications

Taken as a whole, then, the research to date on the impact of government funding on nonprofit organizations suggests that many of the fears that surround this relationship have not been borne out in practice. Clearly, dangers to agency independence, pursuit of agency purposes, and internal management style may result from involvement with public programs, but these dangers do not appear to be so severe as to argue for dismantling the partnership that has been created. More troubling, in fact, may be the concerns on the public side—that reliance on nonprofits to deliver publicly financed services can undermine public objectives and inflate costs. Perhaps the safest conclusion is that this relationship has involved excesses on both sides because of a failure to examine it closely or to develop a reasonable set of standards to guide it. By bringing this relationship into clearer empirical and theoretical focus, as this and the preceding chapters have sought to do, it may be possible to move toward the more balanced assessment that is desperately needed.

More generally, several broad implications flow from the discussion in this and previous chapters on the scope, theory, and consequences of government-nonprofit ties.

Retention and Strengthening of "Nonprofit Federalism"

Perhaps the most important of these implications is that the partnership that has been forged in this country between government and the nonprofit sector is worth preserving and strengthening. Had we not already invented this mechanism for delivering needed services, we would likely be thinking about inventing it now, rather than subjecting it to serious strain, as has recently been the case.

What "nonprofit federalism" offers is the opportunity to combine the service-delivery advantages of voluntary organizations with the revenue-generating and democratic priority-setting advantages of government. In many cases, moreover, this mechanism makes it possible to match publicly generated funds with privately generated ones to provide a better service than either side could provide on its own. This is not to say that all services should be distributed through this mechanism since there are disadvantages as well. But a strong case can be made for promoting this approach as one important element of the nation's service-delivery system.

Accommodation by Government of the Organizational Needs of Nonprofit Organizations

"Nonprofit federalism" has advantages as a form of service delivery in large part because of certain distinctive characteristics of nonprofit agencies. These characteristics reflect the role that private, nonprofit organizations have traditionally played not so much as contributors to efficiency as mechanisms for promoting other important social values, such as group and individual freedom, diversity, a sense of community, civic activism, and charity. These features have long made it in the national interest to protect and nurture the voluntary sector even if there were costs involved.

The nonprofit sector also offers a number of more practical advantages in the delivery of human services, however. Among these advantages are the following:

- A significant degree of flexibility resulting from the relative ease with which agencies can form and disband and the closeness of governing boards to the field of action.
- Existing institutional structures in a number of program areas resulting from the fact that voluntary agencies frequently begin work in particular areas prior to the development of government programs in these areas.
- A generally smaller scale of operation, providing greater opportunity for tailoring services to client needs.
- A degree of diversity both in the content of services and in the institutional framework within which they are provided.
- A greater capacity to avoid fragmented approaches and to concentrate on the full range of needs that families or individuals face, to treat the person or the family instead of the isolated problem.
- Greater access to private charitable resources and volunteer

labor, which can enhance the quality of service provided and "leverage" public dollars.

Whether intentionally or not, involvement in government programs can threaten some of these inherent advantages of nonprofit agencies. For example, such involvement often creates a tension for nonprofit agencies between their service role and their advocacy role, between their role as deliverers of government-funded services and their role as critics of government and private policies. Such involvement can also put a strain on other important features of the organizations, such as their reliance on volunteers, their sense of independence, their frequently informal and nonbureaucratic character, and their direction by private citizens along lines that these citizens think appropriate. Since many of these features are the ones that recommend nonprofit organizations as service providers in the first place, it would be ironic if government programs seriously compromised these features. What this suggests is the need for some forbearance on the part of government with respect to some aspects of the relationship between the two sectors, and for structural features that help to strengthen rather than weaken the distinctive elements of the nonprofit sector. Among other things this might include:

- Payment schedules on grants and contracts that avoid costly cash-flow problems for nonprofit organizations.
- Avoidance of undue interference with the nonservice functions of the organizations.
- The use of challenge grants or other funding devices that reward agencies for the use of volunteers or the generation of private-sector funds to supplement public resources.
- Continued encouragement of private giving, which is crucial for the preservation of an element of independence and flexibility for nonprofit agencies.

Recognition of the Need for Government Involvement and of the Legitimate Accountability Requirements of Government

If the partnership between government and the nonprofit sector gains strength from the involvement of the nonprofit partner, it also gains strength from the involvement of the governmental partner. Indeed, the whole thrust of the "voluntary failure" theory outlined in chapter 2 is that the voluntary sector, for all its advantages, has certain limitations that make sole reliance on it unwise. In particular, four major considerations make government involvement desirable even when voluntary associations are involved.

Financial: While private giving and voluntary activity remain vitally important, it seems unreasonable to expect that these sources can be counted on to generate the levels of support needed to sustain the kinds of services, including human services, that our advanced industrial society has come to require in order to make the most effective use of human resources. This was a lesson taught at considerable cost through the late nineteenth and early twentieth centuries in most of the advanced industrial societies of the world, including our own, and it remains relevant today.

Equity: Not only is government in a better position to finance needed services, it is also in a better position to ensure the equitable distribution of those resources among parts of the country and segments of the population. Private charitable resources may or may not be available where the need for them is greatest. In the absence of some mechanism like government, it is extremely difficult to channel the available resources reliably to the areas and populations that need them the most. In addition, sufficient nonprofit agencies with the experience and capability to provide certain services may not be available in particular locales, making it necessary to rely on direct public provision instead.

Diversity: While the nonprofit sector has a number of advantages as a service provider, it also has a number of disadvantages. For example, private voluntary agencies have been known to intrude more than some people might like into personal religious or moral preferences. Similarly, established agencies can sometimes monopolize the flow of private philanthropic dollars, limiting the resources available to newer or smaller groups. Finally, there are purposes for which existing institutions are considered inappropriate or are unreliable, and for which public stimulation of the creation of new institutions is in the public interest. For all of these reasons, there is an argument for a government role to ensure a sufficient degree of diversity in the service-delivery system, including the funding of for-profit providers.

Public Priority-Setting: A central tenet of a democratic society is that the public should be able to set priorities through a democratic political process and then muster the resources to make sure those priorities are addressed. Complete reliance on private-sector initiative and action robs the public of that opportunity and leaves the setting of priorities in the hands of those with the most control over private resources.

The fact that government has a crucial role to play in the government-nonprofit partnership means, of course, that government has certain legitimate expectations to place on nonprofit organizations. At a minimum, these include requirements for basic financial accountability in the expenditure of public funds and adherence to the purposes for which the funds are authorized. Beyond this, involvement in government programs also appropriately carries with it an obligation to be nondiscriminatory. The key, however, is to find a balance that protects the legitimate public interest in accountability without undermining the characteristics that make nonprofits effective partners of government.

The Need for Improvement in the Management of the Partnership

Although a substantial financial "partnership" has emerged in the human services area between government and philanthropic institutions, this partnership remains, in many senses, one in name only. For the most part, the resource allocation processes in these two sectors proceed independently, and often in ignorance, of each other. Public-sector organizations have little clear idea of the uses to which private philanthropic dollars are being put, and the charitable sector frequently has only imperfect knowledge of, and limited influence over, the allocation of public funds. Even basic information about the scope and structure of the private, nonprofit delivery system is unavailable in most locales, making coherent policymaking difficult.

While this diversity and lack of coherence is one of the strengths of the current pluralistic delivery system, it also has significant costs in terms of the effective use of limited resources. As governmental resources become even tighter and corporate and other philanthropic institutions begin to play a larger role, it may be appropriate to consider ways to achieve a greater degree of dialogue on questions of resource allocation, division of responsibilities for meeting community needs, and joint public-private ventures. At a minimum, this will require developing a more complete picture of the extent and character of the private, nonprofit delivery system and its interaction with the public sector. Beyond this, it will likely require the establishment of some more formal communication and decision-making apparatus to systematize the flow of information between these two sectors and among the component parts of each. The myth of separation that now characterizes public and private thinking on these issues needs to be broken down and more explicit recognition made of the mixed economy that actually exists. This is not to suggest that a single, comprehensive public-private planning and decision-making apparatus should be created to set priorities and make decisions on all local funds. Such a development would be resisted by all parties, and rightly so. But between this "red herring" and the chaotic situation that now exists in most locales lies ample room for a middle course of cooperation and information sharing that could improve the use of resources and possibly contribute to some fruitful cooperative ventures.

Conclusion

For better or worse, cooperation between government and the voluntary sector is the approach this nation has chosen to deal with many of its human service problems. Although largely overlooked both in treatments of the voluntary sector and in analyses of the American welfare state, this pattern of cooperation has grown into a massive system of action that accounts for at least as large a share of government-funded human services as that delivered by government agencies themselves, and that constitutes the largest single source of nonprofit-sector income. Despite its problems, this partnership has much to recommend it, combining as it does the superior revenue-raising and democratic decision-making processes of government with the potentially smaller-scale, more personalized service-delivery capabilities of the voluntary sector. What is more, the partnership has deep roots in American history, testifying to its fit with basic national values.

While this partnership has deep historical roots and has grown massively in scale, it is hardly without its problems. Its sheer complexity is a guarantee against this, and the presence of quite divergent interests and perspectives between the state and its nonprofit partners only complicates the situation. Having invented this partnership and seen it grow, therefore, we must now make it work.

CHAPTER 9

The Charitable Behavior of the Charitable Sector

The Case of Social Services

Of all the components of the nonprofit or charitable sector, none might be expected to adhere more closely to the dictionary definition of "charity" as "generosity to the poor" (Random House Dictionary 1978) than the social service or human service component. Nonprofit human service organizations owe their origins to the efforts to cope with the poverty and want that accompanied the massive influx of immigrants into American cities in the late nineteenth and early twentieth centuries. Although often combining their efforts to relieve material distress with efforts to instill various religious and moral values, these organizations clearly took the problems of the poor as their principal focus of activity.

Although the development of government social welfare programs in the 1930s brought new resources into the field, it hardly eliminated the need for significant private action. America has long been at best a "reluctant" welfare state, restricting public aid to narrow categories of people and, even then, keeping benefits at minimal levels. The "rediscovery of poverty" in the 1960s provided clear evidence, if any were needed, that the public assistance system created by the New Deal hardly eliminated the need for aggressive, private voluntary action.

At the same time, the needs of the poor have not been the only ones competing for the attention of nonprofit human service organizations. Developments in the social work field were already creating tensions between service to the poor and service to a broader client population during the 1940s and 1950s (Cloward and Epstein 1965). Despite the spurt of interest in the problems of the poor in the 1960s, moreover, a "profound reorientation of purposes" (Gilbert and Sprecht 1981, 1) took place in the social services field in the 1970s and 1980s as a "new social service system" took shape. The principal feature of this reorientation was a shift in focus away from the narrow goal of reducing poverty and economic dependency toward the broader goal of enhancing human development (Kamerman and Kahn 1976, 3). Under the new approach, social services of the sort provided by nonprofit human service agencies came to be viewed as something appropriate not simply for the poor, but for a broad cross section of the population as well.

How have nonprofit human service agencies coped with the pressures that have resulted from this broadening of the human service client base? To what extent have they remained true to their historic missions? To what extent have they shifted their attention from the poor to broader segments of the population? To the extent such a shift has occurred, what accounts for it? Who, in fact, is served by nonprofit social service agencies and who foots the bill?

The purpose of this chapter is to answer these questions. In the process, however, the chapter also seeks to explore a number of more basic theoretical issues about the character of nonprofit organizations, issues that an analysis of client focus throws into bold relief. In particular, by examining whom nonprofit social service agencies serve it is possible to shed interesting empirical light on the relative explanatory power of four alternative theories that have been advanced to explain the existence or behavior of the nonprofit sector: the market failure/government failure theory, the voluntary failure theory, the supply of charitable entrepreneurs theory, and organization theory. In addition, it is possible to gauge the validity of the argument that government support has distorted the client focus of nonprofit agencies.

To carry out these objectives, the discussion here falls into four major sections. The first section defines what I mean by the nonprofit social service sector and provides some basic background information on its scope and scale. The next section reviews what is known about the client focus of this set of organizations, drawing particularly on an extensive survey that I directed in 1982 and repeated in 1985–86. In the third section we turn our attention to the alternative theoretical concepts that can help explain the existing pattern of client focus and to a test of these concepts using the empirical evidence from the survey. The last section reviews the central conclusions and implications that flow from this work.

Human Service Nonprofits: An Overview

"Social services" or "human services" are inherently amorphous terms. In the British context, these terms are used to refer to the entire range of people-oriented services and benefits, including basic income support for the elderly and the unemployed (Brenton 1985). In the United States, the term *social services* is used slightly more narrowly. In particular, for our purposes here we will focus on agencies providing what the U.S. Census of Service Industries terms "social and legal services." This excludes hospitals, schools, and arts, culture, and recreation institutions, but includes agencies that provide direct income and other material support, individual and family services, day care, residential care (except for nursing homes), job training, mental health and addiction services, and nonhospital health care, as well as agencies that engage in community organizing, advocacy, community development, research, and public education. We will refer to the organizations that fall within this field as the "nonprofit human service sector."[1]

Perhaps reflecting the diversity of the field, nonprofit human service organizations constitute the largest single component of the charitable nonprofit service sector[2] in terms of numbers of organizations. According to the 1987 *Census of Service Industries,* which provides the most recent available data, 75,612 organizations fall within the nonprofit human service sector as we have defined it here. This represented an estimated 52 percent of all charitable nonprofit organizations, as shown in table 9.1. The most numerous of the human service nonprofits, as table 9.1 shows, were individual and family service agencies, followed by child day care and residential care.

Taken together, these human service nonprofit organizations had expenditures totalling $36.6 billion as of 1987, as shown in table 9.2. To put this into context, the entire charitable nonprofit service sector (including hospitals, educational institutions, and cultural facilities) had expenditures of $238.7 billion that same year, and government spending on human services as defined here totaled $87.1 billion. Although hardly the largest part of the nonprofit sector in terms of expenditures, the human service organizations of primary concern to us here nevertheless represent a significant industry, equivalent in size to the primary metals and aviation industries.[3]

TABLE 9.1
*Nonprofit Human Service Agencies in Relation to Other Charitable
Nonprofit Organizations*

Type of Organization	Number	Percentage of Total	Percentage of Human Service Organizations
Human services			
Legal services	1,439	1%	2%
Child day care	13,822	9	18
Individual and family services	21,862	15	29
Job training and vocational rehabilitation	5,005	4	7
Residential care	10,474	7	14
Civic[a]	2,021	1	3
Other[b]	20,989	14	27
Subtotal	75,612	52%	100%
Other "charitable" nonprofits			
Health and hospitals	12,370	8	
Education	6,350	5	
Arts, culture, recreation	13,162	9	
Other civic, social	38,394	26	
Subtotal	70,276	48	
Total	145,888	100%	

SOURCES: Higher education data from U.S. Department of Education (1991, 229); remaining data from U.S. Census Bureau (1989a, 13–14).
NOTES: [a]Includes 5 percent of all civic, social, and fraternal associations based on survey results indicating this proportion is engaged in community organizing and advocacy.
[b]Includes 2,414 noncommercial research organizations and 6,736 home health providers and outpatient clinics.

Whom Does the Nonprofit Human Service Sector Serve?

What role does this nonprofit human service sector play in the over-all social welfare system? Do these organizations supplement the public system, filling in significant gaps in public provision? Or have non-profits carved out a particular "market niche"? Who benefits from the activities of the nonprofit human service sector? What distributional consequences does it have?

Unfortunately, the answer to these questions is far from straight-forward. For one thing, the benefits that result from the activities of nonprofit human service agencies are varied. In addition to the *direct benefits* that accrue to the immediate recipients of services, there are a variety of *indirect or community benefits* that accrue to a wide assortment of other people—family members, acquaintances, neighbors, the general public. A drug addiction center may provide direct benefits to poor, inner-city drug addicts, for example, but its chief beneficiaries

TABLE 9.2

*Operating Expenditures of Nonprofit Human Service Organizations in Relation to
Other Charitable Nonprofits*

($ Billions)

Type	Amount	Percentage of Total
Human services		
Legal services	$0.4	
Child day care	2.9	1%
Individual and family services	7.5	3
Job training and vocational rehabilitation	2.8	1
Residential care	6.0	3
Civic[a]	0.4	
Other[b]	16.6	7
Subtotal	$36.6	15
Other "charitable" nonprofits		
Health services	134.2	56
Education	54.5	23
Arts, culture, recreation	5.2	2
Other civic, social	8.2	4
Subtotal	202.1	85
Total	$238.7	100%

SOURCE: Adapted from Hodgkinson and Weitzman (1989, 183).
NOTES: [a]Includes 5 percent of civic, social, and fraternal associations engaged in community organizing and advocacy according to survey results.
[b]Includes 1,946 noncommercial research organizations.

may be middle-class suburbanites whose neighborhoods become more safe as a consequence. Difficult decisions consequently have to be made about whether it is the direct or the indirect benefits that should be included, and if the latter, which ones.

Beyond this, there are problems in deciding who even the direct beneficiaries are. For example, is the principal beneficiary of an adoption service the natural mother, the adopted child, the new parents, or all of the above? If there are differences in the income levels of these various parties, the distributional consequences of the service will vary depending on the definition of the beneficiary used. What is more, some services involve multiple "treatments" whereas others involve far fewer contacts. This poses thorny empirical problems about whether to count the number of "clients" or the amount of contact time with the human service provider in calculating the distributional effects of agency activity. If the typical poor client absorbs far less of an agency's resources than the typical nonpoor client, which method is chosen can have significant implications for the outcome.

Finally, the great diversity in the human service field poses further problems in reaching aggregate judgments about the distributional consequences of the services that are provided. Even when it becomes possible to settle on an appropriate measure of who is being served and by how much in one service field, it is rare to be able to compare another service field in the same terms. Developing a client count for a day care center, for example, is a far different thing from assessing the number of people served by a disaster assistance program. The former may involve daily contact stretching over many months, while the latter may involve one night on a cot in a church social hall during a tornado. Adding together the number of clients in the latter with the number in the former to measure the overall clientele of the nonprofit human service sector and the distribution of the sector's efforts among income groups can therefore be very misleading.

Perhaps because of these difficulties, few analyses of the client base of the nonprofit human service sector exist, and almost none treats the potential distributional consequences.[4]

To shed some empirical light on this issue, the survey of nonprofit human service agencies I organized in the mid-1980s included a specific question on the client focus of agencies.[5] In particular, agencies were asked in the first round survey to indicate what percentage of their clients were poor, defined as below the official poverty line.[6] While this is admittedly still a crude measure for the reasons noted above, it provides at least a partial picture of the distributional impact of these agencies.[7]

Overall Client Focus

Perhaps the central finding that emerges from this survey is that nonprofit social service agencies focus far less extensively on the poor than is sometimes imagined. Thus, of the 1,474 nonprofit human service agencies for which we were able to compile complete data, only 27 percent indicated that most of their clients were poor (that is, having incomes below the poverty line), as shown in table 9.3. Another 20 percent reported some poor clients (that is, between 21 percent and 50 percent of the agency's clientele). Significantly, over half (53%) of the agencies reported "few" (that is, 20% or less) or no low-income clients.

A similar picture emerges from an examination of the service offerings of these agencies. Although the poor have many needs, it seems reasonable to conclude that basic material needs—food, shelter, and financial assistance—would be particularly prominent. Agencies serving the poor could therefore be expected to offer many of these basic material resources. Yet, as table 9.3 also shows, the proportion of agen-

TABLE 9.3
Poverty Focus of Nonprofit Human Service Agencies

Focus	Percentage of Agencies ($n = 1,474$)
Client focus	
Mostly poor (> 50% of clients)	27%
Some poor (21%–50% of clients)	20
Few or no poor (20% of clients or less)	53
Total	100%
Provide material assistance	
Yes	16
No	84
Total	100%

SOURCE: Salamon Nonprofit Sector Project Survey, rounds 1 and 2 (1982, 1985).
NOTE: The sample consists of 1,474 nonprofit human service agencies in twelve metropolitan areas and four rural counties throughout the United States surveyed by mail in 1982, with a follow-up survey in 1984–85.

cies providing material assistance was quite small. In particular, only 16 percent of all human service agencies we surveyed indicated that they provided any direct material assistance of this sort. Quite clearly, the nonprofit human service sector does not appear to be primarily engaged either in providing the kind of material assistance most needed by the poor or in serving the poor in other ways.[8]

Variations among Types of Agencies

Not all types of agencies performed the same in terms of their extent of focus on the poor, however. To the contrary, some types focused more heavily on the poor than did others. In particular, as shown in table 9.4, agencies specializing in employment and training and legal rights and advocacy were far more likely to focus primarily on the poor than agencies specializing in education and research, outpatient health care, or social services. One reason for this finding may be that substantial numbers of day care centers are included among the social service agencies, and these centers tend to have a broader clientele than human service agencies generally. Thus only 24 percent of the day care providers focus primarily on the poor compared to 27 percent of all agencies.

Expenditures versus Agencies

The fact that only 27 percent of the human service agencies focus primarily on the poor still does not tell us precisely what share of the

TABLE 9.4
Agency Field of Service and Client Focus

Principal Field of Service	Percentage of Agencies Whose Clientele Include			
	Mostly Poor[a]	Some Poor[b]	Few or No Poor[c]	Total
Employment, training, income support	53%	10%	37%	100%
Legal rights and advocacy	43	19	38	100
Institutional/residential care	31	19	50	100
Mental health	30	25	45	100
Housing, environment	29	24	47	100
Multiservice	29	25	46	100
Social services	26	19	56	100
Health (excluding hospitals)	23	30	47	100
Education, research	10	12	78	100
All	27%	20%	53%	100%

SOURCE: Salamon Nonprofit Sector Project Survey, rounds 1 and 2.
NOTE: The chi-square test yields a probability of 0.000.
[a]Over 50 percent of clients poor.
[b]20–50 percent of clients poor.
[c]Fewer than 20 percent of clients poor.

resources of the human service sector goes to support the poor since agencies differ markedly in size. The share of resources going to the poor may therefore be greater or less than 27 percent depending on whether the primarily poor-serving agencies are on average larger or smaller than other agencies.

To take account of agency size, we attempted to estimate the actual resources devoted to the poor among the agencies surveyed. To do so, we assumed that agency expenditures were split among agency clientele roughly equally so that the proportion of expenditures going to the poor were roughly equivalent to the proportion of poor people among the agency's clientele. For example, if an agency reported that 50 percent of its clients were poor, then we assumed that 50 percent of its expenditures were allocated to poor clients. This approach probably overstates the share of resources going to the poor since prior research has shown that poor clients of human service agencies tend to receive less personalized and intensive forms of treatment (Hollingshead and Redlich 1965; Cloward and Epstein 1965), but there was no reliable basis for any alternative assumption. Furthermore, as noted above, we excluded from the analysis any agencies that failed to specify the proportion of poor people among their clients, even though it is likely that these agencies serve very few poor people. Once again,

TABLE 9.5

Estimated Share of Nonprofit Human Service Agency Expenditures Devoted to the Poor, by Type of Agency, 1982

(n = 1,399)

Type of Agency (Sample Sizes in Parentheses)	Percentage of Total Expenditures
Legal, advocacy (55)	71.8%
Employment and training (84)	55.4
Social services (462)	43.9
Multiservice (244)	42.1
Health (145)	36.6
Mental health (52)	36.3
Housing (58)	32.6
Institutional care (130)	30.9
Education/research (148)	16.2
All (1,399)	39.5

SOURCE: Salamon Nonprofit Sector Project Survey.

therefore, our analysis probably overstates somewhat the share of all resources going to support services for the poor.

The results of this analysis are reflected in table 9.5. As this table shows, even with the rather generous assumptions detailed above, we estimate that only about 40 percent of the expenditures of the agencies we surveyed went to support services targeted to the poor and that 60 percent went for services to other income groups. Among some types of agencies, however, the proportion of total expenditures devoted to poor people was higher than this—72 percent for legal service and advocacy agencies and 55 percent for employment and training agencies. Interestingly, social service agencies, which ranked well below average in terms of the proportion of agencies focusing primarily on the poor, nevertheless rank slightly above average (44%) in terms of the proportion of all expenditures targeted to the poor. This likely reflects the generally larger size of the primarily poor-serving social service agencies.

Summary

In short, only about a quarter of the nonprofit human service agencies we surveyed focus primarily on service to the poor, although another 20 percent of the agencies reported some (that is, between 21% and 50%) poor clients. In terms of total expenditures, approximately 40 percent of the expenditures of these agencies goes for service to the poor, though this figure may be somewhat exaggerated since it allocates expenditures in proportion to numbers of clients and excludes agencies that failed to report their client focus. Compared to other segments of the nonprofit sector, such as health or higher education, the human service agencies seem to focus more squarely on the poor, but it is still the case that most agencies focus primarily on the nonpoor, and most of the resources go to persons other than the poor.

Explaining Client Focus

How can we explain this pattern of client focus among nonprofit human service agencies? Why is it that so few of these agencies focus primarily on the poor despite a rhetoric of charitable intent? And what light does this shed on the character of the nonprofit human service sector and the theories available to understand it?

To answer these questions, it is useful to examine the characteristics of the poor-serving agencies in our sample in light of a number of theories that have been developed to explain the role, character, and scale of the nonprofit sector. Properly speaking, such an analysis does not constitute a "test" of these theories since the theories were not explicitly designed to explain this particular facet of nonprofit operations. Nevertheless, given the importance of this "charitable" dimension in the public's understanding of the nonprofit sector and in the shaping of government policy toward it, it is still useful to determine what light these theories can shed on the pattern of client focus, and, in turn, what light the evidence of client focus can shed on the explanatory power of the theories.

Four such theories or theoretical perspectives are especially deserving of attention in this regard. Three of these are theories of the nonprofit sector, and one reflects organizational theory more broadly.

Market Failure/Government Failure Theory

Perhaps the dominant theoretical perspective for interpreting the character and role of the nonprofit sector grows out of classical economics, with its emphasis on the inherent limitations of the private market in producing collective goods. The central thesis of this theory is that both the market and government have limitations in producing collective goods—the former because of the "free rider" problem that allows consumers to benefit from collective goods without having to pay for them and the latter because of the requirement for majority support in order to get the government to address the resulting unmet need. The nonprofit sector, according to this theory, exists as an alternative provider of collective goods, satisfying the demands for such goods that are left unmet by both government and the market (Weisbrod 1977).

A relatively low level of nonprofit activity focused on the poor is perfectly consistent with this theory. Since nonprofits come into existence in this view to meet demands for collective goods that are not met by government, it is reasonable to expect that the demands that will be met by the sector will be those of the people with the resources to pay for them. To the extent that the unmet demands that these people have are "charitable" in character and focus on helping the disadvantaged, however, this theory would lead us to expect the most extensive nonprofit attention to the poor where government involvement is lowest. In this view, charitably oriented individuals desiring a level of care for the poor that the general political system has not been willing to support can be expected to utilize the nonprofit sector to help fill the resulting gaps. Other things being equal, the greater the level of private support, therefore, the greater the level of private agency attention to the poor that this theory would lead us to expect. Otherwise the public sector could be expected to be involved. Conversely, the greater the level of government support, the lower the level of private agency attention to the poor that would be expected.

Voluntary Failure Theory

A second body of theory posits a somewhat different dynamic at work between government support and nonprofit service to the poor. In this view, the same "free rider" problem that inhibits the market in providing collective goods also inhibits the voluntary sector in generating private support, particularly for aid to the poor (Salamon 1987b). In addition, the nonprofit sector also has other inherent limitations as a mechanism for meeting human needs, such as its frequent paternalism and its particularism, namely, the tendency of agencies to restrict aid to narrow groups of people defined along religious, ethnic, or racial lines. Left to their own devices, therefore, nonprofit organizations can be expected to provide only limited aid to the poor. To expand on their efforts, they need access to broader sources of funds of the sort that government can provide. In this view, nonprofit service to the poor and government support for service to the poor spring from essentially the same social and economic dynamics. But for nonprofits to be able to act on this impulse, outside support from government is crucial. Far from expecting nonprofits to operate where government does not, therefore, this theory would lead us to find both sectors working in tandem. Far from decreasing as government support increases, nonprofit service to the poor would thus be expected to increase as government support increases.

Supply-Side Theory

A third body of theory views the activities of the nonprofit sector as a response not simply to external "need" or demand, but also to the supply of entrepreneurs who choose to meet that demand through the creation of charitable institutions (James 1987). Historically, religious institutions have been among the most prominent sources of such charitably inclined "entrepreneurs." The common assumption is that sponsorship of nonprofit organizations by religious organizations reflects the altruistic values that religions typically espouse (Wuthnow 1990, 7–9). According to this theory, therefore, nonprofit service to the poor will be closely related to the availability of a pool of religiously inspired individuals who create a set of religiously oriented nonprofit organizations. As a consequence, the more closely a nonprofit is associated with religious activity or religious organizations, the more likely it should be to focus on the poor. An alternative version of this theory, associated with the work of Estelle James (1987), argues that the formation of nonprofit organizations by religious groups has less to do with altruistic sentiments toward the poor than with the desire to retain and attract members by offering them tangible services. Since such groups probably prefer to attract middle- and upper-income adherents, this version of the supply-side theory would lead us to expect a negative relationship between religious affiliation and service to the poor, other things being equal.

Organization Theory

This alternative form of the supply-side theory brings us to a final set of theoretical perspectives on the client focus of nonprofit organizations, which flows from organization theory. Rather than viewing the operation of nonprofit and other organizations as a product simply of the external environment and consumer demand, these theories find the explanation for organizational behavior within the organizations themselves—in the maintenance and enhancement needs of agency staff, in the missions and patterns of task accomplishment that are chosen, and in the operating style that agency managers adopt. In this view, organizations have significant latitude in their choice of client focus, and they choose the one that best meets the professional and organizational goals of the agency (Etzioni 1964; Scott 1974; Dess and Beard 1984). Among the factors likely to explain variations in agency focus on the poor, therefore, are the service focus of the agency (which relates to the professional training and preferences of staff members), the degree of professionalization within the agency, the initial focus of agency efforts (since organizations often find it difficult to change in response to external pressures), and the size and consequent degree of bureaucratization within the agency. Some analysts (Cloward and Epstein 1965; Riley 1981) thus argue that the efforts of social workers to acquire professional status in the 1940s and 1950s led to the adoption of a preferred style of task accomplishment that was rooted in psychological conceptions of family problems, and that led private agencies dominated by social work professionals to turn away from advocacy for improvement in the social environment of the poor toward a much more intensive, interpersonal, therapeutic model of treatment that was more suitable for a middle-class clientele. Similarly, Hollingshead and Redlich (1965) found that professional treatment of neurotics varied widely by social class and economic status. Not only were lower-class neurotics much more likely to be referred to public hospitals instead of private clinics or private practitioners, but they were also far more likely to receive organic forms of treatment, such as shock therapy, drugs, and lobotomies. These findings suggest that an agency's focus on social work and social services and its degree of professionalization will be negatively related to its propensity to focus on the poor. By the same token, Scott (1974, 495) found in a study of agencies serving the blind that the services these agencies offered "are often more responsive to the organizational needs of agencies through which services are offered than they are to the needs of blind persons." This suggests that the larger and more bureaucratized the agency, the less likely it is to focus on the needs of the poor, other things being equal.

Empirical Results

To what extent do these various theoretical perspectives find support in the data on nonprofit client focus available through our survey?

The answer to this question, not surprisingly, is somewhat complex since some of the theories are difficult to translate into operational form and not all the variables that might be useful to test the theories are available in the survey. What is more, the survey treats the agency as the unit of analysis rather than the individual program within an agency. It is therefore quite possible that a set of relationships that might operate at the program level—for example, between funding source and client focus—might be obscured, particularly in large agencies, by data that apply to the agency as a whole.[9]

While it is important to recognize these potential limitations, however, the data we have collected still make it possible to shed some valuable empirical light on the causes of the patterns of client focus and distributional effects that are apparent. In this section we examine these data, focusing on the effects of a number of the individual factors that the prevailing theories suggest may be important, and then presenting the results of a multiple regression analysis intended to sort out the independent effects of the various factors while holding constant the effects of the others.

Social and Economic Context

According to the "market failure/government failure theory" of the nonprofit sector, nonprofits should be expected to focus more heavily on the poor in circumstances where existing government programs for the poor are least effective or adequate. This is so because the nonprofit sector is viewed in this theory as a mechanism for satisfying demands for collective goods that are not satisfied by either the market or government.

One way to test this theory is to look at the behavior of nonprofit organizations in urban and rural settings. Because social welfare programs are typically less generous in rural or small-town settings than in more urbanized areas, this theory would predict that nonprofit attention to the poor would be more pronounced in rural than in urban areas.

As table 9.6 shows, however, our survey data provide little support for this hypothesis. Although the proportion of rural agencies that have some (that is, 21%–50%) poor clients is slightly higher than the comparable proportion of urban agencies, and the proportion with few or no low-income clients slightly lower, these relationships are not statistically significant. This finding is all the more notable in view of the fact that income levels in the rural counties were well below those in the urban areas and the proportions of people in poverty and eligible for welfare were considerably higher.[10]

TABLE 9.6
Client Focus of Urban and Rural Nonprofit Human Service Agencies
$(n = 1,474)$

	Percentage of Agencies		
Client Focus	Urban Agencies	Rural Agencies	All Agencies
Mostly poor	27%	27%	27%
Some poor	20	23	20
Few or no poor	53	50	53
Total	100%	100%	100%

SOURCE: Salamon Nonprofit Sector Project Survey, rounds 1 and 2. See tables 9.3 and 9.4 for sample and definitions.
NOTE: Chi-square probability = 0.173.

Funding Source

A second factor that might explain variations in nonprofit human service agency attention to the poor is the funding structure of the agencies. As it turns out, a strong relationship exists between the funding structure of an agency and its client focus, though the relationship tends to support the "voluntary failure theory" more than the "market failure/government failure theory." Under the market failure theory, as we have seen, nonprofit attention to the poor should be most in evidence where government involvement in aid to the poor is least pronounced. This is the so-called gap-filling theory of nonprofit activity, the notion that nonprofits operate to "fill the gaps" left by government social welfare activity, permitting charitably inclined individuals to provide more relief for poverty and distress than the official government programs provide. The "voluntary failure" theory, by contrast, predicts that nonprofit attention to the poor will be greater where government involvement in assistance to the poor is greater, since government support allows nonprofits to overcome their own inherent limitations as providers of aid to the needy.

As table 9.7 shows, there is a strong and consistent relationship between government support and nonprofit attention to the needy, but in the direction predicted by the "voluntary failure theory" rather than the "market failure/government failure" theory. Thus, the agencies primarily serving the poor averaged 57 percent of their income from government in 1981 compared to only 29 percent for the agencies with no poor clients. Conversely, as the share of income from private charitable sources increases, the focus on the poor goes down, except for the agencies with no poor clients, which seem to operate in a more commercial vein, with close to 40 percent of their income from fees. There is thus little evidence here that private charity is filling in for

TABLE 9.7
Funding Sources and Poverty Focus of Nonprofit Human Service Agencies, 1981

	Average Share of Income for Agencies Serving				
Source	Mostly Poor	Some Poor	Few Poor	No Poor	All Agencies
Government	57%	45%	33%	29%	38%
Private giving	28	33	32	25	31
Dues, fees	8	17	26	38	23
Other	7	5	9	8	8
Total	100%	100%	100%	100%	100%

SOURCE: Salamon Nonprofit Sector Project Survey, rounds 1 and 2.
NOTE: Shares are based on reported aggregate income for all agencies in each group.

inadequacies in the system of public support for the poor. To the contrary, the data seem to suggest that one of the major factors accounting for what limited focus the nonprofit human service sector gives to the poor is the availability of government financial support. By contrast, private charitable support seems to flow more heavily to agencies that are less focused on the poor.

This point can be seen even more clearly in table 9.8, which records the estimated share of income from each source going to support services for the poor and the share of total expenditures on services for the poor that came from each of the major revenue sources.[11] As this table shows, an estimated 47 percent of all government support to nonprofit human service organizations went to support services for the poor. By contrast, only 39 percent of all private giving and 25 percent of all fee income went to support such services. Among the sources of private charitable support, moreover, the only one that provided above average support for services to the poor was United Way.

Reflecting these patterns, table 9.8 also shows that government support is even more important to the financing of services to the poor than it is to financing nonprofit human service activities more generally. Compared to the 38 percent of all income it provides to human service agencies generally, government contributed 57 percent of the estimated costs of services to the poor. By contrast, while private giving accounted for 31 percent of all nonprofit human service agency income, it provided only 22 percent of the income going for services to the poor.

Determining the distributional implications of these findings is complicated by the fact that detailed information is not available on the contributions that different income groups make to these various revenue streams. Generally speaking, however, to the extent that the U.S.

TABLE 9.8

*Sources of Revenues to Support Services to the Poor by Nonprofit
Human Service Agencies*

Revenue Source	Percentage of Total Revenue from Source Going to Services for Poor (1)	Percentage of Support for Poor from Source (2)	Percentage of Support for All Services from Source (3)
Government	47.0%	57.2%	38%
Private giving	39.4	21.7	31
United Way	45.3	7.9	
Other federated	35.2	2.0	
Religious	37.3	1.4	
Individual	36.2	5.9	
Corporations	40.7	1.7	
Foundations	36.5	2.9	
Fees	25.2	13.4	23
Other (investments, etc.)	36.9	7.7	8
Total	39.5%	100.0%	100%

SOURCE: Salamon Nonprofit Sector Project Survey, rounds 1 and 2.
NOTE: Column 1 records the share of the revenue from each source going to the poor. Column 2 records the share of all expenditures on the poor that originate from the indicated revenue sources. Column 3 records the share of all expenditures for all clients that originate from the indicated revenue sources. All data were compiled by allocating the revenues from each source to poor clients in each agency in proportion to the share that the poor represent among the agency's clients. Thus if 30 percent of an agency's clients are poor, it is assumed that 30 percent of the agency's private charitable income, 30 percent of its government income, and 30 percent of its fee income goes to support the poor.

tax structure is mildly progressive (Pechman and Okner 1974), the extensive flow of government support to services for the poor through the nonprofit sector is redistributive in character.[12] The same can probably also be said for fee income, which is most likely to be paid by middle- and upper-income clientele. Although it accounts for only an estimated 13 percent of the cost of nonprofit human service agency services to the poor, and although only an estimated 25 percent of all fee income finds its way into support for such services, there is probably still a meaningful redistributional dimension to this support.

The situation with respect to private giving is more complicated. In the first place, there is some evidence that giving is regressive, namely, that the poor contribute more as a percentage of their income than do the better-off (Hodgkinson et al. 1990, 48–49). In the second place, the better-off receive tax deductions that significantly reduce the actual out-of-pocket cost of their gifts. If these deductions average 30 percent, and if only 40 percent of all private giving goes to support services to the poor and some of this comes from the poor or near-

TABLE 9.9

Religious Affiliation and Nonprofit Human Service Agency Client Focus

Client Focus	Percentage of Agencies by Religious Affiliation		
	Yes	No	All
Mostly poor	25%	28%	27%
Some poor	17	21	20
Few or no poor	58	51	53
Total	100%	100%	100%

SOURCE: Salamon Nonprofit Sector Project Survey, rounds 1 and 2.
NOTE: Chi-square probability = 0.01.

poor, then the redistributive effect of private philanthropy's contribution to human service agencies is open to serious question.

Religious Affiliation

According to the "supply-side" theory of the nonprofit sector, the existence of a need such as continued poverty is not a sufficient explanation for the existence of significant nonprofit activity. Equally important is the availability of a supply of "social entrepreneurs" willing to organize a charitable response. To a significant degree, moreover, such entrepreneurs have historically tended to emerge from one or another religious tradition. This suggests that the presence or absence of a religious connection should help to explain the extent to which a nonprofit organization focuses on the needs of the poor.

Two measures of religious affiliation were available in our survey to assess this dimension of nonprofit activity. One classified agencies according to whether they had "any formal religious affiliation." The other asked whether the agency "belong[s] to or receive[s] funds from any religious federation (e.g., Catholic Charities, Jewish Federation)." Altogether, about 15 percent of the agencies we sampled indicated one or both of these forms of religious ties.

When we related religious affiliation to the client focus of agencies, however, a curious result emerged. While religious affiliation does appear to be significantly related to the extent of poverty focus, the relationship is the reverse of what the "supply-side" theory would predict. In particular, as table 9.9 shows, agencies with a religious affiliation were less likely to have a primarily low-income clientele than agencies without such an affiliation. Thus only 25 percent of the agencies with a religious affiliation reported that most of their clients were poor, compared to 28 percent of the agencies without such an affiliation. By contrast, 58 percent of the religiously affiliated agencies reported few or no low-income clients compared to 51 percent of the remaining agencies. Although it will still have to be tested holding other factors constant, this finding seems to refute the conventional "altruism" view of the relationship between religion and nonprofit organizations and to lend credence to the alternative organization theory view of how this relationship works.

Agency Age

One possible explanation of this unexpected result may be that agencies change their client focus over time. Put somewhat differently, the initial focus of the agency may not be so much on the problems of the poor as on the problems of a particular religious community that happens to start out poor. As the economic circumstances of this community improve, the client focus of the agency may appear to change away from the poor. In this sense, the agency might lose its poverty focus through "natural causes," namely the improvement of the economic status of the "community" on which it focuses its activities.

To the extent this occurs, however, it would run counter to one of the central tenets of organization theory, which holds that organizations tend to resist changes in their basic technologies or approach. Organization theory would thus predict that agencies that start out with a focus on problems of the poor would retain this focus over time.

To test these two possible hypotheses, we grouped agencies by their year of formation. Our expectation was that agencies formed during either of two periods would be most likely to start out being focused on the poor and therefore would be most likely, if the organization theory view holds, to retain that focus today. The first is the period prior to 1930, when the nonprofit sector was the only line of defense against poverty and distress. The second was the period of the 1960s, when poverty was "rediscovered," and voluntary organizations were formed to represent the poor and carry out antipoverty initiatives of various sorts.

When this notion is tested against the data, it finds little empirical support. As shown in table 9.10, agencies formed during the 1960s do seem to be more heavily focused on the poor, but only slightly so. By contrast, the pre-1930 agencies are among the least likely to focus on the poor. Overall, the relationship that exists between agency age and

TABLE 9.10
Agency Age and Client Focus
($n = 1,469$)

	Year Formed—Percentage of Agencies				
Client Focus	Before 1930	1930– 1960	1961– 1970	1971– Present	All
Mostly poor	23%	23%	29%	29%	27%
Some poor	28	23	18	18	21
Few or no poor	49	54	53	53	52
Total	100%	100%	100%	100%	100%

SOURCE: Salamon Nonprofit Sector Project Survey, rounds 1 and 2.
NOTE: Chi-square probability = 0.06.

client focus is not statistically significant. If the two groups of agencies started out their lives strongly focused on the poor, something must have intervened to reduce that focus.

Agency Field of Service

One such possible intervening factor suggested by the literature is professionalization and changing agency operating technology. Cloward and Epstein (1965) and others have argued, as we have noted, that the field of social work underwent a significant metamorphosis in the period following the Great Depression. It became more professional, more preoccupied with the techniques of individualized social "casework," and in the process lost some of its orientation toward the poor and toward advocacy. One reason that the 1930s agencies may be less oriented to the poor than we might have expected, therefore, is that they have taken on the coloration of this dominant profession.

This line of argument may explain the pattern of agency client focus reported in table 9.4. The professionalization argument would lead us to expect that social service agencies would focus less heavily on the poor than agencies providing employment, training, and income support, or legal services and advocacy since it is in the social service agencies that the practice of social casework is most clearly lodged.

As noted above, this is exactly what we found. The primarily social service agencies, which account for 34 percent of all the agencies in our sample, ranked among the lowest in terms of average proportion of clients who are poor. In particular, only 26 percent of the social service agencies focus primarily on the poor while 56 percent report having few or no poor clients. By contrast, over half of the employment, training, and income support agencies, and over 40 percent of the legal rights and advocacy agencies, focus primarily on the poor. What is more, these findings are statistically significant at the 0.01 level of probability (that is, they could have happened by chance less than one time in 100).

Despite these results, however, there is reason to question whether the dynamic that Cloward and Epstein identified in the mid-1960s is still at work as powerfully in the nonprofit sector as of the early 1980s. In the first place, as we have seen, the rather weak showing of social service agencies in service to the disadvantaged seems to be due at least to some extent to the inclusion of numerous child day care centers among the social service agencies. More than other social service providers, agencies that provide day care seem to focus less heavily on the poor. Thus, only 24 percent of the day care providers focus principally on the poor compared to 28 percent of the other agencies. Similarly, 55 percent of the day care providers report few or no poor clients compared to 52 percent of the other agencies. While this relationship is not statistically significant, it suggests that the inclusion of day care providers may be one of the reasons for the relatively limited focus of social service agencies on the poor. What is more, this same point receives even stronger confirmation when we zero in on the agencies providing "individual and family counseling," which is the precise locus of the social casework mode of service. As it turns out, a statistically significant relationship exists between the provision of individual and family counseling and agency focus on the poor, but it is in a direction opposite to what Cloward and Epstein would predict. Agencies providing individual and family counseling are more likely rather than less likely to focus heavily on the poor. Thus, 33 percent of the agencies providing this service focus primarily on the poor compared to only 27 percent of all agencies. Conversely, only 43 percent of the individual and family counseling agencies serve few or no poor clients, compared to 52 percent of all agencies. Given the "ecological fallacy" problem mentioned earlier,[13] it may still be the case that the providers of individual and family counseling within these agencies may not serve the poor. But the weight of the evidence seems to temper the thrust of the Cloward and Epstein thesis. At the very least, some agencies seem able to combine their focus on professional casework services for a general population with attention to the problems of the poor.

Two routes for doing this may be to include within the activities of an agency some focus on social advocacy and the provision of material goods, even though these may not be the principal activities of the agency. Based on our survey data, numerous agencies do this. Thus, while only 4 percent of our sampled agencies were primarily involved in advocacy work, just over 20 percent reported some advocacy activity; and among these the proportion reporting that most of their clients are poor was 38 percent, compared to 27 percent of all agencies. Similarly, while only 6 percent of all the agencies were primarily involved in providing material assistance, 16 percent indicated that they provided some material assistance, and 48 percent of these indicated that most of their clients were poor.

In short, while there is some support for the Cloward and Epstein thesis that professionalization of the social work field has alienated it from the poor, it seems clear that many agencies delivering professional social casework services continue to serve the poor, at least in part, through advocacy and material assistance. Whether these activities represent a serious assault on the problems of the poor, or a thin veneer of activity intended chiefly to provide legitimacy to agencies that are supposed to be charitable but are largely not, is more difficult to say.

Professionalization

One way to shed more light on this issue is to examine the relationship between agency staffing patterns and client focus more directly. If professionalization is associated with loss of interest in the poor, we would expect that the agencies with the most reliance on professional staff would have the lowest levels of focus on the poor.

Unfortunately, our survey did not gather direct information on the professional degrees of agency staff. However, it did gather other information that makes it possible for us to explore this relationship, including information on the size of agency paid staffs and on the ratio of paid staff to volunteers. Generally speaking, this information provides little support to the professionalization thesis. In the first place, it appears that agencies with more paid staff focus more heavily on the poor than do agencies staffed entirely by volunteers or by only a handful of paid staff. This is evident in table 9.11, which relates the staff size of the agencies in our sample to their client focus. A clear, statistically significant relationship is apparent, but opposite to what the professionalization thesis would suggest. In particular, only 10 percent of the agencies staffed wholly by volunteers focused chiefly on the poor, whereas 77 percent reported few or no poor people among their clients. By contrast, among agencies with 100 and over paid staff, the comparable figures are 39 percent of the agencies serving mostly poor clients and only 36 percent serving few or no poor clients. This rela-

TABLE 9.11
Agency Employment Levels and Client Focus

	Percentage of Agencies with Indicated Client Focus			
Paid Staff Size (FTE)[a]	Mostly Poor	Some Poor	Few or No Poor	Total
None	10%	13%	77%	100%
1–2.5	17	20	65	100
3–13	28	20	52	100
14–99	34	23	43	100
100 and over	39	25	36	100
All agencies	27%	21%	52%	100%

SOURCE: Salamon Nonprofit Sector Project Survey, rounds 1 and 2.
NOTE: Chi-square probability = 0.000.
[a]Part-time staff converted to full-time equivalents (FTE).

TABLE 9.12
Staff-Volunteer Ratios and Client Focus

	Percentage of Agencies with Indicated Client Focus			
Staff/Volunteer Ratio	Mostly Poor	Some Poor	Few or No Poor	Total
Low[a]	19%	17%	64%	100%
Medium[b]	30	22	48	100
High[c]	31	25	44	100
Very high[d]	27	17	56	100
All agencies	27%	21%	52%	100%

SOURCE: Salamon Nonprofit Sector Project Survey, rounds 1 and 2.
NOTES: Chi-square probability = 0.000.
[a]Less than 1 staff per volunteer.
[b]1–14 staff per volunteer.
[c]15–100 staff per volunteer.
[d]Over 100 staff per volunteer.

tionship may be due in part to the fact that "informal" organizations are excluded from our survey, but the fact remains that reliance on volunteers instead of paid professional staff does not seem to be associated with attention to the needs of the poor, as is sometimes assumed.

As a second way to check on this relationship, we computed the ratio of paid staff to volunteers in our surveyed agencies. The basic notion here is that what is potentially important in determining agency responsiveness to lower-income clientele is not simply the number of paid staff, which may really be a proxy for the size of the agency, but the extent to which volunteer staff are also incorporated into agency operations. The results, however, reported in table 9.12, provide further support to the conclusion reached above. Thus of the agencies with the lowest paid staff to volunteer ratios, only 19 percent primarily served the poor, whereas 64 percent reported few or no low-income clients. By contrast, among the agencies with medium or high ratios of paid staff to volunteers, about 30 percent focused principally on the poor and 44 to 48 percent reported few or no low-income clientele. In other words, extensive reliance on volunteers instead of professional staff is no guarantee of attention to the poor. Evidently, it is the volunteers who may be alienated from the poor, not the professionals. The one piece of contrary evidence is the finding that the agencies with "very high" ratios of staff to volunteers (that is, in excess of 100:1) tended to be less likely to focus on the poor, but the difference is not great.

As a final check on the relationship between professionalism and client focus, we asked agency directors whether they agreed or disagreed with the statement that "volunteers can be substituted extensively for paid professionals in nonprofit organizations without any significant decline in service quality." Not surprisingly, 80 percent of the respondents disagreed with the observation. Interestingly, however, the agency personnel taking the anti-volunteer position were more likely to represent agencies primarily serving the poor than was the case with those who took the pro-volunteer position. Thus, 30 percent of those who disagreed with replacing professionals with volunteers worked in agencies primarily serving the poor compared to 20 percent of those who favored such replacement. Conversely, over 60 percent of those favoring volunteers over paid staff work in agencies with few or no poor clients compared to 47 percent of those who are more skeptical about the capabilities of volunteers.

Overall, there thus seems to be a strong relationship between professionalization within the nonprofit sector and attention to the needs of the poor. Whether fairly or not, efforts to cope with the serious problems of poverty and distress have come to be seen as requiring more than amateur approaches and volunteer activity. The good news in this is that professionalization may not alienate nonprofit organizations from the problems of the poor as much as some may fear. The bad news is that the costs of mounting a serious attack on the interrelated problems of poverty and despair may be higher than some are willing to pay, whether the approach uses the nonprofit sector or direct public intervention.

Bureaucratization

Quite apart from the level of professionalization of staff, the sheer size of an agency may have an impact on its client focus. According to

TABLE 9.13
Agency Size and Client Focus

	Percentage of Agencies with Indicated Client Focus			
Agency Expenditures	Mostly Poor	Some Poor	Few or No Poor	Total
Small[a]	18%	17%	65%	100%
Medium[b]	30	23	47	100
Large[c]	35	24	41	100
All agencies	27%	21%	52%	100%

SOURCE: Salamon Nonprofit Sector Project Survey, rounds 1 and 2.
NOTES: Chi-square probability = 0.000.
[a]Expenditures under $100,000.
[b]Expenditures of $100,000–$999,999.
[c]Expenditures of $1 million or more.

organization theory, organizations "seek out environments that permit organizational growth and stability" (Dess and Beard 1984, 55). The larger an agency, the greater these pressures must be and therefore the greater the possibility of "goal displacement," of the substitution of the needs of the organization qua organization for those of the clients. To the extent that organizational survival requires moving away from the needs of the poor, agency size will therefore be associated with less attention to the poor.

As reflected in table 9.13, this line of reasoning finds little support in the data from our survey. Far from decreasing as agency size increases, attention to the poor increases. Thus, only 18 percent of the smallest agencies reported focusing most of their attention on the poor compared to 35 percent of the largest agencies. Conversely, among the small agencies, 65 percent reported few or no poor clients compared to only 41 percent among the large agencies. Large size thus does not appear to be an inhibiting factor in making nonprofit agencies responsive to the poor. To the contrary, it is small size that seems to inhibit attention to the poor.

Summary: Regression Results

What are we to make of these findings? To what extent do they refute the organization theory approach outlined earlier, as seems to be the case? Which of the theoretical perspectives on the nonprofit sector finds most support in the data reviewed here?

To answer these questions properly, it is necessary to go beyond the cross-tabulation analysis that has been presented thus far to take account of the interrelationships among some of the variables we have been examining. A strong correlation exists, for example, between

TABLE 9.14
*Expected Relationships between Agency Characteristics and
Extent of Poverty Focus*

Theory	Variable	Expected Relation to Poverty Focus
Market failure/ government failure	Government support (%)	−
	Fee support	+
	United Way support	+
Voluntary failure	Government support (%)	+
	Fee support	−
Supply-side theory	Religious affiliation	+
Organization theory	Social service expenditures	−
	Employment/income support expenditures	+
	Legal services/advocacy expenditures	+
	Pre-1930s formation	+
	Expenditure size	−
	Staff size	−
	Professional/volunteers ratio	−

agency size and the share of agency income coming from government. This is so for the obvious reason that government support tends to come in rather large chunks. It is therefore important to try to sort out whether it is the source of the income or the size of the agency that is really the relevant factor. To the extent that the latter is at work, we will have found a basis for refuting the organization theory perspective, which holds that the larger and more bureaucratized the agency, the greater the maintenance and enhancement pressures and therefore the greater the incentive to extend the reach of the agency beyond the poor. To the extent it is the former, this theory will retain credence.

To sort out these interrelationships, we have developed a multiple regression model that seeks to assess the independent impact of the various factors that our theories suggest as possible explanations of the extent of nonprofit attention to the poor, while holding constant the impact of the other factors.

Table 9.14 summarizes the variables in the model, the theory or theories with which each is associated, and the direction of impact that the various theories suggest will exist between the factor and the extent of agency focus on the poor. Thus, the market failure/government failure theory would lead us to expect that the extent of agency focus on the poor will be positively related to the extent of private support an agency receives, and negatively related to the extent of government support, other things being equal. The voluntary failure theory, by contrast, would lead us to expect a positive relation between govern-

TABLE 9.15

Relationship between Agency Characteristics and Percentage of Poor in Agency Clientele

Factor	Predicted Relation to Client Focus (% Poor)	Actual Regression Factor
Government support (%)	+	0.1612**
United Way support (%)	+	0.2141**
Fee support (%)	−	−0.2498**
Religious affiliation	+	4.6374
Social service expenditures (%)	−	0.0039
Employment/income support expenditures (%)	+	0.2477**
Legal services/advocacy expenditures (%)	+	0.1720**
Pre-1930s formation	+	−4.3978
Expenditures	−	4.4980
Staff size	−	0.0276
Professional/volunteer ratio	−	−0.5466

$R^2 = 19.5\%$
Probability $= 0.0001$

NOTE: ** = Significant at the .01 level.

ment support and the extent of agency focus on the poor. For the supply-side theory, at least in its "religion-as-altruism" version, the key variable is the presence of a religious affiliation, and the expected relation between religious affiliation and attention to the poor is positive. Finally, organization theory posits negative relationships between agency poverty focus and adoption of the social casework method (percent of social services expenditure), agency size (expenditures and staff size), and professionalization (professional/volunteer ratio). This same theory would lead us to expect a positive relationship between the extent of poverty focus and agency involvement in employment and income support as well as legal services and advocacy, and agency age (on grounds that agencies formed prior to the creation of government social welfare programs in the 1930s would be more likely to focus on the poor and to retain this focus today).

Table 9.15 presents the results of this multiple regression analysis. As this table shows, five of the factors we have examined turn out to have a statistically significant independent effect on the propensity of agencies to focus on the poor. Three of these have to do with the sources of agency income—the share coming from government, which is positively related to poverty focus; the share coming from United Way, which is also positively related to poverty focus; and the share coming from fees and charges, which is negatively related to poverty focus. The remaining two factors have to do with the service field in which agencies concentrate. Thus the propensity to focus on the poor is positively related to the share of agency expenditures going into advocacy and the share going into employment and income support (that is, direct material support) activities.

Interestingly, however, once these factors are taken into consideration, there is no significant relationship between poverty focus and agency size, year of formation, religious affiliation, extent of involvement in the provision of social services, or the ratio of paid staff to volunteers. Taken together, these factors lend support to the "voluntary failure" and "organization theory" models of the operation of the nonprofit sector. Far from filling in for the inadequacies of government policies for coping with the problems of the poor, as the "market failure/government failure theory" would predict, nonprofit organizations seem to operate in the same fields as does government and to rely extensively on government support to extend their reach to the poor. Aside from United Way, which provides relatively modest levels of support, private giving is not particularly available to agencies focusing on the poor. Far from creating a conflict between agency survival and attention to the poor, the availability of government support has given agencies a way to avoid such a conflict.

The fact that agency size drops out as an independent explanatory factor once government support is included in the equation reinforces this interpretation. The expectation that large agencies would feel compelled to turn away from the poor in order to ensure their survival turns out not to be supported by the evidence, but this may not be because the basic organizational dynamic is not at work. Rather, the reason appears to be that government support became available to rescue at least some agencies from this dilemma. Thanks to government support, in other words, agencies were able to reconcile their organizational survival needs with at least limited service to the poor. The alternative would have been greater dependence on either fees or private support, neither of which seems congenial to service to the poor.

Finally, the data give little credence to the "supply-side" theories of the nonprofit sector, at least as they relate to the question of who the nonprofit sector serves. Religious affiliation and poverty focus are positively related to each other, as these theories predict, but the relationship is not strong enough to be statistically significant. Religious affiliation thus has no independent effect on the likelihood that agencies will serve the poor.

Conclusions and Implications

These findings have significant implications for the success of the social policies put into effect in the United States in the early 1980s and for the evolution of the nonprofit sector as a consequence. A central premise of these policies was that the private nonprofit sector could make a significant dent in filling the gaps left by cutbacks in government support for the poor. Underlying this premise was the assumption that the nonprofit sector remained oriented toward service to the poor and would redouble its efforts to attend to this obligation as government support declined.

The data presented here, however, suggest a rather different view of the dynamics at work within even the human service component of the nonprofit sector. What these data make clear is that nonprofit human service agencies, whatever else they may be, are first and foremost organizations. As such, they seek to maintain themselves as viable systems. But as nonprofits, they find themselves in a particularly vulnerable position, in what Hasenfeld and English (1974, 100) term a "state of dependency," "dependent on external units for the procurement of resources without having sufficient countervailing powers vis-à-vis these units." To cope with this situation, nonprofit human service agencies have had to develop internal routines, mission concepts, staffing approaches, and definitions of their clientele that allow them to come to terms with the realities of their environment. This has involved a broadening of the concept of social services that has extended the domain of nonprofit human service agencies well beyond the needs of the poor, the development of a mode of task accomplishment congenial to the professionalization of agency staff, and the legitimization of a source of funding—fees for service—that provides some relief from dependence on the vagaries of private largesse.

The upshot of these pressures, however, has been to shift the focus of nonprofit human service agencies to a significant extent away from the poor. As we have seen, fewer than 30 percent of the agencies surveyed reported that the poor constitute half or more of the agency's clientele. By contrast, over half of the agencies reported serving few or no poor clients and over 60 percent of the resources went to the nonpoor. What is more, this pattern held across most of the service fields in which human service agencies operate—social services, mental health, health, institutional and residential care, and even housing and community development. Only employment, training and income support agencies, and legal rights and advocacy organizations differed markedly from this pattern, and these agencies make up a very small proportion of the sector.

The one truly effective countervailing force in the system has been the availability of government funding targeted to the poor. Based on our statistical analysis, it has been the availability of such funding that has allowed or encouraged the nonprofit sector to focus on the poor to the limited extent that it has. Other factors thought to be associated with attention to the poor—such as agency traditions, religious affiliation, private giving, and high levels of voluntarism—turn out to have little or no effect.

Far from distorting the traditional objectives of nonprofit agencies as some have feared, in other words, the recent rise of government support may actually have allowed these agencies to retain a stronger commitment to their traditional charitable goal of service to the needy than would otherwise have been possible.

In view of this finding, the retrenchment in government social welfare spending, and in government support to nonprofit agencies, that took place in the 1980s, far from liberating the nonprofit sector, may have forced it to turn away from those in greatest need. To assess the extent to which this occurred, however, it is necessary to turn from this general analysis of the scope and consequences of government-nonprofit collaboration to an assessment of the scope and consequences of the retrenchment policies of the 1980s and early 1990s.

PART IV

The Impact of Retrenchment

Few developments have affected the nonprofit sector in the United States more profoundly in recent years than the significant reorientation of domestic policy inaugurated by the Reagan administration between 1981 and 1989. Few developments, therefore, are as important to understand and assess.

After five decades of almost continuously expanding government involvement in the provision of human services, the Reagan administration came to power in 1981 committed to a sweeping redirection of the national approach. Rather than expanding governmental protections in the human service field, the Reagan administration sought to narrow them sharply and place more reliance on private action instead. What is more, through its Omnibus Budget and Reconciliation Act of 1981 and its Economic Recovery Tax Act of the same year, the administration made important headway in putting this program into effect, cutting sharply into the resources made available for a wide range of domestic programs and severely limiting the revenues available to fuel further growth. In the process, it raised fundamental issues about the roles of government and other institutions in American life and left a legacy of fiscal retrenchment that continues to dominate the national agenda.

For the thousands of organizations that comprise the nation's private, nonprofit sector, this shift in policy has been, at best, a mixed blessing. On the one hand, because the new administration justified its budget cuts and program reforms in important part as an effort to return more of the responsibility for dealing with public problems to private, voluntary groups, it rescued these organizations from the widespread obscurity to which they had been consigned during the long period of governmental growth. On the other hand, however, by failing to recognize the existence of the elaborate system of governmental support for these institutions detailed earlier in this book, it exposed them to serious fiscal pressures that threatened to undermine their ability to meet the new demands being placed on them. In a sense, the Reagan administration based its approach to domestic policy on a fundamental misunderstanding of the realities of government operations and government-nonprofit relations as they existed at the time it took office. It thus posed a serious challenge to precisely the institutions it looked to to make its policies work.

The story of the Reagan administration's impact on the nonprofit sector is not only important for historical reasons, however. It also has continuing, contemporary relevance, both practically and analytically. On the practical level, the fiscal constraints that the Reagan administration and its successor visited on the nonprofit sector in the 1980s continue to shape nonprofit operations today, if for no other reason than the fact that the heavy residue of debt these administrations left in their wake has continued to limit the revival of governmental support. Understanding the origins and structure of these constraints is thus crucial to appreciating some of the pressures with which key elements of the nonprofit sector are still contending today.

Beyond this, however, the story of the Reagan administration's relationship to the nonprofit sector is important as an illustration of how critical it is to understand the actual realities of nonprofit operations examined earlier in this book in order to shape effective public and private policy toward this set of institutions, and how dangerous it is to base policy on simplistic ideology and rhetoric instead. Whatever its presumed values or symbolic importance, the nonprofit sector is also a significant set of institutions with complex ties to other parts of American society. Understanding these ties and the relationships to which they give rise thus becomes essential in shaping effective public and private action. This is all the more important now in view of the results of the 1994 Congressional election, which seems likely to produce a return to the Reagan approach of the early 1980s.

The chapters in part 4 explore various dimensions of this story. Chapter 10 examines the budget and administrative features of the Reagan administration's approach to the nonprofit sector and analyzes them in the context of the opportunity that existed in the late 1970s to place government-nonprofit relations on a more coherent and rationalized basis, an opportunity that the Reagan administration, in my view, systematically failed to seize. Chapter 11 zeros in on the tax portions of the Reagan program and shows why the administration's important Economic Recovery Tax Act of 1981 added to the difficulties that the administration's budget cutbacks were already creating for nonprofit organizations. Chapter 12 summarizes the discussion by examining the Reagan administration's approach to the nonprofit sector against the more general backdrop of the themes and realities introduced earlier in the book. What emerges overall from this discussion is the picture of a set of policies that may have been well intentioned, but that was based more on rhetoric than reality and that misfired badly as a consequence.

CHAPTER 10

The Reagan Revolution and Nonprofit Organizations

The Lost Opportunity

> With the same energy that Franklin Roosevelt sought government solutions to problems, we will seek private solutions. The challenge before us is to find ways once again to unleash the independent spirit of the people and their communities. . . . Voluntarism is an essential part of our plan to give the government back to the people.
>
> —Ronald Reagan, October 1981

In few areas did the Reagan administration enter office with a clearer sense of purpose than in its commitment to voluntarism and private action as a way to respond to national needs. Yet in few areas were its concrete achievements more difficult to discern. Committed to a new approach to public problems stressing private initiative instead of public action, the administration never managed to convert that commitment into a serious program of action. In the process, it lost an important opportunity that existed in 1980 to develop an improved partnership between government and voluntary organizations as an alternative to purely governmental solutions to social problems.

The story of the Reagan administration's performance in the area of private-sector initiative and voluntary action is not only important in its own right, however. It is also important for what it can tell us about how the administration performed where its goals were not simply to cut spending, but to launch a program of genuine policy change.

To tell the story, this chapter first examines the nature of the opportunity facing the administration, then reviews the administration's response, and finally analyzes the available evidence on the impact of the administration's policies on private voluntary agencies.

The Opportunity

The unusual opportunity that confronted the Reagan administration in 1981 to improve the relationship between government and voluntary institutions in American life and chart a new course for dealing with the nation's social problems arose from a growing dissatisfaction with the actual operation of the widespread government-nonprofit relationship that had developed over the previous two decades. As noted in previous chapters, this relationship took shape in ad hoc fashion with little attention to the careful demarcation of responsibilities. What is more, the fragmented structure of government programs splintered agency attentions while government administrative procedures created enormous bureaucratic strains. Complicating the life of nonprofit organizations further was a growing concern about the viability of the philanthropic base of the nonprofit sector. For one thing, the 1969 tax act represented a significant assault on private foundations, potentially requiring them to cut into their endowments to make charitable distributions. For another, the continued liberalization of the "standard deduction" on the income tax forms meant that fewer and fewer taxpayers had a financial incentive through the tax system to contribute to nonprofit organizations. By the latter 1970s, over 70 percent of all taxpayers were using the standard deduction rather than itemizing their deductions and thus benefiting from the deduction for charitable contributions. Whether for these or other reasons, between 1969 and 1979 private giving as a share of gross national product declined from 2.1 percent to 1.8 percent (AAFRC 1981, 31).

In the face of these challenges, the nonprofit community began to organize a response. The first and most important element of this response was the formation in 1973 of a private, blue ribbon Commission on Private Philanthropy and Public Needs chaired by John Filer, chairman of Aetna Life and Casualty Company. The Filer Commission undertook a detailed inquiry into the health and characteristics of the nation's nonprofit sector, focusing particularly on the declining base of charitable support and the growing role of government. While acknowledging the dangers that the growth of government posed to the autonomy and character of the nonprofit sector, the commission in its 1975 report urged not that public support be constrained, but that private assistance be encouraged and expanded. Accordingly, the Filer Commission called for the establishment of a permanent national commission on the nonprofit sector, the expansion of corporate philanthropy, and a series of tax changes designed to encourage charitable giving (Commission on Private Philanthropy and Public Needs 1975, 18–27).

While the Filer Commission focused on nonprofit funding, a second effort, housed at the Washington-based American Enterprise Institute for Public Policy Research (AEI), sought to redefine the role of voluntary organizations and other so-called mediating structures such as neighborhood, church, and family within the modern welfare state. Rejecting ultra-conservative hostility to government involvement in serving community needs, this "mediating structures" project developed a way to square the conservative preference for voluntary institutions with existing government-guaranteed protections for those in need. It did so by proposing a much more explicit partnership between government, voluntary organizations, and other mediating institutions, under which government would strive at a minimum to avoid harming such institutions in its policies and seek "wherever possible" to "utilize mediating structures for the realization of social purposes." Thus, for example, proposals were advanced to underwrite the activities of tenant associations in managing inner-city housing, to encourage home-based care for the aged, and to rely on existing community institutions to handle foster care. As the leaders of this project summarized the thinking behind such proposals, "We suggest that the modern welfare state is here to stay, indeed that it ought to expand the benefits it provides—but that *alternative mechanisms are possible to provide welfare services*" (Berger and Neuhaus 1977, 1; Woodson 1981; Egan et al. 1981).

Unfortunately the proponents of this "mediating structures" paradigm took too little account of the extent to which existing government program structures already used mediating institutions for the realization of social purposes, emphasizing instead the ways in which government harmed such institutions. Nevertheless, by virtue of its explicit acceptance of federal welfare responsibilities and its commitment "not to revoke the New Deal but to pursue its vision in ways more compatible with democratic governance," the AEI project offered a bridge between the conservative and liberal traditions and a program of action around which a conservative president might muster liberal support.

The process of developing a private-sector agenda begun by the Filer Commission and the "mediating structures project" benefited also from two developments occurring toward the end of the decade. The first was the formation in 1979 of a major new national association, Independent Sector, intended to represent all segments of the philanthropic community—funders as well as service organizations—in national policy deliberations and to foster greater awareness of and appreciation for the role of the "third sector." Potentially, Independent Sector provided a vehicle for mobilizing support behind voluntary action of the sort that the AEI "mediating structures" project had developed. At about the same time, the conservative Heritage Foundation produced its own analysis of the status of philanthropy in America and reached many of the same conclusions as the Filer Commission (Butler 1980). The result was to give a conservative stamp of approval to a program of action originally formulated by a moderate-liberal coalition of business, foundation, and voluntary agency leaders.

By the time the Reagan administration took office in early 1981, therefore, the pieces were in place—both analytically and politically—for a significant redirection of national policy that could place greater reliance on voluntary organizations, rationalize government's relationships with them, and foster a more sensible partnership between government and philanthropic institutions in carrying out public purposes. A consensus had tentatively formed around four key elements of the redirection: first, increased financial support for programs that rely on "mediating institutions" to carry out public purposes; second, tax changes to encourage private charitable giving;[1] third, a set of management reforms to ease the burdens that existing federal programs often imposed on nonprofit providers; and fourth, increased use of challenge grants and similar devices to encourage organizations to supplement public support with private resources.

To be sure, these strands of thought had yet to coalesce into a coherent program of action. Also, voluntarism still provoked a degree of cynicism among liberals, while conservatives frequently had trouble squaring their fondness for the concept of voluntary organization with their hostility to some of the more activist neighborhood groups that had formed in the 1960s. Nevertheless, the sense of shared concern was striking, insofar as it spanned a considerable range of ideological and political persuasions, and even social and economic positions. Some of the thinking was reflected in the policy initiatives of the Carter administration—particularly in its urban policy, emphasizing as it did the need for a "new partnership" between public and private institutions. However, most of the ideas had hardly been tapped in any serious way. They were thus available for adoption by a new administration, particularly one committed to what the 1980 Republican platform termed the restoration of "the American spirit of voluntary service and cooperation, of private and community initiative."

The Reagan Response

Against this backdrop, the Reagan administration's handling of the nonprofit sector constitutes a significant lost opportunity. Instead of forging a new coalition in support of a positive program of cooperation between government and the voluntary sector, the administration relied primarily on exhortation and on the expected success of its economic program to suffuse the country with voluntaristic spirit. The problem, however, was that the administration's tax and budget actions had serious negative implications—apparently never clearly thought out—for the overall health of the nonprofit sector. Insofar as the administration acted at all with specific regard for this sector, the actions—chiefly establishment of a task force—must be judged tepid at best and wrong-headed at worst. Meanwhile, the administration pushed a set of administrative changes widely perceived as threatening to the nonprofit sector. Thus, the lost opportunity is at least in part attributable to the simple fact that the administration's real priorities clearly lay elsewhere, in the major program of spending cuts, tax reductions, and defense buildup. But the situation is also in part attributable to an unwillingness to face up to the complex realities that characterized existing government-nonprofit relations, exacerbated by the hostility of a few individuals in the administration to particular types of organizations. To see this, it is useful to examine briefly the three major kinds of actions the administration took that touched most directly on the voluntary sector: spending and tax action, the formation of a Presidential Task Force, and changes that occurred or were proposed in other facets of the government's relations with the nonprofit sector.

Spending and Tax Cuts

Although the primary motivation for the combination of spending and tax cuts embarked on in 1981 was clearly economic, the cuts came to be defended as well for the contribution they could make to the restoration of voluntarism and private action. This defense was rooted in the conservative theories mentioned earlier, which regard the growth of government as seriously jeopardizing the position of the voluntary sector by robbing it of its "functional relevance." From here it was an easy step to the conclusion that the best way to revitalize the voluntary sector was simply to get government out of the way. In this sense, spending and tax cuts would create a new opportunity for the resurgence of the voluntary sector.

The scale of the opportunity to be thus created for the philanthropic sector was quite substantial, however. In the initial budget proposed for the period FY 1982 to FY 1985, the administration would have cut federal spending in program areas in which nonprofits are active by the equivalent of $115 billion in real terms below what would have been spent had FY 1980 spending levels simply been maintained. The bulk of the cuts would have come in the fields of social services, employment and training, and housing and community development, where we projected that overall federal spending would have declined by 57 percent in real terms between FY 1980 and FY 1985 (Salamon and Abramson 1982a, 26).

By reducing government service provision, these spending cuts promised to increase demand for the services of nonprofit organizations. Never acknowledged, however, was that they would simultaneously reduce the revenues these organizations had available to meet even the preexisting level of demand. In particular, we estimated that by FY 1985, after adjusting for inflation, the administration's proposed reductions in federal spending would have reduced the federal support to nonprofit social service organizations by 64 percent below what it was in FY 1980. For community development organizations the drop would have been 65 percent, and for education and research organizations, 35 percent (Salamon and Abramson 1982a, 51). In addition, some of the programs most clearly oriented toward stimulating private, nonprofit action—such as the community action program, neighborhood "self-help" housing, and some of the demonstration programs under the Comprehensive Employment and Training Act— were targeted for the sharpest cuts. Under the circumstances, the administration's protestations of support for nonprofit organizations and public-private partnership came to have an exceedingly hollow ring to leaders within the philanthropic community, and the potential support within this community for the administration's efforts began to slip quickly away.

The other prong of the administration's economic recovery program—the tax cuts—also had a hidden hook for the voluntary sector. An extensive body of research has found that, among taxpayers who itemize their deductions, higher tax rates are associated with a greater willingness to give to charity and lower tax rates with reduced propensities to give (Taussig 1967; Schwartz 1970, Feldstein 1975; Morgan, Dye, and Hybels 1977; Clotfelter and Steurle 1981). Because charitable contributions are tax deductible, the real "cost" of giving is the difference between what the taxpayer gives and what he or she would have owed the government in the absence of the gift. For someone in the 70 percent tax bracket, for example, the net cost of giving a dollar to charity is only thirty cents, whereas for someone in the 40 percent tax bracket, the cost is sixty cents. In other words, as tax rates fall, the real cost of giving rises, and ample evidence attests that this real cost rise discourages giving.

Preoccupied as it was with the macroeconomic consequences of its tax-reduction proposals, the Reagan administration gave scant attention to these potential negative impacts on charitable giving. What is more, it opposed the proposals advanced by the philanthropic community to offset some of the potentially harmful effects by instituting an above-the-line charitable deduction for nonitemizers and liberalizing the foundation payout requirement—both proposals advanced by the Filer Commission and supported by the Independent Sector and a broad coalition of voluntary groups. Although both measures passed over administration objections, the above-the-line charitable deduction passed only in watered-down form, with a phase-in provision, a cap, and a termination date. As a result, even after taking account of the increased income the tax act would leave private individuals, we estimated that the 1981 tax act would reduce individual charitable giving approximately $10 billion over the 1981–84 period below what would have existed under prior law (Clotfelter and Salamon 1982; see also chap. 11).

Task Force on Private-Sector Initiatives

Recognizing somewhat belatedly that a menu of spending and tax cuts hardly added up to a positive program for encouraging nonprofit action, the Reagan administration moved in late 1981 to create a Presidential Task Force on Private Sector Initiatives to "promote private sector leadership and responsibility for solving public needs and to recommend ways of fostering greater public-private partnerships" (Public Papers of the President of the United States 1982, 885). Chaired by Armco Steel President William Verity, this task force was to bring together several dozen private-sector leaders to work closely with administration officials in developing an action program. As the president put it at the end of his speech announcing the formation of the task force: "I'm not standing here passing this off to you as solely your task, and the government will wash its hands of it. We intend a partnership in which we'll be working as hard as we can with you to bring this about" (886).

Translating this promise into action, however, turned out to be far more difficult than was initially supposed. Despite the president's apparent personal commitment to the concept, "private-sector initiatives" never caught on as a serious policy effort. Although a special White House Office for Private Sector Initiatives was established, it was more a part of the White House public relations operation than a part of its policy operation, and was at any rate divorced from the budget decision making going on in the Office of Management and Budget (OMB) and the Treasury. Nor did the task force itself ever really jell as a shaper of policy; instead, it functioned the way the White House Office did, as an outreach effort to the press, outside groups, and local officials. If the leadership of either the task force or the White House Office ever seriously addressed the theoretical and policy issues formulated by the Filer Commission, AEI, the Heritage Foundation, and Independent Sector, there is little evidence of it in the actions taken. Indeed, the task force leadership pointedly rejected an offer from the American Enterprise Institute to develop a more explicit program of action built around the "mediating structures" paradigm. The major activity involved amassing a data base of innovative private-sector initiatives and organizing counterparts to the president's task force in local communities across the country (Berger 1984). Although these efforts usefully publicized the concepts of voluntarism and private action to solve public problems, and therefore buttressed the administration's effort to change public thinking about the role of government and involve private-sector leaders in public problem solving, the tangible effects were fairly limited. *Newsweek* (1982) was thus exaggerating only in part when it pointed to the delivery of five thousand copies of Pat Boone's record "Lend a Hand" to radio stations across the country as one of the most substantive accomplishments of the effort.

Administrative Changes

Contributing further to the administration's lack of credibility as the supporter of an effective program of voluntarism and public-private partnership were a number of administrative actions that served to erode further its relations with the voluntary community. The first was the administration's decision to eliminate the government's principal vehicle for promoting community-based voluntary organization, the Community Services Administration (formerly the Office of Economic Opportunity). The second was to appoint as the head of ACTION, the government's voluntary action agency, a particularly ardent conservative who early on began an effort to stop funds from going to liberal, activist organizations. Simultaneously, as part of its budget program, the administration sought to eliminate or significantly scale back the postal subsidy for nonprofit organizations, which would have seriously hampered their direct mail fund-raising efforts.

Even more significant for the voluntary sector were two further administrative developments. The first was an effort to restrict access to the federal government's annual workplace charitable drive—the Combined Federal Campaign (CFC). The largest workplace charitable solicitation in the nation, the CFC functioned from its inception in 1957 through the mid-1970s as a mechanism for raising funds for a small number of large charities, such as United Way, the Red Cross, and the American Lung Association. In the 1970s, however, a variety of independent charities, many of them minority run or advocacy oriented (such as the Black United Fund and Planned Parenthood), managed to secure access to the CFC and thus challenged the dominance of the established charities. With United Way support, the Reagan administration moved to reverse this trend, developing a draft executive order that would bar from the CFC any charity that provided abortion or abortion counseling, or that engaged in lobbying or litigation on public policy issues. Leaked to the press in late 1981, this draft executive order sparked a prolonged battle between the Office of Personnel Management (which supervises the CFC) and a broad coalition of independent charitable organizations. This struggle led ultimately to issuance of a slightly revised presidential executive order in February 1983, which a U.S. District Court then declared unconstitutional. In the process, the administration added considerably to the apprehensions of the more liberal elements of the voluntary community.

Even more widespread apprehensions were created by yet another administrative move: an effort launched by the counsel of the Office of Management and Budget to rewrite the accounting principles applicable to voluntary organizations as well as to many other contractors with government. Concerned that public funds were going to support advocacy activity, OMB proposed to revise its Circular A-122, which sets guidelines for organizations that receive government support. Under the proposed revised rules, organizations that engage in "political advocacy" would have to isolate all funds and resources used for this purpose from those used to fulfill their government contracts, if the government contract represented as much as 5 percent of their budget. An organization that engaged in "political advocacy" might therefore have had to maintain separate offices and administrative structures—one for the government contract work and one for the advocacy activity. Not surprisingly, the reaction from the philanthropic community was exceedingly hostile, and the administration once again found itself in the middle of an intense battle with many of the organizations that might naturally have been its allies.

Not content simply to ignore the AEI "mediating structures" agenda, the administration thus seemed determined to violate the AEI's basic principle that "public policy should cease and desist from damaging mediating structures." Whether this was conscious policy or simply the working out of the uncoordinated preferences of individual administration appointees, the cumulative effect on the voluntary sector was unmistakably chilling. As Brian O'Connell, president of the broad-based Independent Sector, pointed out in testimony before a subcommittee of the House Government Operations Committee in early 1983, the administration's combination of rhetorical support for voluntarism and budget policies hostile to the charitable sector had made many leaders of voluntary organizations "skeptical, if not cynical, about the president's interest." "Against this uneasy backdrop," O'Connell continued, the administrative changes proposed by the administration, particularly the proposed change in the rules governing political advocacy, "have changed the skepticism and cynicism to bewilderment and hostility" (1983b, 5).

The Impact

Aside from the question of whether the Reagan administration failed to take actions that might have capitalized effectively on the opportunity that seemed to exist to improve the federal government's relations with the voluntary sector and to develop a new approach to coping with domestic problems, it is important to analyze the actual impact of the actions the administration did take. It is necessary to ask, in other words, not simply whether the Reagan program failed to help nonprofits but also whether it did them real damage. For this purpose, we draw on two principal bodies of data: first, an analysis of the implications for nonprofit organizations of the actual changes in federal spending approved by Congress and the president for the period between FY 1980 and FY 1984;[2] and second, a major survey we conducted of nonprofit human service and arts agencies in late 1982 and early 1983 to determine how government budget cuts were affecting nonprofit agencies and how the agencies were responding.

Federal Budget Changes

In FY 1980 the federal government spent $148.3 billion on programs in fields where nonprofit organizations are active.[3] This figure represented slightly more than one-fourth of all federal expenditures and one-third of all nondefense expenditures. About 35 percent of these expenditures went for health services; about 25 percent for needs-tested income assistance; about 20 percent for "social welfare" (including social services, employment and training, and community development); about 15 percent for education; and the remaining 5 percent for international assistance, arts and culture, and conservation.

As a result of the Omnibus Budget and Reconciliation Act of 1981, the level of federal spending on these programs declined in real terms by about 5 percent between FY 1980 and FY 1982 after adjusting for inflation. Excluding Medicare and Medicaid, which continued to grow, the drop was a much larger 13 percent. Following these significant reductions in FY 1982, however, Congress generally resisted the further sharp cuts in these program areas proposed by the administration for FY 1983 and FY 1984. At the same time, health care finance programs continued to grow. The result is that, by FY 1984, total federal spending on programs of relevance to nonprofit organizations was down 3 percent below FY 1980 levels with health included, and by 15 percent with health excluded (table 10.1). In short, although less extreme than the administration originally proposed, a significant reduction occurred in federal support in a variety of program areas (particularly social welfare, education, and the environment) likely to affect the demand for nonprofit services.

The reductions just outlined had implications for nonprofit revenues, not just for service demands. In particular, if we assume that the share of each program's resources going to nonprofits in FY 1984 was roughly equivalent to the share they received in FY 1980, then the federal budget changes enacted as of the start of 1984 translate into overall reductions in nonprofit support from the federal government of between 1 and 2 percent in FY 1982 and FY 1983, and an actual increase of 3 percent in FY 1984, as noted in table 10.2. However, these figures are somewhat misleading because they largely reflect the impact of the continued growth of Medicare, and to a lesser extent Medicaid, reimbursements to hospitals. With health care excluded, the value of federal support to the remaining types of nonprofit organizations dropped an estimated 27 percent between FY 1980 and FY 1984.

Impact on Nonprofits

Whether these reductions in federal spending actually show up in the balance sheets of nonprofit organizations cannot be determined

TABLE 10.1

Changes in Federal Spending in Fields Where Nonprofit Organizations Are Active, FY 1984 vs. FY 1980
(In constant 1980 $)

Program Area	Outlays (1980 $ Billions)		Percentage Change
	FY 1980	FY 1984[a]	FY 1984 vs. FY 1980
Social welfare	$28.5	$18.6	−35%
Social services	7.3	5.7	−22
Employment and training	10.3	4.1	−60
Community development	10.8	8.8	−19
Education and research	22.0	17.1	−22
Elementary, secondary	7.0	5.4	−23
Higher	10.4	6.9	−34
Research	4.7	4.8	+2
Health	53.0	63.2	+19
Medicare, Medicaid	49.1	60.0	+22
Health services	4.0	3.1	−23
Income assistance	36.4	37.2	+6
International aid	6.9	7.3	+4
Arts and culture	0.6	0.5	−17
Environmental	0.7	0.4	−43
Total	$148.3	$144.2	−3%
Total excluding Medicare, Medicaid	$99.2	$84.2	−15%

SOURCE: Author's calculations based on federal government data from Office of Management and Budget and Congressional Budget Office documents. Figures for FY 1984 are estimates reflecting congressional actions on the FY 1984 budget. Actual FY 1984 spending may differ as a result of changes in economic conditions, different spending rates, and supplemental appropriations.
NOTE: [a]In FY 1980 dollars.

TABLE 10.2

Estimated Changes in Nonprofit Revenues from the Federal Government, FY 1980 vs. FY 1984, by Type of Organization

Type of Organization	Outlays (1980 $ Billions)		Percentage Change
	FY 1980	FY 1984[a]	FY 1984 vs. FY 1980
Social services	$6.5	$4.2	−35%
Civic	2.3	1.8	−22
Education and research	5.5	4.6	−16
Health	24.9	30.2	+21
Foreign aid	0.8	0.6	−25
Arts and culture	0.4	0.2	−50
Total	$40.3	$41.6	+3%
Total, excluding Medicare, Medicaid	$16.7	$12.2	−27%

SOURCE: Author's calculations based in part on federal government data from Office of Management and Budget and Congressional Budget Office documents. Data for FY 1984 are estimates based on congressional action in the FY 1984 budget as of the beginning of the fiscal year.
NOTE: [a]In FY 1980 dollars.

from top-down budget analysis alone. Too many other factors can intervene along the way. For example, state and local governments may have decided to offset or intensify federal cuts through their own funding decisions; local delays may have occurred in putting the cuts into effect because of ongoing contractual arrangements; the share of program resources going to support nonprofit service delivery rather than delivery by state or local government agencies may have changed. To gain a clear view of actual impacts, we conducted a major survey of nonprofit charitable service organizations, exclusive of hospitals and higher educational institutions, in sixteen localities across the country. The localities were selected to provide a reasonable cross section of the nation in terms of region, size, economic circumstance, urban and rural character, and philanthropic tradition (for further details, see chap. 5 and Salamon 1995).

The first conclusion that emerges from this survey confirms our earlier finding that government plays a substantial role in the financing of nonprofit activities in this country. Sixty-two percent of the organizations responding to our survey reported receiving some government support in 1981, and government accounted for a significant 41.1 percent of their total revenues.[4] This makes government the largest single source of revenues for these organizations, with the other two major sources—fees and service charges (28%) and private giving (20%)—far behind. What is more, even among the types of agencies in which the government share of total support is smallest, the proportion of agencies receiving some government assistance was substantial. In fact, except for education (chiefly private elementary and secondary education), well over half of all the nonprofits we surveyed in every field received some government support. Government budget decisions are thus very relevant to a sizable segment of the nonprofit community, even though the impacts of the decisions vary markedly.

Between 1981 and 1982, the organizations we surveyed reported a 6.3 percent reduction in their government support (table 10.3). Among some types of agencies, however, the loss of government support was even larger: 29 percent for legal services organizations, 16 percent for housing and community development organizations, 13 percent for employment and training agencies, and 9 percent for social service organizations. By contrast, government cutbacks were far less pronounced among institutional/residential care, health, mental health, and arts and culture agencies. In fact, the institutional/residential care institutions registered an overall increase in the value of their government support, reflecting in all likelihood the continued growth of the federal Medicaid program. When this information is combined

TABLE 10.3

Real Changes in Nonprofit Revenues and in Support from Government by Type, Age, and Size of Agency, 1981–1982

Type of Agency	Percentage Change in Government Support	Percentage Change in Total Agency Expenditures
By primary service area		
Legal services/advocacy	−28.8%	−15.5%
Housing/community development	−15.6	+1.9
Employment/training	−12.7	−6.3
Social services	−8.8	−4.0
Multipurpose	−8.1	−1.7
Education/research	−7.3	+0.6
Culture/arts/recreation	−1.3	+5.7
Health care services	−1.3	+3.3
Mental health	−0.1	+6.5
Institutional/residential care	+4.1	+4.4
By age (year formed)		
Pre-1930	−2.6	+1.9
1930–60	+1.3	+2.3
1961–70	−12.7	−4.5
1971–82	−6.7	+1.5
By size (expenditures)		
Small (<$100,000)	−1.8	+9.7
Medium ($100,000–$1 million)	−4.9	+2.7
Large (>$1 million)	−6.7	−0.4
All Agencies	−6.3%	+0.5%

SOURCE: Nonprofit Sector Project Survey, round 1.
NOTE: In comparing the columns the reader should bear in mind that since government funds accounted on average for about 40 percent of total revenue for these organizations, a 6.3 percent reduction in government support will translate into only a 2.4 percent reduction in total agency income.

with the data on changes in government funding by agency age (in the same table), it is clear that the reductions in government support were most marked among agencies created in the 1960s. In other words, it was the "Great Society" agencies that seem to have suffered most under the Reagan administration. These impacts are all the more notable in view of the fact that the survey was carried out in late 1982, before the full results of the federal budget changes had shown up.[5]

The evidence, outlined above, of the impact of government budget cuts on nonprofit agencies tells only part of the story of the consequences of this administration's policies toward the nonprofit sector. To understand the rest of it, we need to see what happened to the nongovernment sources of income for these agencies since one of the central tenets of the administration's Economic Recovery Program was

TABLE 10.4

Changes in Revenue for the Average Nonprofit Agency,
1981–1982, by Source

Source	Income from Source, FY 1981 (In 1981 Dollars)	Change in Income from Source, 1981–82	
		Amount (In 1981 Dollars)	Percentage
Government	$295,665	−$18,530	−6.3%
Corporations	21,639	+1,261	+5.8
Foundations	24,253	+1,262	+5.2
United Way	38,165	+712	+1.9
Religious and other federated funders	19,317	+703	+3.6
Direct individual giving	42,747	+3,387	+7.9
Fees, charges	200,001	+13,251	+6.6
Endowment, investments	32,097	+1,323	+4.1
Other	40,134	+891	+2.2
Unallocated	3,595	−599	N/A
Total	$717,613	+$3,661	+0.5%

SOURCE: See table 10.3.
NOTE: N/A = not applicable.

that some or all of the loss of government support could be made up through private charitable contributions.

On the surface, the evidence of overall change in nonprofit expenditures seems to support this optimistic expectation (table 10.3). In particular, although the real value of total government support to these organizations declined by about 6 percent between 1981 and 1982, overall organization expenditures increased by 0.5 percent, even after adjusting for inflation. Real increases occurred in several of the nongovernment sources of support, particularly direct individual giving, fees and charges, foundations, and corporations, all of which grew by more than 5 percent even after adjusting for inflation. Given the economic downturn that had begun when our survey was conducted, this was a notable achievement.

Examination of the absolute dollar amounts in table 10.4, however, makes it clear that the real explanation of the capacity of the nonprofit sector to close the funding gap left by federal budget cuts was not the increases that occurred in private charitable contributions. Rather, the major part of the explanation was the increase that occurred in income from fees and service charges. Almost 60 percent of the income that enabled the average agency to close the gap left by federal budget cuts and achieve a modest 0.5 percent overall real gain came from such fees, and another 6 percent came from endowment and investment

TABLE 10.5

Changes in Real (Inflation-Adjusted) Support for Selected Types of Nonprofit Organizations, 1981–1982, by Source

Type of Agency	Government	Corporations	Foundations	United Way	Religious and Other Federated Funders	Direct Individual Giving	Fees, Charges	Endowment, Investments	Other	Total
Legal services	−29%	+11%	+3%	+5%	+5%	+4%	+19%	−12%	−7%	−16%
Employment/training	−13	+9	−29	−9	+5	+18	+1	−11	+5	−6
Social services	−9	+1	−2	+4	+3	+4	+4	−3	−6	−4
Multipurpose	−8	+25	−3	+1	+3	+7	+4	+14	−10	−2
Education/research	−7	+2	+14	−3	+7	+7	+3	−1	+5	+1
Housing, community development	−16	+19	+7	−5	+3	+50	+45	+37	+4	+2
Health care	−1	+2	+2	0	−12	−2	+7	+16	0	+3
Institutional/residential care	+4	−4	+34	+4	+11	+23	+5	+9	0	+4
Arts, culture	−1	+3	+8	+4	−2	+11	+9	+3	+5	+6
Mental health	0	+16	−6	−2	+49	−20	+29	+2	+130	+7
All agencies	−6%	+6%	+5%	+2%	+4%	+8%	+7%	+4%	+2%	+1%

SOURCE: See table 10.3.

income. Thus, earned income, which comprised 55 percent of the nongovernmental income of these agencies in 1981, made up 65 percent of the increase in revenues for the average agency between 1981 and 1982. Private giving from all sources, which comprised 45 percent of the nongovernmental income of these agencies in 1981, accounted for only 35 percent of the increase. In other words, the philanthropic share of agency income actually declined.[13]

Reflecting this situation, not all types of agencies were able to make up for the government cuts. In general, agencies that focus chiefly on the poor and that have the least access to fee income did the worst (as is apparent from table 10.5). Thus, legal services, employment and training, social services, and multiple service agencies all had above-average reductions in government support and below-average increases in fees and charges. These agencies were also at the high end of the scale in terms of reliance on government support to start with. Although such agencies did manage to increase their private charitable support, the increases were not sufficient to recoup losses in government support. For these types of agencies, therefore, the expectations of the Economic Recovery Program clearly did not work: far from allowing these agencies the support needed to expand their services to fill the gaps left by government cutbacks, the available philanthropic support did not even allow the agencies to maintain prior levels of activity.

A quite different picture emerged for the six types of organizations that posted real increases in expenditures between 1981 and 1982 (mental health, arts and culture, institutional care, health, and housing). Typically, these organizations either experienced relatively modest reductions in government support, or relied on government support less than average, or both; they also had access to above-average increases in fees and charges. The one exception is the housing and community development organizations, which started the period with extremely high reliance on government support, experienced sharp reductions in that support, but were nevertheless able to generate alternative sources of support from virtually all other sources. In the process, we hypothesize, they probably somewhat altered their program mix, turning to fee-generating activities such as provision of day care services and the like.

The picture that emerges from this analysis of changes in the funding base of the nonprofit, charitable service sector thus casts doubt on both the doomsayers and the Pollyannas. Because the federal cuts were less severe than originally proposed, because not all agencies were equally dependent on government support to start with, and because many agencies managed to increase fees and charges significantly, some types of agencies—particularly those in health-related areas and arts and culture—managed to achieve real growth in expenditures between 1981 and 1982 and to move the average for the organizations examined here slightly into the black. At the same time, however, agencies in fields where the government cutbacks were most noticeable and where access to additional fee income is limited ended up worse off despite some real increases in private philanthropic support. Finally, although the charitable service sector as a whole managed to hold its own between 1981 and 1982, it was not in a position to expand its services to fill in for the much larger reduction of direct government services in these fields.

Conclusion

The Reagan administration entered office with a significant opportunity to redefine the way services are delivered in the American version of the modern welfare state and to forge a new model of partnership between government agencies and voluntary groups. Both the political and intellectual roots of such a reorientation of policy had been laid in the 1970s, and a coalition of leaders in the philanthropic and nonprofit communities was eager to push this agenda along. Instead of seizing this opportunity, however, the administration was content to rely mostly on rhetoric, while putting uncritical faith in the workings of its economic program to revitalize the nonprofit sector. In the process, the administration exposed this sector to a period of considerable fiscal strain. Faced with reduced government support—and unable to cover costs from private charity—those agencies in a position to do so turned increasingly to their commercial activities, expanding their reliance on fees and charges. Agencies not in a position to pursue this course found themselves unable to sustain even prior levels of activity, let alone expand enough to meet new demands created by government retrenchment. By emphasizing the importance of private-sector initiatives and voluntary action, the Reagan administration put the philanthropic sector on the agenda of American politics in a forceful way. But by pursuing a serious assault on a broad range of domestic programs that help to sustain the sector financially, without accompanying this with a positive program of action, the administration set back its own private-sector agenda and discredited voluntarism further as a serious policy alternative.

CHAPTER 11

The Impact of the 1981 Tax Act on Individual Charitable Giving

On August 13, 1981, President Reagan signed into law the Economic Recovery Tax Act of 1981, one of the central pillars of the economic program he had unveiled six months earlier. Among the provisions of this law were an across-the-board reduction of 25 percent in marginal tax rates for individuals over three years, a reduction in the maximum tax rate on individual income from 70 to 50 percent, liberalized depreciation allowances, sizable reductions in estate taxes, an "above-the-line" charitable deduction for nonitemizers to be phased in over a period of years, and a provision to index tax rates beginning in 1985.

The purpose of this chapter is to assess the impact of this new tax law on individual charitable giving. This impact is worth exploring not simply because of the magnitude of the resources involved, but even more so because of the special role that charitable giving plays in the private, nonprofit sector of American life, and because of the special implications it consequently has for the administration's overall economic strategy.

The nonprofit sector is a vast amalgam of organizations, ranging from museums, arts societies, universities, and civic clubs, to social welfare agencies, neighborhood organizations, public interest groups, and churches. Historically supported largely from private sources, these organizations have come to rely increasingly over recent years on government support and commercial revenues and fees. Of the $85.3 billion in expenditures that nonreligious nonprofit organizations reported in 1977, for example, only $19.1 billion, or 22 percent of the total, came from private giving.[1] Yet, it is still private contributions that give these organizations their distinctive character as independent, private institutions performing essentially public purposes. With private giving so small a share of nonprofit revenues, therefore, anything that threatens private giving threatens the very essence of the nonprofit sector.

The potential impact of the 1981 tax act on private giving takes on special meaning, however, in the context of the broader economic strategy being pursued by the Reagan administration. One of the central tenets of this strategy, of which the tax act is a pivotal part, is that the role of government should be reduced and the private sector encouraged to fill whatever real gap in services occurs as a result. To the extent that the tax act turns out to discourage such private action by discouraging private giving, it would pose a significant challenge to this strategy and add further strain to nonprofit organizations already burdened by budget cutbacks. Under these circumstances, it becomes all the more urgent to assess what the impact of this act on charitable giving is likely to be.

This chapter addresses the effect of the 1981 tax act on individual giving. It makes no attempt to predict the effect of the law on contributions by corporations, estates, or foundations.[2] This approach is dictated by the limited economic analysis of the giving behavior of these other three sources and is justified by the fact that individual giving accounts for some 84 percent of total private giving. At the same time, however, this focus probably understates the potential negative impact of the 1981 tax law on charitable giving. This is so because the new tax law contains three features that are likely to discourage these other forms of giving. In the first place, bequest giving is likely to be adversely affected by the act's virtual elimination of taxation of estates, which will significantly reduce the tax incentives for charitable bequests. In the second place, corporate giving is likely to be adversely affected by the new law's massive reform of depreciation rules, which will reduce taxable corporate profits and lower corporate tax liabilities. Finally, giving by foundations is likely to be reduced because of the law's easing of the so-called payout requirement imposed on private foundations by the 1969 tax act.

The provisions of the act most likely to influence individual giving are the tax rate cuts, the new charitable deduction for nonitemizers,[3] and, beginning in 1985, the indexing of tax rates. The body of the chapter is organized into three major sections. The first section discusses the analytical problem in assessing the impact of taxes on individual giving. The second section describes the data and methodology used in the present study. The third section presents the results of the simulation, focusing on the level and distribution of contributions resulting from the 1981 tax act and then examining separately the impact of the above-the-line charitable deduction. A brief concluding section summarizes the findings and their implications.

The Relationship between Taxes and Giving

Any tax change such as the 1981 tax act has multiple effects on giving, some of which operate in opposite directions. For example, the tax rate reductions that are a principal feature of the 1981 law will automatically increase after-tax income, which should encourage giving. However, lower tax rates also mean an increase in what economists term the "price of giving," the net, out-of-pocket cost of giving a dollar to charity. Because charitable contributions are deductible from income in computing tax obligations, it does not really cost those who itemize their deductions a full dollar to contribute a dollar to charity. In fact, the higher the tax bracket, the lower the real cost of giving. For a taxpayer in the 70 percent tax bracket, for example, the actual, out-of-pocket cost of giving a dollar to charity (the price of giving) is really 30 cents, since 70 cents would have gone to the federal government anyway. Reduce the tax rate to 50 percent, and the price of giving that same dollar to charity rises to 50 cents, an increase of 67 percent.

By reducing the maximum tax rate on unearned income from 70 percent to 50 percent, cutting marginal tax rates by 25 percent between 1981 and 1984, and indexing tax rates after 1985, the 1981 act promises to have effects of precisely this kind. At the same time, however, the act will permit those who do not use the standard deduction to claim deductions for their charitable contributions while still taking the standard deduction. This provision, which goes into effect in stages between 1982 and 1986, will lower the price of giving for these taxpayers, and thus encourage giving.

In addition to these tax-rate effects, charitable giving is also affected by inflation and economic growth, which increase before-tax income, shift some taxpayers into higher tax brackets, and induce some taxpayers who now take the standard deduction to itemize their deductions instead, reducing their cost of giving and thus encouraging them to give more. These effects are particularly important in the case of the 1981 tax act because of the role this act is supposed to play in a broader economic strategy that its advocates claim will contribute significantly to overall economic growth.

To capture the full effects of the 1981 tax act on charitable giving, therefore, it is necessary to sort out and assess a wide assortment of relationships, and take account of the interactions among them. To do so, it is helpful to differentiate two broad kinds of effects that are at work. The first are *price effects*, which influence the cost of giving. Included here are changes in tax rates, as well as changes in income that move taxpayers into different tax brackets or affect their decisions on whether to itemize deductions. The second are *income effects*, or features that affect the income available for charitable giving. Included here are changes in general economic conditions that affect the level of before-tax income, and changes in tax rates that affect the level of after-tax income. A complete assessment of the impact of the 1981 law must take both of these kinds of effects into account.

To do this, a simulation model of charitable giving behavior by taxpayers was developed based on economic analysis of individual giving and using conventional simulation techniques. These techniques draw on econometric evidence from a literature spanning more than a decade.[4] These studies have established the existence of strong, independent links between levels of giving, on the one hand, and changes in the tax-defined price of giving and in income levels, on the other.

To say that giving levels are affected by income and the price of giving is not, of course, to say that no other factors are involved, or even that these two factors are the most important. Individuals give to charitable purposes for a variety of reasons. Since such contributions have a net cost even for taxpayers in the highest tax bracket, the primary motivation for most taxpayers is probably other than tax related, involving philanthropic impulses, a desire to do good, feelings of attachment to particular causes or institutions, and numerous other reasons as well.

In addition, existing relationships among giving, income, and tax rates can change over time in response to changes in social climate, national leadership, or other factors. Analyses such as the present one, which project from previously observed levels for these quantities into the future, must therefore be seen less as predictions of what will happen than as projections of what would happen if these patterns of interaction were to hold under the new circumstances that are projected.

Methodology and Data

To carry out this analysis, four tasks had to be accomplished. First, we had to draw on a suitable model for relating individual giving to changes in income and tax rates. Second, we had to build into this model a way to estimate the effect of rising incomes on individual propensities to itemize deductions, in order to do justice to the full effects of the 1981 law and its projected economic consequences on giving behavior. Third, we had to build in adjustments for the maximum tax on earned income since the elimination of the differentiation between earned and unearned income was one of the principal features of the new law. Finally, we had to locate suitable data and adjust them to make them comparable. Appendix A to this chapter outlines how these four methodological tasks were handled.

Simulation Results

Three sets of results flow from our analysis of the impact of the 1981 tax act on individual charitable giving. The first of these relates to the aggregate impact of the act on the overall level of individual giving. The second relates to the variation in this impact among different income groups. And the third relates to the consequences that result for different types of recipient organizations. We examine each of these sets of results in turn.

Because of the attention it has attracted, moreover, we also detail in a separate section how the above-the-line charitable deduction would affect giving if it were fully operational as of 1984. To do this, the 1984 projections were recomputed as if full deductibility for nonitemizers were in effect by that date. In fact, of course, full deductibility is not scheduled to go into effect until 1986. By that date, however, the 1981 law's provision for indexing tax rates, which will affect giving negatively, will also be in effect. Since we have not estimated the effects of indexing, the result under full deductibility presented here should be viewed as suggestive only and not as an indication of the full effects of the 1981 law on giving in the period after 1984.[5]

Aggregate Impacts

Table 11.1 shows projected total amounts of individual giving for the years 1981–84 under two basic assumptions regarding the income and price elasticities of contributions. Under the assumption of con-

TABLE 11.1

Projected Individual Giving, 1981–1984, 1981 Tax Act

vs.

Pre-1981 Law, Two Functional Forms, in 1980 Dollars

($ Billions)

| Year | Constant Elasticities | | | Variable Elasticities | | |
	Pre-1981 Law	1981 Tax Act	Difference	Pre-1981 Law	1981 Tax Act	Difference
1981	$41.0	$40.7	−$0.3	$41.6	$41.2	−$0.4
1982	41.9	39.9	−2.0	42.8	39.9	−2.9
1983	45.5	41.7	−3.8	46.4	41.3	−5.1
1984	48.3	44.4	−3.9	49.2	43.4	−5.8
Total	$176.7	$166.7	−$10.0	$180.0	$165.8	−$14.2

stant income and price elasticities for all households, individual giving for the four years, adjusted for inflation, is projected to be $10.0 billion less under the 1981 tax act than under the previous tax law, with the disparity growing from $0.3 billion in 1981 to $3.9 billion in 1984. Under the assumption that price and income elasticities vary by income level, the projected difference between the two laws is $14.2 billion. In other words, the 1981 tax act will likely depress individual giving compared to what it would have been under the old law. It is important to note, however, that the absolute level of real giving is projected to increase in either case. If one takes the previous level of contributions as the yardstick for comparison—the $40.3 billion level in 1980, for example—giving appears to increase under the 1981 law. It is in comparison to the hypothetical extension of the previous law that the 1981 tax act fares poorly.

Taken together, these aggregate projections imply that individual giving as a percentage of personal income will continue under the new law the pattern of decline it has exhibited since at least the mid-1970s. As table 11.2 shows, this pattern is projected to be reversed by 1984, in part because of the expansion of the partial above-the-line charitable deduction in that year. It is far from certain that this turnaround will persist even after full deductibility is in effect, however, because of the potential impact of the indexing provisions that are scheduled to go into effect in 1985.

Variations among Income Classes

Possibly more important than the overall impact of the 1981 tax act on aggregate levels of charitable giving are the significant variations in

TABLE 11.2

Individual Giving as a Percentage of Personal Income,
1976–1980 Actuals and 1981–1984 Projections,
1981 Tax Act vs. Pre-1981 Law

Year	1981 Tax Act	Pre-1981 Law
1976	1.92%	1.92%
1977	1.91	1.91
1978	1.91	1.91
1979	1.89	1.89
1980	1.84	1.84
1981*	1.85	1.86
1982*	1.78	1.87
1983*	1.80	1.97
1984*	1.86	2.03

NOTE: * = estimates.

TABLE 11.3

Projected Distribution of Individual Giving by Income Groups,
1981 Tax Act vs. Pre-1981 Law, 1981–1984, in Constant 1980 Dollars
($ Billions)

Income Group	Projected Giving, 1981–1984		Difference
	Pre-1981 Law	1981 Law	
Lower[a]	$15.3	$15.4	+$0.1
Middle[b]	82.6	81.1	−1.5
Upper[c]	78.8	70.2	−8.6
Total	$176.7	$166.7	−$10.0

NOTES: [a]Includes taxpayers with incomes under $6,000, who accounted for about 30 percent of the taxpayers in 1978.
[b]Includes taxpayers with incomes $6,000 to $25,000, who accounted for about 55 percent of all taxpayers in 1978.
[c]Includes taxpayers with incomes $25,000 or more, who accounted for about 15 percent of all taxpayers in 1978.

impact among income classes. These variations result largely from the fact that the 1981 law reduces tax rates facing upper-income taxpayers more than those for middle- or lower-income taxpayers. As a result, the giving behavior of upper-income taxpayers can be expected to be affected more by the new tax law than that of lower- and middle-income taxpayers, many of whom will be affected by the new deduction for nonitemizers.

Table 11.3 confirms this expectation. What it shows is that a dispro-

TABLE 11.4
Projected Shares of Individual Giving by Income Class
under the 1981 Tax Act

Income Class[a]	1980	1984	Percentage Change 1980–1984
Lower	9.0%	9.3%	+3.3%
Middle	45.7	50.1	+9.6
Upper	45.3	40.6	−10.4
Total	100.0%	100.0%	

NOTE: [a]See notes to table 11.3.

portionate share of the reduction in individual giving associated with
the new law as opposed to the old is concentrated in the upper income
brackets. Representing 15 percent of all taxpayers and 44 percent of
all individual charitable contributions in 1978, the taxpayers in these
brackets account for over 85 percent of the reduction in individual
giving associated with the 1981 law as compared with the pre-1981 law
over the 1981–84 period.

Put somewhat differently, the 1981 tax act significantly shifts the
burden of giving among income groups over the 1981–84 period compared to what it was in 1980. As reflected in Table 11.4 the share of
individual giving for the bottom 30 percent of all taxpayers is projected to increase 3.3 percent between 1980 and 1984 under the 1981
law; and for the middle 55 percent of all taxpayers, it is projected to
increase 9.6 percent. By contrast, the share contributed by the 15 percent of all taxpayers in the highest income brackets is projected to decrease by 10.4 percent.

Resulting Variations in Impact among Recipients

What makes these variations in the impact of the 1981 tax act
among income classes particularly important is the fact that different
income groups distribute their contributions differently among various kinds of charitable activities. Generally speaking, lower-income
groups give proportionally more of their charitable gifts to religious
organizations than do the rich, while the rich give proportionally more
to educational and cultural institutions. By altering the distribution of
charitable giving among different income groups, therefore, the 1981
tax act may have quite uneven implications for different types of charitable organizations.

TABLE 11.5

Estimated Individual Contributions to Various Types of Charitable Organizations,
1981–1984, 1980 vs. 1981 Tax Law Projections, in Constant 1980 Dollars
($ Billions)

Types of Organization	1980[c]	Projected Giving, 1981 Tax Law				Percentage Change 1980–1984
		1981	1982	1983	1984	
Religious	$24.53	$24.94	$24.85	$26.02	$27.78	+13.2%
Other charitable[a]	5.82	5.87	5.74	6.00	6.38	+9.6
Educational	1.53	1.49	1.33	1.38	1.45	−5.2
Hospitals	.65	.63	.57	.59	.62	−4.6
Other[b]	7.75	7.75	7.37	7.70	8.17	+5.4
Total	$40.29	$40.71	$39.89	$41.71	$44.41	+10.2%

NOTES: [a]"Other charitable organizations" here includes such organizations as community chests, American Red Cross, and American Cancer Association.

[b]"Other organizations" includes "literary, educational and scientific foundations, libraries, museums, and zoos."

[c]The allocations among recipient types reported here are not comparable to those reported in *Giving U.S.A.* because of differences in definitions of types of organizations used.

Table 11.5 reports the results of such an analysis using the basic simulation model and data originally compiled by the Treasury for 1962. The table compares the amount of giving that five different types of charitable organizations received in 1980 to what they can expect under the 1981 law over the 1981–84 period. As expected, the impact of the new tax law differs significantly among these different types of organizations. In particular, these projections indicate that religious organizations will absorb 79 percent of the real increase in individual giving projected under the 1981 law during 1981–84. As a result, individual giving to religious organizations is expected to increase by 13.2 percent in real dollar terms between 1980 and 1984. By contrast, individual giving to educational institutions and hospitals is projected to decline by about 5 percent below 1980 levels in real dollar terms during this period.

The Impact of the Above-the-Line Charitable Deduction

Among the many features embodied in the 1981 tax act, and in the simulation results presented above, one deserves special attention because of the interest it attracted within the philanthropic community during the debate over the 1981 bill. This is the provision allowing the 70 percent of all taxpayers who do not itemize their deductions to claim a separate "above-the-line" deduction for their charitable contributions anyway. As it was finally incorporated in the 1981 tax act, this

TABLE 11.6

Effect of the Charitable Deduction for Nonitemizers Illustrated for
1984, in Constant 1980 Dollars

($ Billions)

Tax Provision	Projected Giving in 1984			Difference from Pre-1981 Law
	Nonitemizers	Itemizers	Total	
1981 law with the Following Portion of Nonitemized Giving Deductible				
25%	$14.0	$30.4	$44.4	−$3.9
100%	18.0	30.4	48.3	0
Pre-1981 law	12.7	35.5	48.3	

NOTE: Constant price and income elasticities are assumed. Sums of components may not equal totals due to rounding.

above-the-line deduction was scheduled to go into effect gradually over the period 1982–1986. Because the analysis here extends only until 1984, it picks up only a partial picture of the potential impact of this feature, and even then only in the 1984 tax year, when 25 percent of the first $300 in contributions by nonitemizers becomes deductible.[6] This approach was taken because of the gross uncertainty of economic projections so far into the future and because the 1981 tax law contains a provision that would index tax rates beginning in 1985, adding a new level of complexity to the analysis and complicating the task of ferreting out the separate impact of the above-the-line charitable deduction when it goes fully into effect in 1986.

Because of the importance of this above-the-line charitable deduction, however, it is useful to assess its fully operational potential impact by itself. To do so, we recomputed the 1984 results as if the charitable deduction were fully in effect in that year. Although these results thus differ in character from the projections of the actual 1981 law presented above, they nevertheless allow us to focus on this one important provision.

As reflected in table 11.6 a fully operational above-the-line deduction would have a significant effect on giving levels in 1984. In particular, it would increase contributions by nonitemizers from $14 to $18 billion and would virtually offset the $4.8 billion reduction in giving that other features of the 1981 law produce relative to pre-1981 law. By comparison, the partial version of this feature actually incorporated in the 1981 law offsets only about $0.9 billion of this $4.8 billion reduction.

Because nonitemizers are primarily concentrated among middle- and lower-income taxpayers, the above-the-line charitable deduction

TABLE 11.7

*Projected Changes in Shares of Individual Giving by Income Class
under the 1981 Tax Law, 1984 vs. 1980, with Partial and Full
Deductibility of Gifts by Nonitemizers*

Income Class[a]	Projected Change in Share, 1984 vs. Actual 1980	
	With Partial Deductibility[b]	With Full Deductibility
Lower	+3.3%	+3.3%
Middle	+9.6	+12.9
Upper	−10.4	−13.7

NOTES: [a]See notes to table 11.3.
   [b]Actual law as enacted.

also has a potential distributional impact. In particular, as shown in table 11.7, if this provision were fully operational in 1984 it would further alter the distribution of giving away from upper-income taxpayers toward middle- and lower-income taxpayers. Put differently, most of the increase in giving that would result from this feature if it were fully operational in 1984 would come from middle- and lower-income taxpayers.

Reflecting this, finally, a fully operational above-the-line charitable deduction in 1984 would also alter the results for particular types of organizations. In particular, religious giving under this circumstance would climb 23.9 percent as opposed to 13.9 percent, while levels of giving to educational institutions and hospitals would remain unchanged.

Conclusions

The Economic Recovery Tax Act of 1981 has already taken its place as one of the most controversial and hotly debated pieces of economic policy in our nation's history. However, the debate over this act largely ignored one of its more important, if indirect, potential consequences: its impact on the rate of private, charitable giving and hence on the strength and viability of the whole private nonprofit sector of national life. This neglect is especially ironic in view of the fact that one of the central tenets of the economic philosophy reflected in the tax act was the belief that fewer social functions should be vested in government and more reliance placed on private institutions to cope with national needs. Yet the evidence developed here indicates that, in certain parts of the nonprofit, charitable segment of the private sector, the tax bill was likely to work in the opposite direction, discouraging private giving and thus limiting the capability of private nonprofit institutions to assume an expanded role.

Our projections suggest that aggregate contributions by individuals would decline, relative to the pre-1981 tax law, between 1981 and 1984. When the new deduction for nonitemizers was fully phased in, however, total giving would rise, but probably not to the level it would have reached under the previous act, especially since indexing would by then be in effect. The distribution of that giving would also be affected by the act. The 1981 tax act significantly raised the "price" of giving for upper-income taxpayers. This plus the new incentive for nonitemizers redistributed the burden of giving from those with upper incomes to those with middle and lower incomes. This in turn was likely to lead to disproportionate growth in giving to religious organizations relative to charities favored by the rich, in particular, colleges, universities, and hospitals.

Appendix: Methodology

The basic estimating equation used in the econometric studies of charitable giving cited above takes the form

$$G = AY^a P^b X^f e^u, \qquad (1)$$

where G is dollars of contributions made, Y is adjusted gross income net of taxes due if no contributions were made, P is the price of giving, X is a vector of other determinants of giving, u is a disturbance or error term, A and e are constants, and a, b, and f are estimated elasticities. Applying this model to the present data yields an equation that predicts one year's contributions as a function of a previous year's contributions, and changes in net income and price:

$$G_{ijt} = G_{io}\left(\frac{Y_{ijt}}{Y_{ijo}}\right)^a \left(\frac{P_{ijt}}{P_{ijo}}\right)^b, \qquad (2)$$

where G_{ijt} is predicted average giving for taxpayers in income bracket i, tax status j, in year t. Net income is defined as

$$Y_{ijt} = AGI_{it} - TAX_{ijt} \qquad (3)$$

and is calculated separately for itemizers and nonitemizers, with taxable income for the latter being more at each income level by the average excess deduction claimed by itemizers. Price is defined, following previous empirical work in this area, as the weighted average of the price of giving gifts of cash and assets:

$$P_{ijt} = C_i(1 - M_{ijt}) + (1 - C_i)(1 - M_{ijt} - 0.5MC_{ijt}), \qquad (4)$$

where C_i is the estimated proportion of gifts from the income bracket made in cash, M_{ijt} is the marginal tax rate on ordinary income, and MC_{ijt} is the marginal tax rate on capital gains income. This formulation takes from previous work the assumption that the ratio of appreciation to basis for gifts of assets averages 50 percent. Given the values of net income and price, contributions in equation (1) are calculated in constant dollar terms, translated into current dollars, and summed for itemizers and nonitemizers and by tax status and income class to provide aggregate contributions.

By expressing equation (1) in logarithmic form, the behavioral parameters can be estimated by standard linear regression methods. In this form, the equation used here is taken from Clotfelter and Steuerle (1981, 425):

$$\ln(G + 10) = -1.27\ln P + .78\ln Y + .26MRD$$
$$+ .20DEP + .38A_{30-39} + .56A_{40-49} + .69A_{50-59} \qquad (5)$$
$$+ .90A_{60-64} + 1.20A_{65+} - 3.27.$$

In this equation, G, P, and Y are defined as above; A_{30-39}, A_{40-49}, A_{50-59}, A_{60-64}, and A_{65+} are dummy variables for age groups 30–39, 40–49, 50–59, 60–64, and 65 and older, respectively; and MRD and DEP are dummy variables for taxpayers who are married and who have dependents, respectively. The price elasticity is -1.27, and the income elasticity is .78, with standard errors of .05 and .02, respectively, and R^2 of .47. This equation reflects the most recently estimated parameters for overall individual giving and are in the moderate range of the estimates generated for these elasticities in prior research. This constant elasticity behavioral model underlies the basic simulations presented in this chapter.

Because of the importance of these parameters for simulation, however, it is useful to consider an alternative case in which the income and price elasticities vary over the income range. In alternative simulations presented in this chapter, we do this by taking elasticities estimated separately by income class.[7] In these estimates, the price elasticity varies from $-.945$ for the lowest income groups to -1.779, while the income elasticity varies from .393 to 1.089.

Predicting Itemization Status

An important part of the effect rising incomes are expected to have on charitable giving results from the likelihood that the number of taxpayers itemizing their deductions will increase over time if the standard deduction (zero rate bracket) is kept constant. Because it minimizes their tax liabilities, taxpayers virtually always choose to itemize when their deductible expenditures exceed the established standard level. The last 15 years have witnessed periodic increases in the proportion of taxpayers itemizing, punctuated by sharp decreases when the standard deduction is increased. As incomes, expenditures, and prices rise, it is not difficult to predict that the proportion of taxpayers whose deductible expenditures exceed some given dollar amount will tend to increase.

In order to reflect this behavior, itemization behavior was modeled as a function of average income and the zero rate bracket. In specifying the form of the relationship, it was necessary to choose a functional form that would yield predictions of the proportion of itemizers between 0 and 100 percent. The form chosen is a logistical model, which predicts the odds of itemizing as a function of the ratio of average AGI to the zero rate bracket. The following equation was estimated using 1978 data:

$$\ln\left(\frac{I_i}{1 - I_i}\right) = c + d \ln\left(\frac{AGI_i}{ZRB}\right), \tag{6}$$

where I_i is the proportion of bracket i's taxpayers who itemized, AGI_i is average AGI for the bracket, and ZRB is the zero bracket amount for married taxpayers filing jointly ($\$3,200$ in 1978, more in later years). The estimated value of d was 1.3 (standard error = 0.12), and the R^2 was 0.89. This is the elasticity of the odds in favor of itemizing with respect to the ratio of income to the zero bracket amount. The equation implies, for example, that an increase in this ratio from 5 to 5.5 (10%) will tend to result in a 13 percent increase in the odds of itemizing, or an increase in the proportion of itemizers from 39 to 42 percent.[8]

Accounting for the Maximum Tax on Earned Income

Under the pre-1981 tax law, so-called earned income is subject to a lower maximum tax rate than other income. One of the principal aims of the administration's tax bill was to eliminate the distinction between "earned" and "unearned" income by reducing the top marginal tax rate on "unearned" income from 70 to 50 percent. Since this change could increase by two-thirds the net price of giving faced by a dividend-receiving high-income taxpayer (from 0.3 to 0.5), this aspect of the tax bill has great potential importance for charitable contributions. Because of the provisions of the present maximum tax, however, the effect of the change is unlikely to be this simple. In order to calculate marginal tax rates under the previous law, it is important to account for several important features in the calculation of the maximum tax. Under the maximum tax, taxable income is allocated to earned and unearned taxable income based on the proportion of earned income in *AGI* (Adjusted Gross Income). The "unearned" portion of taxable income is "stacked" on top of earned income, becoming subject to the highest marginal tax rates.[9] Tax liability is

$$TAX = T(Y_{50}) + .50 \, (ETY - Y_{50}) + [T(Y^*) - T(ETY)], \quad (7)$$

where $T(Y)$ is income tax as a function of taxable income, ETY is earned taxable income, Y_{50} is the top taxable income subject to the 50 percent marginal tax rate, and Y^* is total taxable income.

$$ETY = \frac{E}{E + U} \, Y^*,$$

where E and U are earned and unearned income, respectively, and

$$Y^* = E + U - D,$$

where D is total deductions, including itemized charitable contributions. Differentiation of equation (7) yields the result that the decrease in taxes due to an additional dollar of deductions is

$$M^* - (M_e - .50) \frac{E}{E + U},$$

where M^* is the marginal tax rate on total taxable income and M_e is the marginal rate that would apply to the last dollar of earned taxable income under normal treatment.

In order to calculate tax and marginal tax rate under the maximum tax, it is necessary to estimate the proportion of earned and unearned income by income bracket. This was done by defining earned income as the sum of wages and salaries plus 30 percent of income from businesses, farms, partnerships, and small corporations.[10]

Data

The primary source of data for the analysis reported here is the Internal Revenue Service's annual *Statistics of Income*, which summarizes income, deductions, and related data reported on individual tax returns. Information is also available for selected years regarding the

TABLE 11.8
Income and Price Assumptions
($ Billions)

Year	Gross National Product (GNP)	GNP Price Deflator
1980 actual	$2,626	177.4
1981	2,922	193.6
1982	3,160	208.9
1983	3,524	221.5
1984	3,883	232.5

SOURCE: *Budget of the United States Government* (1983, 2-5, 2-7).

distribution of gifts by recipient group and by form of the gift. Distributions of taxpayers by filing status are also available.

While this source is an invaluable tool, it has a number of limitations. In the first place, the most recently published data available to us were for the 1978 tax year. These data therefore had to be "aged," using standard techniques, to bring them up to date. Average household income in current dollars was assumed to increase at the rate of per capita national income. Projected price levels were used to express dollar amounts in terms of constant 1980 dollars. In all cases, the administration's economic assumptions from the 1983 budget are used for projection (see table 11.8). The distribution of taxpayers among filing statuses (e.g., single, married filing jointly) was assumed to remain constant over the period.

In the second place, the *Statistics of Income* reports only aggregate data grouped by income class rather than data for individuals. Fortunately, past research has demonstrated that using aggregate data produces estimates quite close to those obtained using individual data.[11] However, to improve the sensitivity of the analysis, separate simulations were run for taxpayers in each of the five filing statuses and, within each of these, for itemizers and nonitemizers separately.

The third limitation of the *Statistics of Income* is that it provides data on the charitable contributions only of those who itemize their deductions. For nonitemizers, data on charitable contributions were taken from a University of Michigan survey on giving conducted in 1973. These data were aged to make them applicable to 1978 income classes.[12]

Fourth, because appreciated assets are taxed differently from regular income (they are taxed at special capital gains rates), reported contributions had to be divided between cash and other assets and each had to be analyzed separately. This was done using a distribution based on the 1975 *Statistics of Income* (table 2.4, p. 52), which provided the most recent data available on the breakdown of gifts.

Finally, the most recent year for which information is available on the distribution of gifts by recipient group is 1962. In that year the *Statistics of Income* (table E, p. 6) included a breakdown of contributions among five types of recipients: religious organizations, other charitable organizations, educational institutions, hospitals, and other organizations.[13] As above, it was assumed that the proportionate breakdown for each real income level did not change over time, so that the 1962 distributions were interpolated to apply to the 1978 income brackets.

CHAPTER 12

Government and the Voluntary Sector in an Era of Retrenchment

The American Experience

A curious paradox dominates the recent history of the non-profit or voluntary sector in the United States. For almost fifty years prior to the mid-1970s, the nonprofit sector largely disappeared from American public debate, as attention focused instead on the role of government in responding to human needs. Yet during this period, the private, nonprofit sector expanded as never before, growing in both scale and scope. By contrast, during the 1980s attention to the voluntary sector soared. Yet during this period, the sector experienced extraordinary economic strains.

It is the purpose of this chapter to unravel this paradox and to explore the implications it holds for the changing relationships between government and voluntary organizations in America. To do so, it is necessary to examine some of the basic characteristics of the American voluntary sector and its relationships with government, because much of the apparent paradox of recent American policy toward the voluntary sector results from a misunderstanding of how this sector operates and how it fits into the American version of the welfare state. Indeed, few aspects of American society have been more consistently overlooked or more poorly understood. This is unfortunate not only because it leads to poor policy, but also because it obscures a model for the provision of welfare state services that has great relevance for other nations as well.

The purpose of this chapter, therefore, is to address the following questions: How does the American voluntary sector operate? What role does it play in the American welfare state? How has this role been affected by recent national policy changes? And what implications flow from this for the future evolution of the voluntary sector in the United States as well as elsewhere in the world?

To answer these questions, we focus here, as in previous chapters, on the "public-benefit service" portion of the American not-for-profit sector, that is, on organizations that share four crucial characteristics:

1. They are privately controlled but are not profit-seeking businesses and therefore are exempt from federal income taxation;

2. They are primarily dedicated to assisting a broad public and not just the immediate members of the organization;

3. They are eligible to receive tax-exempt charitable gifts from individuals and corporations; and

4. They provide services, as opposed to distributing funds to other service providers.

This definition includes hospitals, universities, museums, arts groups, day care centers, nursing homes, foster care agencies, family counseling centers, neighborhood development groups, advocacy organizations, and many more. It does not include three other sets of tax-exempt organizations: (1) professional associations, labor unions, social clubs and other organizations that exist primarily to serve the immediate members of the organization; (2) churches, synagogues, mosques, and similar entities that are chiefly involved in sacramental religious activities; or (3) funding intermediaries such as private foundations and fund-raising groups, though the activities of these organizations show up in the revenues of service organizations.

Eight Observations

My work at the national level and in sixteen local field sites suggests eight major observations about the recent history of these organizations and the impact on them of recent policy changes.

1. The evolution of the voluntary sector in the United States defies conventional theories, particularly conventional conservative theories, about the relationship between voluntary organizations and the state.

According to conventional accounts, a fundamental conflict exists between voluntary organizations and the state. Government social welfare activities, according to this view, crowd out private, voluntary ones and leave voluntary organizations functionally obsolete. As government grows, therefore, private, nonprofit activity can be expected to shrink, at least in the fields where the two are both involved (Nisbet 1962; Berger and Neuhaus 1977; Kerrine and Neuhaus 1979; for further discussion see Salamon and Abramson 1982b).

In fact, little conflict of this sort has occurred in the United States. Although the growth of public institutions has put some pressures on many private, nonprofit ones in the field of higher education, in most fields—including higher education—the private, nonprofit sector remains a major presence despite the very rapid growth of government. As of 1980, for example, the public-benefit, service portion of the American nonprofit sector alone had expenditures of approximately $116 billion. This represented about 5 percent of the gross domestic product and a slightly larger share of national employment. In fact, nonprofit organizations account for about one in every five service industry workers. And in many fields its dominance is even greater. Thus nonprofits represent 54 percent of all general hospitals, 53 percent of all museums, 70 percent of all four-year colleges, and over 50 percent of all social service agency employees. In many localities, the expenditures of the nonprofit sector outdistance those of city and county government, despite the American tradition of substantial local self-government.[1] Quite clearly, the American nonprofit sector has hardly withered away with the growth of the modern welfare state.

Not only is the American nonprofit sector large, but also much of its growth has occurred in recent years, during which governmental social welfare activity also grew very rapidly. The survey we conducted of nonprofit organizations other than hospitals and higher education institutions revealed, for example, that two-thirds of the organizations in existence as of 1982 had been created since 1960, during the so-called Great Society era (Salamon 1984a, 17). This growth significantly extended the structure of the American voluntary sector, adding to the traditional sectarian organizations numerous organizations with roots in the anti-poverty, civil rights, consumer, environmental, and related movements of the 1960s and 1970s. In short, the expansion of the American welfare state has hardly displaced the voluntary sector. To the contrary, the sector has experienced some of its most impressive growth during precisely the era of most rapid governmental expansion.

2. *The continued expansion of the nonprofit sector in the face of governmental growth is in substantial part a consequence of the way the welfare state has evolved in the American context.*

One of the major problems with the conventional image of the relationship between government and the voluntary sector is its failure to take account of how government operates in the American setting, and in many other countries as well. In the human service field at least, government—particularly the federal government—does very little itself in the United States. What it does, it does through other institutions—state governments, city governments, county governments, banks, manufacturing firms, hospitals, higher education institutions, research institutes, and many more. The result is an elaborate pattern of *third-party government,* in which government provides the funds and sets the directions but other institutions deliver many of the services, often with a fair degree of discretion about who is served and how (Salamon 1981; see chap. 1).

This pattern of government action is a product of the conflict that has long existed in the United States between the desire for public services and hostility to the governmental bureaucracies that provide them. "Third-party government" has emerged as a way to reconcile these competing perspectives, to increase the role of government in promoting the general welfare without unduly enlarging the administrative apparatus of the state. Where existing institutions are available to carry out a function—whether it be extending loans, providing health care, or delivering social services—they have a presumptive claim on a meaningful role in whatever government program might be established. Indeed, government has often created such institutions where none existed in order to carry out a public purpose without extending the governmental bureaucracy.

This pattern of government action has also resulted from America's pluralistic political structure. To secure political support for a program of government action, it is frequently necessary to win at least the tacit approval, if not the whole-hearted support, of the key interests with a stake in the area. One way to do this is to ensure them a piece of the action by building them into the operation of the government program. Thus, private banks are involved in running the government's loan guarantee programs, private medical insurers and hospitals in the operation of the health programs, and state and private social service agencies in the provision of federally funded social services.

By virtue of their "public" or charitable objectives, and their presence on the scene in many of the fields where government involvement has occurred, private, nonprofit organizations have been natural candidates to take part in this third-party system. What is more, government support has consciously stimulated the creation of nonprofit organizations in a number of fields, elaborating the basic structure of the sector and encouraging its expansion into new fields. In the process, an extensive government-nonprofit partnership has taken shape, extending the reach of the voluntary sector and underwriting its operations in important part.

This elaborate partnership takes a variety of different forms—outright grants from the federal government to nonprofits; federal grants to state and local governments which then enter into purchase-of-service contracts with nonprofits; payments to individuals to reimburse them for services provided to individuals; and many more. Perhaps because of this complexity, the system has never been carefully charted. Yet it is immense. According to estimates we have developed, the federal government alone provided approximately $40 billion in aid to the private, nonprofit sector in 1980 (Salamon and Abramson 1982a, 42–43). As detailed more fully in chapter 6, this represented over one-third of the funds that the federal government spent in service fields where nonprofit organizations are active. And in some fields, such as social services, research, arts and humanities, and health, half or more of all federal spending went to support services provided not by government agencies but by private, nonprofit groups!

An even clearer picture of the extent of government reliance on nonprofits to deliver publicly financed services emerges from work I and a group of colleagues have done in sixteen localities of different sizes throughout the United States, and that covers state and local as well as federal spending (see chap. 6). What these data show is that, on average, about 40 percent of the money government spends on services in five key human service fields goes to private, nonprofit providers. By comparison, public agencies absorb about 38 percent of the funds, with the balance delivered by for-profit firms. This means that nonprofits actually deliver a larger share of the services that government funds than do government agencies themselves. And in some fields, such as social services, nonprofits absorb over half of the funds government spends.

In short, one of the major reasons the expansion of the welfare state has not displaced nonprofit organizations in the United States is that government has turned extensively to nonprofit organizations to de-

TABLE 12.1
Sources of Support of Nonprofit Human Service Agencies,
Exclusive of Hospitals and Universities, 1981

Source	Share of Nonprofit Income
Government	41%
Fees, service charges	28
All private giving	20
United Way	5
Other federations	3
Direct individual	6
Corporate	3
Foundations	3
Endowment	5
Other	6
Total	100%

SOURCE: Salamon (1984a).

liver publicly financed services. In the fields where the two sectors are involved, nonprofits are often the principal providers of government-financed services. It is this government-nonprofit partnership that forms the core of the human service delivery system in the United States.

3. Government is the principal source of nonprofit-sector income.

Given the extent of government reliance on nonprofit organizations to deliver publicly funded services, it should come as no surprise to learn that government, not private charity, is the principal source of the income of private, nonprofit organizations in the United States. Compared to the $40 billion they received from the federal government in 1980, for example, nonprofit service organizations received only $25.5 billion from all sources of private giving combined, including corporations, foundations, United Way, religious federations, direct individual giving, and bequests (American Association of Fund-Raising Counsel 1981). This point emerges even more forcefully from the survey we conducted of some 3,400 nonprofit organizations exclusive of hospitals and higher education institutions (table 12.1). Government accounted for 41 percent of the revenues of these organizations as of 1981 (see chap. 4). The second largest source of support, accounting for 28 percent of total revenues, was fees and service charges. Private giving accounted for only 20 percent of the revenues. In short, the government-nonprofit partnership has not only become a dominant feature of the American version of the welfare state, but also it has become the central financial fact of life of the nation's substantial voluntary sector.

4. Government-nonprofit collaboration is in no sense a new development in the United States; rather, it has roots deep in American history.

Within some portions of the voluntary sector, the expansion of government support has been viewed as an unfortunate deviation from the nonprofit sector's historic pattern of independence from government. In fact, such cooperation is in no sense a new phenomenon in the United States; it has roots deep in American history. For example, some of the nation's premier private, nonprofit institutions—such as Harvard University, Columbia University, Dartmouth College, and the Metropolitan Museum of Art—owe their origins and early sustenance to government support (Whitehead 1973; Nielsen 1979). As early as 1890, 57 percent of all public expenditures on aid to the poor in New York City went to support services provided through nonprofit organizations (Warner 1894). So widespread was the practice of government support for private hospitals in the late nineteenth and early twentieth centuries that an American Hospital Association report referred to it in 1909 as "the distinctively American practice." Until late in the nineteenth century, nonprofit organizations were viewed in America as part of the public sector, not the private sector, because they served "public purposes" (Stevens 1982; for further details see chap. 6).

While this pattern of government-nonprofit cooperation has deep historical roots, it has expanded in scope and scale in the period since President Roosevelt's New Deal of the 1930s, and particularly during the 1950s and 1960s, as the scope of government activity grew. Thus Medicare, the federal health insurance program for the elderly established in 1965, made government reimbursement of private hospitals the cornerstone of the nation's health care system. The Social Security Act Amendments of 1967 opened the door for state and local contracting with nonprofit providers under the federal government's new social service program. The Economic Opportunity Act of 1964 led to the creation of a network of federally funded nonprofit organizations to orchestrate local anti-poverty efforts. Through these and other actions, the existing pattern of government-nonprofit cooperation mushroomed in scale and complexity. But the basic contours of the relationship had been set decades, indeed centuries, before.

*5. The extensive pattern of government-nonprofit partnership that
has taken shape in the United States has important advantages as an
alternative to direct governmental provision of welfare services—but it also
poses significant problems of management and coordination that became
increasingly evident during the 1970s.*

Compared to a system of direct government service provision or
one placing sole reliance on voluntary action, the extensive pattern
of government-nonprofit cooperation that has evolved in the United
States has much to recommend it. It combines government's advantages as a mobilizer of resources with the private, nonprofit sector's
advantages as a deliverer of services. Potentially at least, it makes it
possible to set priorities and raise funds for the solution of community
problems through a democratic political process while avoiding exclusive reliance on large-scale governmental bureaucracies to deliver services. And it takes advantage of the smaller scale and dedication of
voluntary agencies without leaving the determination of service priorities exclusively in the hands of the wealthy. Beyond this, it helps to
sustain a network of institutions that engage private citizens in the solution of community problems, and thus promotes an important national value stressing pluralism and private action. In all likelihood,
had this system of service provision not evolved in this country long
ago, Americans would be busily inventing it now.

For all its potential strengths and advantages, this system of
government-nonprofit partnership has also had its problems. For one
thing, despite its scale and importance, it has evolved in ad hoc fashion, with little systematic understanding of the roles and responsibilities of the respective partners and little public awareness that the partnership even exists. As the scale of interactions has increased, tensions
and confusions have resulted. Nonprofit organizations, for example,
have sometimes been distressed by the accountability and paperwork
requirements imposed by government and by the impact of government regulations on their operations (U.S. Senate 1980). There has
also been concern about the potential dilution of board control of
agencies as government contract officers have come to play a larger
role in agency operations, and about the tendency of government to
encourage professionalization and bureaucratization of nonprofit organizations. The sheer fragmentation of government program structures has also caused problems, making it difficult for nonprofits to
fashion integrated approaches to human problems. For their part,
government officials have frequently found it difficult to exercise ade-

quate control over the spending of public funds, and often find it necessary to support the range of services that the existing network of
agencies can provide even when it is not fully consistent with what the
legislation or community needs may require (DeHoog 1985).

As these strains intensified in the 1970s, they were joined by concerns about the apparent erosion of the private philanthropic base of
the voluntary sector. Between 1969 and 1979, for example, private
giving as a share of gross national product declined from 2.1 to 1.8
percent in the United States (American Association of Fund-Raising
Counsel 1981). In part, this was a result of the impact of inflation. But
in part also it was the by-product of a series of changes in the tax system that liberalized the so-called standard deduction, causing fewer
people to itemize their deductions and thus reducing the value of the
special tax deduction that is provided for charitable contributions.[2] At
the same time, there was mounting evidence that a 1969 change in
the laws governing private foundations, coupled with adverse market
conditions, was eating into the assets of private foundations, threatening this source of private charitable support as well (Commission on
Private Philanthropy and Public Needs 1975). Under these circumstances, leaders of the voluntary sector became increasingly concerned
about the future of their set of institutions.

Concerns about the future of the voluntary sector surfaced at a time
when public confidence in government as a mechanism for solving social problems—never very strong in America—was again at ebb tide.
The Vietnam War, escalating inflation rates, hostility to the social regulation of the 1960s and 1970s, and backlash against the social policies
of the Great Society all contributed to a climate of reaction against
the welfare state. Since the public had little awareness of the existing
partnership between government and the voluntary sector, this hostility to governmental programs provided a potential reservoir of support for greater reliance on private action.

*6. In response to the pressures and concerns that surrounded the voluntary
sector and the growing disenchantment with government during the 1970s, an
interesting opportunity arose to strengthen the nonprofit sector and rationalize
its relationships with government.*

Stimulated by the problems identified above, important efforts were
made during the 1970s to examine the status of the voluntary sector
and to rethink its role in national life. As detailed more fully in chapter
9, these efforts took place on both the political Right and the political

Left, and created an interesting opportunity to upgrade the status of the voluntary sector and improve the existing ad hoc pattern of government-nonprofit ties.

Among the most important of these efforts, four deserve special mention here. The first was the formation in 1973 of a blue-ribbon Commission on Private Philanthropy and Public Needs (the Filer Commission), inspired by John D. Rockefeller III and composed of important business, government, and philanthropic leaders. During its two-year life, the commission assembled a massive body of new information on the voluntary sector and formulated a voluntary-sector agenda that endorsed continued governmental support to the voluntary sector but also called for changes in the tax laws to increase the incentives for private charitable giving (Commission on Private Philanthropy and Public Needs 1975). Complementing the work of the Filer Commission was the "mediating structures" project of the business-oriented American Enterprise Institute, which issued a series of reports during the mid-1970s calling for a more explicit and active policy of governmental utilization of "mediating structures" such as voluntary organizations to carry out public objectives (Berger and Neuhaus 1977). The third event was the formation in 1979 of Independent Sector, a new national association representing the various components of the nonprofit sector—service agencies, fundraisers, foundations, corporate giving programs—and devoted to strengthening the sector's role in national life. Finally, in 1980 the far-right Heritage Foundation issued its own report on private philanthropy (Butler 1980), that reached many of the same conclusions as the Filer Commission, and thus added a strong conservative voice to the defense of a set of institutions that during the 1960s and early 1970s had acquired a decidedly liberal following as well.

By the time the Reagan administration took office in 1981, an unusual consensus had formed among at least some leaders on both the political Left and the political Right in favor of strengthening nonprofit and voluntary groups and broadening and rationalizing existing relationships between such groups and government (Salamon 1984b). To be sure, the strands of analysis and insight had yet to be drawn together into an integrated program of action. What is more, voluntarism still engendered considerable skepticism on the political Left while conservatives sometimes found it hard to reconcile their enthusiasm for the theoretical concept of voluntary organization with their hostility to many of the actual liberal, neighborhood, and public-interest groups that had formed in the 1960s. Nevertheless, the degree of consensus was still quite surprising, especially in view of the wide divergence of political perspectives it embraced. Coupled with growing disaffection with traditional welfare state policies, the pieces were therefore in place—both politically and analytically—for a significant policy initiative featuring an expansion of the role of voluntary groups and a more explicit policy of government-nonprofit cooperation. Here was a unique opportunity indeed for an administration committed, as the 1980 Republican Party platform put it, to the restoration of "the American spirit of voluntary service and cooperation, of private and community initiative."

7. The Reagan administration adopted policies that threatened to dismantle, or at least significantly reduce, the prevailing pattern of government-nonprofit cooperation.

Although strongly committed conceptually to encouraging the voluntary sector, the Reagan administration did precious little to build on the consensus that had developed during the 1970s in support of a positive program of cooperation between government and nonprofit groups. To the contrary, the administration subsumed its policy toward the voluntary sector under its overall economic program, which called for substantial cuts in government spending and in tax rates in order to stimulate economic growth. In a sense, the administration retreated to the traditional theories that viewed government and the nonprofit sector as competitors. With this theory, it was easy to jump to the conclusion that the best way to help the nonprofit sector was to get government out of its way and let the private sector "pick up the slack."

What this approach largely overlooked, however, was that government and the nonprofit sector are not inherently in conflict in the American setting, and that an extensive partnership links the two. The same budget cuts that increased the need for nonprofit action threatened to reduce the revenues that private, nonprofit groups had available to meet even existing needs. In fact, the administration's initial budget proposals would have reduced the support that private, nonprofit organizations received from the federal government by some $33 billion—about 20 percent—below its 1980 levels during the period 1982–85. For some types of organizations, moreover, the projected loss of federal support would be considerably more severe. Thus, under the administration's initial proposals, federal support to nonprofit social service organizations would be 64 percent lower in Fiscal Year (FY) 1985 than it had been in FY 1980, after adjusting for inflation. Community development organizations would have lost 65 percent of their federal support, and education and research organizations 35 percent (Salamon and Abramson 1982a, 30, 51). Because government represents a large source of income for these organizations, these reductions posed a significant challenge to existing agency operations. In short, while encouraging voluntary organizations to do more, the Reagan administration, through its budget proposals, was forcing them to do less. What is more, thanks to the program of tax cuts and a stringent set of administrative changes outlined in more detail in chapter 9, the administration also challenged the sector's private philanthropic base. Committed to a budget strategy designed to reduce government spending but wedded to a political theory that obscured the existing pattern of government-nonprofit cooperation, the Reagan administration thus found itself encouraging the voluntary sector at the rhetorical level while undermining its position at the programmatic level, and not really appreciating the conflict between the two. In the process, the administration alienated substantial segments of the voluntary community, undermined emerging liberal support for a voluntary-sector agenda by tying this agenda to a retreat from public responsibilities, and thus squandered an important opportunity to develop a positive program of change that would strengthen the nonprofit sector and improve the prevailing pattern of government-nonprofit cooperation.

8. As a result of the budget reductions proposed by the Reagan administration and partially enacted by Congress, nonprofit organizations have been forced to seek alternative sources of funding or to reduce their operations. Generally speaking, the sector has responded not by becoming more charitable but by becoming more commercial.

The U.S. Congress ultimately approved only a portion of the cuts in human service spending proposed by the Reagan administration in 1981. Nevertheless, this reduced federal support to nonprofit organizations substantially below the levels that existed as of 1980, the year before Mr. Reagan came to power. In particular, outside of the health field, where spending grew, nonprofit organizations lost a total of approximately $23 billion in federal support—about $4.6 billion a year—over the five years 1982–86, compared to what they would have received had 1980 spending levels been maintained. By 1986, federal support to nonprofit organizations outside of the health field was thus 28 percent below its 1980 level, after adjusting for inflation (table 12.2). In some fields, such as social services and community develop-

TABLE 12.2

Changes in Federal Support of Nonprofits, FY 1986 vs. FY 1980, in Constant FY 1980 Dollars

Type of Organization	FY 1980 Federal Support ($ Billions)	Change, FY 1986 vs FY 1980	
		($ Billions)	Percentage
Social services	$6.5	$−2.6	−40%
Community development	2.6	−1.1	−44
Higher education	2.7	−0.6	−21
Other education/research	2.9	+0.2	+7
Health	25.0	+5.8	+23
Foreign aid	0.8	−0.1	−8
Arts, culture	0.4	−0.2	−41
Total	$40.8	+$1.5	+4%
Total without Medicare, Medicaid	$16.7	−4.8	−28%

SOURCE: Abramson and Salamon (1986). Columns may not add to totals due to rounding.

TABLE 12.3

Changes in Nonprofit Support from Government, by Type of Agency, 1981–1982, in Inflation-Adjusted Dollars

Type of Agency	Percentage Change in Government Support
Legal services/advocacy	−28.8%
Housing/community development	−15.6
Employment/training	−12.7
Social services	−8.8
Mixed	−8.1
Education/research	−7.3
Culture/arts	−1.3
Health services	−1.3
Mental health	−0.1
Institutional/residential	+4.1
All agencies	−6.3%

SOURCE: Salamon Nonprofit Sector Project Survey, round 1.

ment, the value of federal support by 1986 had dropped over 40 percent below what it had been in 1980 (Abramson and Salamon 1986).

As table 12.3 shows, federal cuts did begin to affect the balance sheets of the nation's private, nonprofit organizations during the early 1980s. Based on a survey I organized of all such organizations except for hospitals and universities, government support for nonprofit service providers declined by 6 percent overall between 1981 and 1982 after adjusting for inflation. And in some fields the reductions were severe. Thus, legal services and advocacy organizations lost 29 percent of their government support between 1981 and 1982; housing and community development organizations 16 percent; employment and training organizations 13 percent; and social service organizations 9 percent.

Despite these losses in government revenue, however, the nonprofit sector as a whole registered an overall increase in total income of 0.5 percent over this period, even after adjusting for inflation. What made this possible was not growth in private charitable support, as the Reagan administration had hoped. Although private charitable income grew, it offset no more than a quarter of the government losses (Salamon and Abramson 1985). By contrast, 70 percent of the replacement income came from additional service charges and fees. The nonprofit sector managed to recover from government cuts chiefly by charging their clients more for their services or by instituting fees where none formerly existed.

While this shift from government to essentially commercial income is not necessarily harmful to the nonprofit sector, it raises important questions about the future of this set of institutions and about their role in the American welfare state. Conceivably, the more voluntary agencies must rely on service fees to survive, the more they will be forced to tailor their services to clientele who can pay for them and the less they will be able to focus on those in greatest need. This is particularly troubling in view of two additional facts that emerge from our surveys. In the first place, far fewer of these agencies focus primarily on the poor and needy than might have been expected. Of the human service agencies we surveyed, less than 30 percent reported that poor people comprise the majority of their clients, and about half reported that poor people comprise less than 10 percent of their clients. In the second place, the agencies overwhelmingly agreed that government support has played an important role in inducing them to focus more on the poor than they had done previously. The clear implication is that as government support declines, agency attention to the poor may wane.

Some evidence of this is apparent in the variations in agency ability to bounce back from government budget cuts. In particular, while on average the agencies we surveyed registered an 0.5 percent gain in income between 1981 and 1982, agencies serving the poor ended up with a significant overall decline. Generally speaking, the agencies with the best access to paying clients (e.g., health agencies) did best in response to the recent budget cuts while those with the least access (e.g., employment agencies) did worst (Salamon 1984a). As the nonprofit sector shifts from governmental to commercial sources of income, therefore, the structure of the sector is likely to change as well.

Beyond questions about what the nonprofit sector does and whom it serves, the shift to greater reliance on fee income also raises questions about the basic rationale for the nonprofit form of organization. This is particularly problematic in view of a challenge that has been posed to the nonprofit sector in the United States by the small business community, which is jealous of the tax advantages enjoyed by nonprofit organizations. As nonprofits move more actively into commercial activities, and as they come to rely more heavily on fees for service to finance their operations, the more serious the challenge is likely to become from profit-making agencies.

Conclusion

The American voluntary sector stands at an important crossroads in its development. More than its counterparts in many other countries, this set of organizations has maintained a substantial role despite the growth of the welfare state. It has done so, however, not so much in opposition to government as in cooperation with it. The resulting pattern of government-nonprofit partnership in the provision of welfare state services stands in stark contrast to the direct governmental provision of services that is the central feature of the welfare state in many western nations.

As a system of service provision, this pattern of government-nonprofit partnership has much to recommend it, combining as it does the capacity to generate resources and set priorities through a democratic political process and the ability to deliver services through smaller, locally oriented, private nonprofit groups. It thus makes welfare state benefits available as a matter of right while still preserving a useful degree of competition and pluralism in the service-delivery structure.

Despite its scale and importance, this pattern of government-nonprofit partnership is very poorly understood in the United States. Government-nonprofit cooperation took shape not as a matter of conscious policy but as an adaptation to powerful political realities—the political strength of the voluntary sector, the widespread public hostility to governmental bureaucracy, and the general tepidness of public support for welfare services. Not surprisingly, strains developed in this partnership during the period of rapid expansion of the 1960s and 1970s.

Although serious efforts were made during the 1970s to face up to these problems and come to terms with them, these efforts were short-circuited by the budget and tax program of the Reagan administration, which, in the name of strengthening the voluntary sector, subjected it to severe economic pressures and made voluntarism and the voluntary sector a euphemism for governmental retrenchment. Ironically enough, while other countries were enlarging cooperative ties between government and voluntary organizations of the sort that have long existed in the United States, American policy was unwittingly moving in the opposite direction.

Whether it will be possible to revive the political support that was emerging for a conscious policy of strengthening the voluntary sector and rationalizing government-nonprofit cooperation remains to be seen. But this partnership offers a useful model for the organization of welfare state services, both in the United States and elsewhere.

PART V

Future Trends

The policies of the Reagan administration are not the only forces shaping the future evolution of the nonprofit sector at the present time. Also important are a variety of demographic and economic developments both in this country and abroad. Some of these are having a generally positive impact on the nonprofit sector, increasing the demand for its services or otherwise expanding its base of support. Others are more negative in their effect, reducing the resources available to the sector as a whole or to some of its constituent parts, or otherwise constraining their ability to function as before.

This section examines these broader forces shaping the future evolution of the nonprofit sector both in the United States and abroad. Chapter 13 sets the stage for this discussion by identifying five major developments likely to affect the evolution of the nonprofit sector in the years ahead. These include a variety of demographic developments likely to expand the need for nonprofit services as well as shifts in the scope and structure of public assistance that are likely to expose nonprofit organizations to increased competition for resources.

Chapter 14 details some of the consequences that have already flowed from the dramatic changes of the 1980s. Most importantly, it focuses attention on a pervasive "marketization" of welfare that seems to be one of the most salient heritages of these years. This is evident not only in a vast expansion of the dependence of nonprofit organizations on fee and service income, but also in the dramatic expansion of for-profit competition in many traditional fields of nonprofit activity.

Finally, chapter 15 broadens the focus to the global scene where even more dramatic changes have taken place in the role and visibility of nonprofit organizations. As this chapter makes clear, the rediscovery of the nonprofit sector that occurred in the United States in the 1980s is really part of a broader global phenomenon reflecting a pervasive crisis of the state and significant changes in education and communications. For the nonprofit sector to take its appropriate place on the global scene, however, it will have to be approached with the same realism and careful analysis that recent events have demonstrated are needed domestically as well. And nowhere will this be more important than with respect to the relationships between nonprofit organizations and the state that are the principal focus of this book.

The Voluntary Sector and the
Future of the Welfare State

The future of the voluntary agency is indissolubly tied
to the future of the welfare state, and both are increasingly perceived to be in crisis.
— Ralph Kramer, 1980

Two alternative paradigms vie for the attention of scholars
and practitioners in defining the role of the voluntary sector in the
future of the modern welfare state: the paradigm of competition and
the paradigm of partnership. The paradigm of competition is the paradigm of the law, of economic theory, and of conservative social
thought. Stressing the uniqueness of the voluntary sector, it posits an
inherent conflict between voluntary organizations and the state and
views the growth of the latter as a threat to the viability of the former
(see, e.g., Nisbet 1953; Berger and Neuhaus 1977; Weisbrod 1977).
The paradigm of partnership is the paradigm of practice and of liberal
pragmatism. Acknowledging the special characteristics of the voluntary sector, it stresses instead the areas of overlap and potential cooperation between voluntary organizations and the state.

Previous chapters have examined the applicability of these two paradigms to the realities of the American welfare state as it had evolved
through the early 1980s. This work revealed that an elaborate partnership between government and the voluntary sector forms the core of
the modern welfare state and constitutes the principal financial fact of
life of the modern voluntary sector. However, recent developments
have challenged this partnership in rather fundamental ways. In response, some (for example, Butler 1985) have beckoned the nonprofit
sector back to its essentially voluntary roots in line with the paradigm

of competition, while others (such as Crimmins 1985) have nudged it toward a more entrepreneurial future. What is lacking is an assessment that explicitly relates the future of the voluntary sector to recent trends in the modern welfare state, although Gilbert (1983) has made a significant start toward this goal. It is the purpose of this chapter to outline at least the major components of such an assessment.

The central argument here is that powerful forces are leading the voluntary sector away from its recent role as a partner in public service toward greater integration into the private, market economy. To help the reader understand this development, the discussion in this chapter is divided into three parts. I begin by reviewing three major conclusions that flow from my earlier work on the recent pattern of government-nonprofit relations in the American welfare state. Next, I explore some of the salient trends in the operation of the American welfare state. Last, I examine the implications of these trends for the future character and role of the voluntary sector.

Prevailing Realities

The central fact of life of the American welfare state as it had evolved by the 1970s was a widespread pattern of partnership between government and the voluntary sector. Facing major new responsibilities in a context of continued public hostility to the bureaucratic state, government at all levels turned extensively to existing and newly created private, nonprofit organizations to help it carry out expanded welfare state functions. As a consequence, through direct and indirect grants and third-party payments, government support easily surpassed private charity as the major source of private, nonprofit sector income.

This partnership between government and the nonprofit sector was not, moreover, a recent development, as some accounts of the sector suggest. Rather, its roots lay deep in American history. Summarizing the historical record, Waldemar Nielsen (1979, 47) points out that "collaboration, not separation or antagonism, between government and the Third Sector . . . has been the predominant characteristic" through much of our history.

Not only does this pattern of partnership have deep historical roots, it also has a strong theoretical rationale. Unfortunately, this rationale has been obscured by prevailing theories of the welfare state and of the voluntary sector, which emphasize, respectively, a hierarchically structured state and a voluntary sector filling in for "market failures" where government has yet to act. But as I have argued elsewhere (Salamon 1987a and chap. 2), these theories overlook the fragmented character of the American state, its widespread reliance on third parties to carry out public functions, and inherent weaknesses in the voluntary sector that make collaboration between government and the voluntary sector a productive partnership for both.

Recent Trends

Whatever its historical roots and theoretical rationale, the collaborative relationship between government and the voluntary sector confronts immense challenges in the years ahead. Important developments now under way seem likely to change the character of the voluntary sector and remove the partnership between government and the nonprofit sector from its place as the central organizing principle of the American welfare state. This section examines five of these developments.

Resource Constraints

The most obvious change in the operation of the American welfare state in recent years has been the imposition of a significant restraint on its provision of resources. While the Reagan administration was far less successful than it had hoped to be in reducing budgetary outlays for human service programs, it did manage to halt a twenty-year pattern of rapid growth, and the Bush administration generally continued to hold the line. Thus, after adjustment for inflation, federal spending on a wide array of human service programs as of fiscal year 1990 was a mere 5 percent above the level it had reached in fiscal year 1980, and most of this was due to growth in health expenditures. Indeed, if we exclude the two major federal health programs, Medicare and Medicaid, spending on the remaining human service programs was 7 percent lower in 1990 than it had been in FY 1980 (Salamon and Abramson 1992). Inevitably, this decline translated into fiscal constraints on the private, nonprofit sector. Excluding Medicare and Medicaid, the real value of federal support to nonprofit organizations declined 25–30 percent between 1980 and 1986, and by FY 1990 nonprofit organizations still ended up with about 10 percent less federal support than they had received in fiscal year 1980. Thus a considerable period of rapid growth was reversed. With rare exceptions, the states were not able to compensate for the federal restraint. On the contrary, in many areas, federal contraction brought state contraction along with it (Nathan, Doolittle, and Associates 1987; Salamon, Musselwhite, and De Vita 1986).

Perhaps even more significant than the cuts in federal social welfare spending achieved during the Reagan era is the legacy of restraint imposed by the federal budget deficit created during this period. Although estimates of the size of the future deficit vary widely, there is little basis for optimism about the potential for major domestic spending increases in the foreseeable future. The one potentially countervailing factor is the splintering of the Soviet bloc after 1989 and the opportunity that this creates to reduce defense spending and free up resources for social programs. Given the size of the deficit, however, even under this scenario there is little basis for optimism about the potential for major domestic spending increases in the foreseeable future.

From Categorical Aid to Universal Entitlements

In addition to the overall pattern of restraint, important changes have taken place in the composition of social welfare spending. In particular, the retrenchment hit hardest on the so-called discretionary spending programs and the means-tested welfare programs aimed at the poor and near poor. In contrast, the so-called entitlement programs, especially those targeted at the middle class, saw considerable growth. In the process, a significant shift occurred in the structure of federal welfare spending—away from categorical programs aimed at the needy, toward general entitlement programs available to significant portions of the middle class.[1]

The data in table 13.1 provide evidence of this shift, comparing the pattern of federal spending for Social Security, Medicare, and other retirement programs—the major entitlement programs—with other domestic spending. As the table shows, after adjustment for inflation, federal spending on the entitlement programs increased 38 percent between fiscal year 1980 and fiscal year 1990, while spending on the rest of the domestic budget declined by 10 percent. In this ten-year period, spending on these middle-class entitlement programs therefore increased from 47 percent of the domestic budget to 57 percent.

To be sure, the Reagan administration made efforts to cut back on entitlement payments to middle-income groups under a number of federal programs, including food stamps and college student aid. But some of these changes have been reversed, and coverage under other

TABLE 13.1

Growth of Federal Entitlement and Other Domestic Programs, FY 1980–1990, in Inflation-Adjusted Dollars

($ Billions)

Program	FY 1980 Outlays	FY 1990 Outlays (in FY 1980 Dollars)	Percentage Change 1980–1990
Entitlements			
Social Security	$118.5	$154.8	+31%
Medicare	32.1	61.0	+90
Other retirement	31.7	35.5	+12
Subtotal, entitlements	182.3	251.4	+38
Other domestic programs	208.1	186.6	−10
Total domestic programs	$390.4	$438.0	+12%
Entitlements as a percentage of domestic programs	46.7%	57.4%	

SOURCE: Computed from figures in U.S. Office of Management and Budget (1991).

programs has been extended. For example, coverage under the federal government's Medicaid program, which originally was limited to welfare recipients, was recently expanded to allow states to cover the aged poor as well as pregnant women and children under five years of age in families whose income is as much as 85 percent above the poverty line, whether the families are on welfare or not (Pear 1988). Reflecting these changes and other developments, Medicaid expenditures have continued to grow despite rather vigorous cost-control efforts. More generally, the recent reality has been one not of across-the-board restraint but of cutbacks falling most heavily on the most vulnerable, while support for the broad middle class shows considerable growth.

From Producer Subsidies to Consumer Subsidies

A third important trend in the structure of the American welfare state is a marked shift in emphasis away from aid delivered through producers of services to aid delivered through consumers. This trend is only the most recent manifestation of a broader pattern of government operation of which government reliance on nonprofit organizations is one part. This pattern involves the transformation of government from a direct producer of services into a financier or arranger of service provided by others (Salamon 1981; and chap. 1). Paying nongovernmental third parties, including nonprofit organizations, to

TABLE 13.2

Changes in the Forms of Federal Assistance to Nonprofit Organizations between FY 1980 and FY 1986

	Percentage of Total Support	
Form	FY 1980	FY 1986
Producer subsidies	47%	30%
Consumer subsidies	53	70
Total	100%	100%

SOURCE: Computed from data in U.S. Office of Management and Budget (1988).

deliver publicly financed services has been one way of accomplishing this transformation. Paying the consumer of services directly and letting him or her decide what provider to use is simply a more extreme version of the same idea.

While the shift from producer subsidies to consumer subsidies or vouchers is rooted in the broad movement toward third-party government, it has more proximate origins in the efforts by conservatives to "privatize" the public sector. As one advocate (Butler 1985, 43) has observed, "From the privatizers' perspective, the voucher is a useful device to make private-sector alternatives financially available to low-income citizens." According to advocates of privatizing, the great advantage of vouchers is that they rely on the market rather than on the government or the producer to determine the allocation of resources, and thus they presumably increase efficiency and cut the important political link tying service providers, politicians, and bureaucrats together in support of public expenditures (Butler 1985; Savas 1987). This same line of argument has recently been endorsed as well by a group of pro-government moderates who view reliance on market-oriented incentives as a useful way to help "re-invent government" (Osborne and Gaebler 1992), a view that gained considerable currency in the Clinton administration.

The extent of the shift toward voucher-type arrangements is quite striking. Looking only at federal assistance to the nonprofit sector, table 13.2 shows that the amount of federal aid that reached nonprofit organizations through voucher payments to individuals (that is, through Medicare) grew between fiscal year 1980 and fiscal year 1986 from 53 percent of all federal assistance to 70 percent. During this same period, producer subsidies that nonprofits received from the federal government—either directly or via state and local governments— fell from 47 percent of the total to 30 percent. In other words, while the total volume of federal support in constant 1980 dollars remained the same, consumer subsidies grew just about enough to offset the decline in producer subsidies (U.S. Office of Management and Budget 1988).

In addition to the expansion of voucher-type programs and the contraction imposed on direct-service programs, reliance on so-called tax expenditures to subsidize human services is increasing. Like voucher payments to individuals, tax expenditures—that is, exemptions in the tax law for certain kinds of activities—channel government aid through the consumers of services. The main difference between tax expenditures and voucher payments is that the former operate through the tax system rather than the expenditure side of the budget. Not incidentally, they also tend to deliver their benefits disproportionately to the better-off, whose tax liabilities are more substantial to start with. Thus, in the field of day care, while the federal budget cut the real value of federal spending for the Title XX social services program (the chief producer subsidy for day care as well as other social services) from $2.7 billion in fiscal year 1980 to the equivalent of $2.0 billion in fiscal year 1987, the federal tax credit for child and dependent care expenses increased more than 400 percent in inflation-adjusted terms, from $700 million in fiscal year 1980 to $3.2 billion in fiscal year 1987 (U.S. Office of Management and Budget 1988). In other words, by 1987 the federal government was "spending" more on day care through consumer subsidies in the tax system than it was expending on day care and more than a dozen other social services through the producer payments provided by the Social Services Block Grant. Further shifts in the pattern of government support for day care are evident in state efforts to switch day care funding for welfare recipients from the Social Services Block Grant, a producer-oriented discretionary program whose funding levels have been declining, to the Aid to Families with Dependent Children Program, an entitlement program whose funding levels have proved harder to cut. These and similar developments in other fields add up to a significant overall trend that, while relatively unheralded, has important implications for the evolution of government-nonprofit relations.

Demographic Developments

Beyond these programmatic shifts, important changes have also occurred in the basic demography of the welfare state and in the demands for its services. Some of these demographic changes are manifest in the trends noted earlier. Others have yet to make their full effects felt. Four of these changes seem particularly likely to have significant long-term consequences.

The Graying of the Population. One of the most dramatic changes confronting the American welfare state is the continued growth in the number and proportion of elderly persons. Between 1960 and 1980, the number of persons aged sixty-five and older increased by 50 percent, while the overall population grew by just over 25 percent. If this trend continues over the next forty to fifty years, the proportion of the population that is sixty-five and older will double. Moreover, among the elderly, the proportion that is over seventy-five is also projected to grow, so that it will reach 50 percent of the elderly over the next forty to fifty years. This demographic fact of life has already found expression in the growth of federal support to the elderly. Given the potent political power that the elderly can wield, there is every reason to expect continued pressures for expansion of the welfare state benefits they receive.

The Changing Social and Economic Position of Women. Another recent change that has powerful implications for the character of the American welfare state is the transformation in the role of women. While this transformation has many dimensions, one of the most important is the surge in female labor force participation. Between 1960 and 1980, the labor force participation rate of women increased from 30.5 percent to 50.1 percent. Even more dramatic, the labor force participation rate for married women with children under the age of six rose from 18.6 percent in 1960 to 45.1 percent in 1980. That same year, the labor force participation rate for separated women with children under six reached 55.2 percent. For divorced women with children under six, it grew to 68.3 percent. Aside from its social and economic effects, this development signals a substantial increase in the need for day care.

Changes in Family Structure. Significant changes have also occurred in family structure. In 1960, there was one divorce for every four marriages. By 1980, there was one divorce for every two marriages. During this period, the number of children involved in divorces almost tripled, from 463,000 in 1960 to almost 1.2 million in 1980. Since divorce typically brings a significant loss in economic status, this development suggests increased demands on existing human services. What is more, a very significant increase also occurred in the proportion of births to unmarried women. Between 1960 and 1980, the proportion of such births jumped from 5.3 percent to more than 18 percent. Among nonwhites, it rose from 22 percent to 48 percent. Although the proportion of births to unmarried women was lower among whites, the absolute number of such births was almost equal—320,000 whites and 346,000 nonwhites for a total of 666,000 as of 1980, compared to 224,000 twenty years earlier (U.S. Census Bureau 1986).

Emergence of an Urban Underclass. The fourth recent demographic development of great importance to the evolution of the American welfare state has been the emergence of a sizable cadre of hard-core inner-city poor persons, which some scholars perceive as a veritable urban underclass. As University of Chicago sociologist William Julius Wilson (1987, 7–8) has put it, "Regardless of which term is used, one cannot deny that there is a heterogeneous grouping of inner-city families and individuals whose behavior contrasts sharply with that of mainstream America. . . . Today's ghetto neighborhoods are populated almost exclusively by the most disadvantaged segments of the black urban community, that heterogeneous grouping of families and individuals who are outside the mainstream of the American occupational system. Included in this group are individuals who lack training and skills and either experience long-term unemployment or are not members of the labor force, individuals who are engaged in street crime and other forms of aberrant behavior, and families that experience long-term spells of poverty and/or welfare dependency. . . . The term *ghetto underclass* . . . suggests that a fundamental social transformation has taken place in ghetto neighborhoods, and the groups represented by this term are collectively different from and much more socially isolated than those that lived in these communities in earlier years."

From Cultural to Economic Explanations of Poverty

The last development in the evolution of the American welfare state worth mentioning involves a significant change in our thinking about the causes and solutions of poverty. The central change involves a loss of faith in the traditional dogma of professional social work, with its emphasis on casework and individualized services as a cure for poverty and distress. During the 1960s, this doctrine was translated into public policy through the 1962 amendments to the Social Security Act and, later, through portions of the Economic Opportunity Act. The central premise of this doctrine was that poverty was the product of a "culture of poverty" that could be broken only by the provision of a variety of supportive services. Attention consequently focused on the individual, whose maladjustment or aberrant behavior was perceived as being largely responsible for the persistence of poverty.

Whether this services strategy received a fair test or not, it now enjoys little sustained enthusiasm either from the left or from the right. Conservatives view the growth of supportive services during the 1960s as at best wasteful and at worse destructive of the work ethic and fundamental values of self-reliance. Liberals now question the tendency of the culture-of-poverty theory to degenerate into a new form of "blaming the victim," since it tended to focus on correcting the behavior of the poor, rather than the social and economic circumstances that were responsible for their plight.

This latter critique has gained added force as awareness of the impact of international economic changes on the availability of traditional manufacturing jobs in the United States has grown. Now that unionized production workers—not just racially stereotyped ghetto dwellers—have found themselves exposed to structural unemployment and distress, attention has come increasingly to focus on the underlying economic causes of poverty. Even some presumably cultural phenomena, such as the rise of households headed by females and out-of-wedlock births among blacks, have been reinterpreted in strongly economic terms that emphasize the negative impact of chronic joblessness on stable family life. According to this line of thought, what accounts for the deterioration of black family life in urban ghettos is not lax morals or a deteriorating sense of responsibility but a concrete decline in the pool of marriageable—that is, employed—black men (Wilson 1987).

Implications for the Nonprofit Sector

The changes in the American welfare state just outlined have important implications for the evolution of the private, nonprofit sector. Of course, how these implications play out depends on factors that are difficult to predict. But some of the main pressures in the system are already evident.

Overall Sector Growth

One of the most obvious yet often overlooked implications of the trends just discussed is that the private, nonprofit sector is not likely to wither away in the foreseeable future. The prevailing demographic trends alone suggest a significant increase in the demand for the kinds of services that nonprofit organizations have traditionally provided, including day care, nursing home care, family counseling, and hospital services. Moreover, the demand is growing not only among the poor—the traditional target group of charitable organizations—but also among the broad middle class. That is the meaning of the jump in labor force participation rates among women with children under six, of the growth in the numbers of elderly people and in the income support and medical assistance to help sustain them, and of other, similar trends. Assuming a reasonable degree of responsiveness and efficiency on the part of nonprofit providers, there is every reason to expect that the nonprofit sector will capture a significant share of the expanded "business" that seems likely to result. At the same time, the growth seems likely to be concentrated in particular portions of the sector—the portions in which growing demand coincides with growing resources. Most likely, this coincidence will occur in the areas of services for the aged, health care, the arts and recreation, and day care for children.

Commercialization

If there is thus reason to expect considerable growth in the size and scale of the nonprofit sector in the foreseeable future, there is also reason to expect that this growth will occur through greater integration of the voluntary sector into the market economy. In part, this development reflects the expansion of the paying market for human services as a product of the demographic developments detailed earlier. In part, it also reflects the shift in government human service expenditures for the poor from producer subsidies to consumer subsidies. By explicit design, this shift moves the provision of human services even for the poor into a commercial-type market.

One important consequence of this development, which Neil Gilbert (1983, 23) has chronicled in *Capitalism and the Welfare State*, is the "penetration of profit-oriented agencies into the welfare state." As chapter 14 shows, such penetration has become epidemic in such fields as specialty hospital care, home health, nursing home care, and social services. Equally important, however, is the penetration of the mechanics of the market into the operation of nonprofit organizations. This development is evident in the growth of fee-for-service income in the funding structure of the nonprofit sector.

Like the expansion of government support, such commercial income is by no means a new phenomenon for nonprofit organizations. For example, in the early 1900s, the Charities Aid Society of New York operated both a wood yard and a laundry that charged fees for their services and generated income for the organization (Brandt 1907). Similar examples are evident in the settlement house movement of the Progressive Era. But, it is clear that the scale of such support has grown substantially in recent years. For example, as chapter 4 noted, private nonprofit human service agencies, exclusive of hospitals and higher education institutions, already received 30 percent of their income from service fees in 1981, more than from all sources of private giving combined (for further details, see Salamon 1995). This figure was even higher among some types of organizations, such as institutional care facilities and arts organizations. Perhaps even more significantly, a larger proportion of these nonprofit agencies received income from service fees than from any other single income source.

More important, as government support declined in the early 1980s, nonprofit organizations turned increasingly to fee income to finance their activities. In fact, such income accounted for 55 percent of the replacement income that the nonprofit sector generated in the 1980s, which enabled the sector to overcome its loss of government support and post an overall gain in income (see chap. 14 and Salamon 1993, 25).

The developments discussed earlier strongly suggest that this trend is likely not only to continue but to accelerate. In the process, it seems likely that the process of transformation that affected the nonprofit hospital between 1885 and 1915 is well under way for a broad array of nonprofit human service agencies today. As historian David Rosner (1982, 6) has noted, that transformation involved a switch from small community institutions to large bureaucratic organizations staffed by professionals, supported by fees, oriented to paying customers, and "focused less on patients' overall social and moral well-being and more on their physical needs alone." Whether other segments of the non-profit sector will join hospitals in becoming "once charitable enterprises" is hard to tell, but the pressures in that direction are unmistakable. (For further detail, see chapter 14.)

Reorganization of Assistance to the Needy

While it seems likely that a significant share of the activity of traditional human service agencies will assume an increasingly commercial cast, both subsidized and unsubsidized, it is also possible that other institutions will assume increased responsibility for the traditional charitable mission of the nonprofit sector. In other words, while nonprofit organizations move increasingly toward the higher end of the human services market, other institutions may be developing a sense of responsibility and a service rationale targeted on those left behind. These developments are even more speculative and uncertain than the ones just identified, but some of the main lines of potential evolution are beginning to be visible.

The key to this change is the growing realization that the traditional skills of the human service sector may be increasingly irrelevant to the problems facing the urban poor. As long as the prevailing conceptions attributed a significant share of the responsibility for poverty to the personal maladjustments of the poor, traditional social work practice and traditional social welfare agencies had a significant role to play in the alleviation of poverty. But, as newer conceptions that attribute poverty to the maladjustments of the economy take hold, new solutions seem called for. In this emerging view, the solution to social distress is identical to the solution to economic distress—access to a decent job. Under these circumstances, the employer rather than the social worker becomes the pivot of social policy.

Fortunately, trends in the labor market are creating powerful economic incentives for business interest in the job situation of the urban poor. These trends suggest the real possibility of a significant shortage of trained labor in the years immediately ahead (U.S. Department of Labor 1988). As one educator (Hornbeck 1988) recently put it, "For the first time in our history, we are facing a situation where we can no longer afford the economic luxury of throwaway kids. We could never afford the moral luxury of throwaway kids, but only recently have the economic costs become prohibitive."

To the extent that these observations prove correct, they suggest a reorientation of antipoverty and charitable activity toward the preparation of skilled workers for the labor market. Private, nonprofit organizations may play a role in this effort, but, except for the community-development corporations, these organizations have a limited track record in this area. More likely is an increase in the focus on partnership arrangements involving the business community and the public school system. Equally likely is increased reliance on penal institutions and the criminal justice system in general to ease the transition of the inner-city poor into the work force of the future. Finally, business enterprises themselves will play an increasing role, utilizing on-the-job-training and employment guarantees to tighten the link between the inner-city poor and the world of work.

For-Profit/Nonprofit Competition and the Challenge to Tax Exemption

Taken together, the developments just cited will further intensify the competition between the for-profit and nonprofit sectors and weaken the traditional rationale for nonprofit tax-exempt status. Of course, increased competition between the sectors and loss of tax-exempt status do not necessarily go hand in hand. Competition between for-profit and nonprofit organizations does not need to provoke a challenge to the tax-exempt status of the nonprofit sector. While tax-exempt status gives nonprofit organizations certain advantages, it also exacts certain costs, such as limitations on the generation and distribution of profit. Thus, it is quite conceivable that the competition between nonprofit and for-profit organizations will increase without posing a serious challenge to the tax-exempt status of the sector. However, for this to occur, the sector will have to clarify the relative advantages and disadvantages of tax-exempt status and develop a rationale for tax exemption that takes account of the sector's changing role.

Implications for Nonprofit Managers

The changes identified above have implications not only for the nonprofit sector. They also have implications for the individual nonprofit manager. Four such implications seem especially deserving of comment.

Market Savvy

First, the trends elaborated above make it clear that nonprofit managers must increasingly add to their already large repertoire of skills a more sophisticated awareness of the market trends in the fields in which they are operating. As their organizations become more sensitive financially to shifts in consumer demand and to competitive pressures arising from other providers, nonprofit managers must find ways to stay on top of the market conditions facing them. Increasing use of advertising, market surveys, "industry analyses," and the like will consequently be necessary as managers seek to define and maintain a suitable market niche for their organizations.

Personnel Management Challenges

The pressures pushing nonprofit managers to take more account of market forces will also put special strains on human resource management within nonprofit organizations. As these organizations go "up-scale" in client focus, they will likely encounter pressures from staff to upgrade pay and other working conditions. At the same time, the pressures of competition will force nonprofit organizations to seek cost-cutting possibilities, perhaps by keeping wages for nonprofessional staff low. To the extent this occurs, however, it will reduce one of the principal advantages of the nonprofit sector as a place to work—the relative "flatness" of nonprofit organizations, the relative lack of strict hierarchy, and the resulting sense of solidarity among workers who consider themselves participants in a shared mission.

Similar tensions may also arise between paid staff and volunteers. The more nonprofits become engaged in fee-for-service work, the more the rationale for volunteers to give their time to the organization for free will be strained. To be sure, hospitals have escaped this di-lemma and retain a significant voluntary corps, but the task of defining and promoting the role of the volunteer still seems likely to become more problematic for nonprofit managers in the world that seems destined to lie ahead for them.

The Threat to Organizational Missions

Underlying these marketing and personnel management pressures is a more basic challenge that the forces identified here pose for non-profit managers in the years ahead. This is the fundamental challenge of maintaining a distinctive sense of organizational mission. Mission orientation is, in a sense, the fundamental distinguishing characteristic of nonprofit organizations. Where for-profit organizations acquire their organizational raison d'être fundamentally from the pursuit of profit, nonprofit organizations get theirs from the pursuit of a mission, a purpose that binds the agency's personnel, supporters, and benefi-ciaries together in common purpose. The most important task of a manager in such organizations is to protect and embody the agency's mission while adapting as necessary to the pressures of the external world. A manager who makes it possible for an agency to survive as an organization but at the cost of undermining its central mission inevi-tably purchases short-term victory at the cost of long-term viability. So, too, however, a manager who holds so rigidly to a particular concep-tion of an agency's mission and modus operandi that he or she fails to adjust to external realities can end up with no organization to protect over the long run. The successful manager is the one who strikes a reasonable balance between these internal and external pressures.

What the analysis presented here suggests, however, is that this balance is likely to grow increasingly hard for nonprofit managers to achieve in the years ahead as the pressures to adapt to the market grow increasingly intense. While becoming more "market savvy," therefore, nonprofit managers will have to take care to nourish the sense of "mission" within their agencies.

Preserving the Advocacy Role

Among the missions of the nonprofit sector likely to be placed under particular strain by the developments outlined here is the advocacy role these organizations have traditionally performed. One of the great strengths of the nonprofit sector is its function as a source of criticism of government and the market sector, and hence as a source of innovation in policy. As organizations become more enmeshed in the competitive market economy, it is likely that their managers will lose both the time and the incentive for this kind of advocacy work. This is so because advocacy can often lead to adverse publicity in addition to absorbing the time and energy of agency staff. Nonprofit managers struggling to attract clients to their agencies may therefore be inclined to downplay their advocacy role lest they antagonize potential customers or dissipate agency energies in "do-good" causes that do little for the "bottom line." Some observers of nonprofit social service agencies have argued that this is precisely what happened to them as professional social workers committed to "casework" took over from an earlier breed of community organizers (Cloward and Epstein 1965). It seems reasonable that the commercialization of the nonprofit sector would intensify this tendency, furthering the transformation of nonprofit organizations into service providers rather than policy innovators and social critics.

Conclusion

Whether these implications will materialize as predicted here depends, of course, on the speed with which the developments outlined above proceed, and on the way nonprofit managers react to them. Properly fortified with a sense of the mission of the nonprofit sector and the values that are critical to its continuance, nonprofit managers may fend off some of the pressures that are looming. But this will require a high level of self-consciousness within the sector and a concerted effort to revitalize the value base on which the sector rests. While there is only very limited evidence of the prospect of such a development, some encouraging signs are apparent—in the renewed calls to service on the part of the Clinton administration and in the surge in nonprofit activity that is apparent at the international level (Salamon 1994 and chap. 15). Whatever the reaction, however, it seems clear that the first step must be to understand the basic challenges that exist, and these challenges are now confronting the nonprofit sector not from the side of government, but from the side of the private market.

CHAPTER 14

The Marketization of Welfare

*Changing Nonprofit and For-Profit Roles in
the American Welfare State*

That the challenges being posed for American nonprofit organizations by the social, economic, and fiscal trends identified in
chapter 13 are far from hypothetical is already evident in a subtle, but
potentially fundamental, shift that seems to be under way in the basic
structure of the American social welfare system.

At the heart of this shift is what might be called the "marketization
of welfare," the penetration of essentially market-type relationships
into the social welfare arena. Much more is involved here than the
continued expansion of for-profit firms into the "social market" identified by Neil Gilbert in the early 1980s (Gilbert 1983). Although that is
clearly part of the story, an equally important part is a striking expansion of commercial activity on the part of nonprofit firms, blurring
the distinction between nonprofit and for-profit providers and raising
serious questions about who will serve those in need.

The purpose of this chapter is to examine these changes in the
structure of the American social welfare system during the 1980s by
drawing on a variety of new data sources that bring these shifts into

far better focus than has previously been possible.[1] The discussion falls into five parts. The first section outlines the basic structure of the American social welfare system as it took shape between 1930 and the 1970s. The second section describes the significant policy changes that affected this system during the 1980s. In the third and fourth sections, attention turns to the effect of these changes on the structure of the U.S. social welfare system, focusing first on the changing funding base and resulting shifts in the basic composition of the nonprofit sector and then on the changing balance among nonprofit, for-profit, and government providers, especially in four major subfields: hospitals, nursing homes, home health, and social services. The fifth section concludes with some implications that seem to flow from these structural shifts and the consequences they may have for our social welfare system.

Background: Public and Private Welfare in the American Welfare State

The Growth of Government

Perhaps the major development in American social welfare policy between the Great Depression of the 1930s and the Reagan Revolution of the 1980s was the substantial expansion in the role of the state. Although government has long played a more important role in the social and economic life of our nation than popular rhetoric would lead us to believe, prior to the New Deal of the 1930s, the principal line of defense for those in need was private action and private voluntary groups. Not until the Great Depression decisively broke popular faith in the capacity of private action alone to remedy serious economic ills did significant public action take shape, and even then, progress was rather slow. Although the New Deal set in place a basic system of social insurance and social welfare protections, coverage was patchy and benefit levels rather meager. As late as 1950, therefore, government social welfare spending represented no more than 8 percent of the U.S. gross national product, and 40 percent of this went for elementary and secondary education (Bixby 1988, 22).

It took the assassination of a popular president and the urban riots of the 1960s to change this. Between 1965 and 1972, as a consequence, a series of substantial new initiatives was launched, considerably expanding federal assistance in such fields as health, social services, housing, education, and employment training. By 1980, government social welfare spending had increased six times over its 1950 level in real dollar terms, reaching 19 percent of the gross national product.[2]

The Expanding Partnership with Nonprofit Organizations

Not surprisingly, with so much attention focused on the establishment, and ultimate expansion, of the state role in social welfare, the role of the private, nonprofit sector tended to be ignored. Indeed, judging from both popular rhetoric and scholarly research, it would appear that the nonprofit sector had largely disappeared as a major actor in the social welfare field during this period. This view was reinforced, moreover, by political rhetoric on the Right that criticized government social welfare activity on the ground that it had destroyed the voluntary sector (Nisbet 1962; Berger and Neuhaus 1977) and by political rhetoric on the Left that stressed the inherent weakness of the voluntary sector as a major justification for expanding the role of the state.

In fact, however, the conflict between the state and the voluntary sector was never as sharp as this rhetoric suggested. For one thing, the continued patchy character of the public social welfare system left considerable room for private, nonprofit action. Even more important, the expansion of government involvement in the social welfare field during the 1960s more often took the form of a partnership between government and the voluntary sector than a conflict between the two.

Reflecting a widespread American practice of "third-party government," public authorities often turned to private, nonprofit organizations to carry out the policies they enacted (Salamon 1981). As detailed in previous chapters, this practice took root early in American history, as reflected, for example, in the special levy that the Commonwealth of Massachusetts passed to support Harvard College (Whitehead 1973). By the 1890s, New York City relied on private nonprofit organizations to deliver almost all the aid it provided to the poor (Warner 1894). When state action expanded in the 1930s, and particularly in the 1960s, government support of voluntary organizations expanded as well. Through direct grants, "purchase-of-service contracts," and various reimbursement schemes, government built an elaborate partnership with the nonprofit sector in the delivery of a wide range of human services. For example, Medicare essentially reimburses hospitals for care they provide to the elderly but leaves to the elderly the choice of which hospital to use. Because a preponderance of hospital beds are in private, nonprofit hospitals, these institutions have received the majority of the benefits. Similarly, private, nonprofit universities have benefited from expanded federal support for research, as well as from new programs of scholarship aid and loan guarantees, and social service and community development programs enacted in the 1960s provide grants-in-aid to state and local governments, which, in turn, often contract with local nonprofit organizations to provide such services as "meals-on-wheels" to the elderly, day care, residential care, adoption assistance, and the like.

As of 1980, therefore, nonprofit organizations had become the deliverers of a larger share of government-funded human services than government agencies themselves, as previous chapters have made clear. Far from displacing the nonprofit sector, in other words, the expansion of government activity actually stimulated its growth, enabling nonprofit organizations to carry out far more functions than they had been able to conduct in the past. Instead of withering away, the nonprofit sector emerged in the latter 1970s as a major economic force, with expenditures equal to about 6 percent of the American gross national product and employing approximately one in every 14 American workers.[3]

The Rise of For-Profit Welfare

Although the nonprofit sector was the principal beneficiary of the expansion of state-financed welfare in the 1960s, it was by no means the only beneficiary. The availability of government support, often financed through purchase-of-service contracts, attracted for-profit providers into the field. At the same time, the target population for certain social and human services changed. Once conceived as targeting principally the poor, such services came to be viewed during the 1950s and 1960s as appropriate for, indeed required by, other segments of the population as well, for example, the growing numbers of working women, the elderly, and middle- and upper-income people in need of family counseling, drug treatment, adoption assistance, and other social services (Gilbert 1983).

The upshot of these developments was significantly increased involvement of for-profit organizations in the social welfare field. This was not a wholly new phenomenon, of course. For-profit organizations had long had a significant position in the nursing home industry and among day care providers. But during the 1970s, they gained a foothold as well in a number of other fields in which nonprofit providers

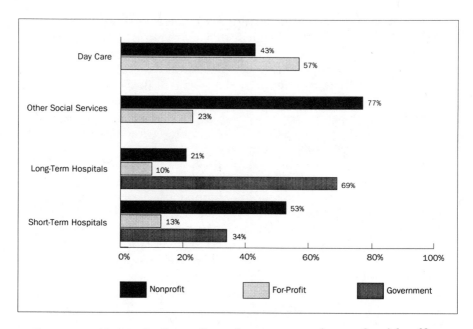

Figure 14.1. Nonprofit, for-profit, and government shares of social welfare providers, by field, 1977. *Source:* Data on day care and social services from U.S. Census Bureau (1981), vol. 1, part 1, tables 2 and 3; data on hospitals from American Hospital Association, *Hospital Statistics,* 1977. Other social services include individual and family social services, job training and vocational rehabilitation services, residential care, and social services not elsewhere classified.

had traditionally held sway. As of 1977, as figure 14.1 shows, for-profit providers accounted for 57 percent of the day care centers, 23 percent of the other social service agencies, 10 percent of the long-term care hospitals, and 13 percent of the short-term hospitals.[4] Although nonprofit organizations still held a larger position in all these fields except child day care, for-profit firms were clearly establishing a presence.

In short, by the latter 1970s, the United States had developed a complex system of social welfare protections providing significant levels of assistance not just to the poor but to the middle class as well and involving an extensive partnership between government and both nonprofit and for-profit providers. Although the government financed a growing share of the services, the actual delivery was handled mainly by private institutions, most of which were nonprofit organizations, but with a significant for-profit presence.

The 1980s Retrenchment

Beginning in the late 1970s, and accelerating in the early 1980s, as we have seen, this system of support was subjected to a serious shock. In the face of increasing federal deficits, the Carter administration began in the latter 1970s to restrain the growth of government social welfare spending. This then gave way during the Reagan administration to a broad-scale assault on the federal government's role in the social welfare field (see chaps. 9 and 11). Between 1977 and 1982, federal social service spending declined almost 30 percent in inflation-adjusted terms, federal education spending declined 33 percent, and federal income assistance spending declined by 5 percent—the latter despite the fact that the country found itself in the middle of a significant recession. Although it was hoped that state and local governments would offset these reductions, in fact the value of state and local spending in these same fields also declined. Only the continued expansion of health expenditures kept total social welfare spending from declining.[5]

In the balance of the decade, Congress resisted further proposed cuts, and some increase in state and local spending occurred. At the same time, the key middle-class entitlement programs, such as Social Security and Medicare, continued to grow. The result, as figure 14.2 shows, is that by 1989 the value of government spending on programs targeted toward the poor remained below what it had been in 1977, while spending in other areas actually grew. Among the losers were income assistance (down 4%) and social services (down 19%). In education, the value of federal spending declined 28 percent, but state and local spending boosted the total. By contrast, federal health spending, fueled by escalating health costs and an aging population, continued its steep rise throughout this period of so-called retrenchment. Such spending grew by 81 percent between 1977 and 1989 even after adjusting for inflation (see fig. 14.2). Despite a steady decline in veterans' payments, pension expenditures (mostly Social Security) also experienced continued growth during this period, rising by some 34 percent after adjusting for inflation. This was due to the automatic cost-of-living increases built into the Social Security program coupled with the continued growth of the elderly population. Alone among the programs at least moderately targeted toward the poor, housing assistance

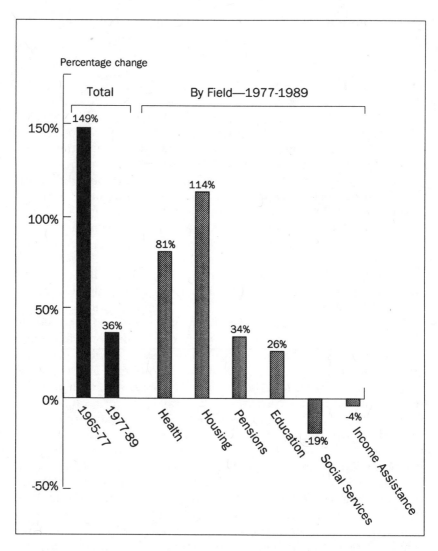

Figure 14.2. Changes in government social welfare spending, 1965–1977 and 1977–1989, overall and by field, in constant 1989 dollars. *Source:* Ann Kallman Bixby (1991).

also experienced significant growth during this period. This reflects, in part, the low base from which it started and, in part, prior commitments.[6]

Altogether, therefore, government social welfare spending did not decline during this period. To the contrary, it increased in real terms by \$253 billion, or some 36 percent. However, 39 percent of this growth is accounted for by health expenditures and another 38 percent by Social Security and other pension payments. These two components thus accounted for 77 percent of all the growth, even though they represented only 60 percent of the spending as of 1977. By contrast, income assistance and other social welfare programs experienced declines. The overall effect was thus to shift the center of gravity of the social welfare system more toward the middle class and away from the poor.

What was the effect of these changes on the nonprofit sector and on the balance between nonprofit and for-profit providers of social welfare assistance? Has private charity filled the gap left by the partial dismantling of the partnership between the nonprofit sector and government? Have for-profit providers, deprived of government support, abandoned the social welfare field? It is to these questions that I will now turn.

The Commercialization of the Nonprofit Sector

Overall Growth

Because government support to the nonprofit sector outdistanced private philanthropic support by two or three to one by the latter half of the 1970s, nonprofit organizations naturally stood to lose considerably from the governmental retrenchment of the 1980s. In fact, however, the nonprofit sector experienced considerable growth over this period, boosting its revenues by 79 percent between 1977 and 1989 after adjusting for inflation.[7] This was more than double the 36 percent increase that occurred in overall government social welfare spending.

To what extent does this record redeem the hopes of the Reagan administration that private giving or state and local spending would fill in for federal cutbacks and thus shield the nonprofit sector and those it serves from harm? The answer, it seems, is not very much.

Commercialization of the Financial Base

In the first place, although private giving did grow—by about 53 percent in inflation-adjusted terms between 1977 and 1989, or about 4 percent a year—its growth actually lagged behind that of most of the

TABLE 14.1
Sources of Nonprofit Growth, 1977–1989, by Type of Agency

| Type | Share of Growth by Source, 1977–1989 | | | |
	Private Giving	Government	Fees, Sales	Total
Health	1%	40%	59%	100%
Education	17	15	68	100
Social services	38	23	39	100
Civic	34	15	51	100
Arts	60	6	34	100
All	15%	30%	55%	100%

SOURCE: See n. 7.

other sources of nonprofit support. Private giving thus accounted for only 15 percent of the overall growth of the nonprofit sector between 1977 and 1989, as shown in table 14.1.

The major source of nonprofit growth during this period was service fees and other essentially commercial income, including sales of products. This source already accounted for 47 percent of nonprofit income as of 1977. Between 1977 and 1989, however, it grew by 93 percent, or almost twice as fast as private giving. And it did so starting from a larger base. As a consequence, this one source accounted for 55 percent of all the growth of the nonprofit sector during this period.

Fee income not only grew disproportionately as a source of overall nonprofit income, it also extended its reach within the sector. As of 1977, fees and other commercial income were largely concentrated in the health and education areas of the nonprofit sector. By contrast, these sources represented less than 20 percent of the income of social service and civic organizations. Between 1977 and 1989, however, nearly 40 percent of the growth of social service organization income and 51 percent of the growth of civic organization income came from fees and other commercial sources. This made such commercial income the largest single source of growth for these types of organizations as well, as table 14.1 also shows.

The remaining 30 percent of the growth of the nonprofit sector between 1977 and 1989 resulted from increased government support. As we have seen, government social welfare spending continued to grow during the 1980s. However, this growth was largely confined to the fields of health and pensions. The growth of health spending in particular helped fuel a significant 77 percent expansion of overall government support to the nonprofit sector, despite the decline of government social service support that occurred.

TABLE 14.2
Shares of Nonprofit Expenditure Growth by Type of Agency, 1977–1989

Type	Share of Expenditures, 1977	Share of Growth, 1977–1989
Health	52%	60%
Education	28	22
Social and legal services	12	9
Arts	4	3
Civic	4	2
Unallocated		4
Total	100%	100%

SOURCE: See n. 7.

Changing Composition of the Nonprofit Sector

Because not all types of organizations had equal access to these various sources of income, the decade of the 1980s produced significant shifts in the composition of the nonprofit sector. Most notable, perhaps, was the disproportionate growth in the health field. As table 14.2 shows, health organizations, which accounted for 52 percent of all nonprofit revenues as of 1977, absorbed 60 percent of the growth of the sector between 1977 and 1989. By contrast, social and legal service organizations, which accounted for 12 percent of all revenues at the start of the period, claimed only 9 percent of the growth. The decade of the 1980s thus witnessed a further shift in the center of gravity of the nonprofit sector away from social services and toward health.

Furthermore, given the composition of the new streams of revenue available even to the social service and civic organizations, it seems likely that a similar shift from services targeted toward the poor to those targeted toward customers able to pay took place within the social services field. Although it is difficult to determine the extent of any such shift from the data available, the fact that so much of the income fueling growth in this field came from fees and charges certainly suggests that this was the direction of change.

Summary

In short, the decade of the 1980s seems to have altered both the structure and the financial base of the nonprofit sector. In the first place, the continued growth of government support for health providers, especially hospitals, plus the expansion of fee income from insurance and direct patient payments, enabled the health component of the nonprofit sector, already dominant, to claim a disproportionate share of the growth that occurred. Second, and possibly more important, the reduction in government support for other types of nonprofit organizations and the relatively slow growth of private giving made it necessary for other nonprofit agencies as well to turn increasingly to fees and other commercial income to sustain their operations. Although some portion of this increased fee income may have come from insurance reimbursements, it still involved more of a market-type relationship than when government or private charity was the source. Such commercial income accounted for well over half the growth in overall nonprofit income during this period. What is more, it was the principal source of growth of every major type of organization except for arts organizations, and even among those organizations, commercial income dominated the sources of operating, as opposed to total, income. The result was not only a further shift in the center of gravity of the nonprofit sector toward health but also a decisive turn toward the market, a fundamental "marketization" of the nonprofit sector.

Shifting Nonprofit and For-Profit Roles

In addition to the shifts they produced within the nonprofit sector, the changes in government policy during the 1980s also helped encourage some significant shifts in the balance between nonprofit and for-profit providers. The nature of these shifts is in some sense surprising, however. Because for-profit firms were originally attracted to the social welfare field by the availability of government funding, there was reason to expect that the decline in government support would lead to a wholesale for-profit retreat. In fact, however, the for-profit role seems to have expanded quite dramatically. One reason for this is that government support did not decline across the board, as we have seen. To the contrary, it expanded in certain fields, and for-profit providers have been effective in positioning themselves to benefit from this growth. In the second place, as the social welfare field has grown increasingly commercial, for-profit firms have enjoyed certain advantages in going after the resulting "business." The result has been a very substantial expansion in the market share controlled by for-profit firms in virtually every social welfare field. A look at four major fields—hospital care, home health, social services, and nursing home care—will make this clear.

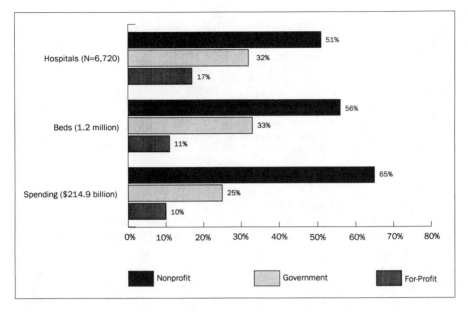

Figure 14.3. Nonprofit share of hospital industry, 1989. *Source:* American Hospital Association, *Hospital Statistics, 1990–91* (1991), tables 2A and 2B.

Hospitals

Of all the components of the American social welfare system, the largest by far is health care. Almost one in four dollars of government social welfare spending goes for health care, and an even larger amount of private spending goes into this field. As of 1988, health care accounted for 11 percent of the American gross national product—a total of $540 billion in spending (Office of National Cost Estimates 1990, table 13).

Of all the components of health care, hospital care is by far the largest and the one in which nonprofit organizations are most prominent. Close to 40 percent of all health spending goes for hospital care—a total of $212 billion in 1988. By comparison, private practitioners (dentists and physicians) received 25 percent of the total, and nursing homes, 8 percent.

Of the 6,720 hospitals registered with the American Hospital Association as of 1988, 51 percent are nonprofit hospitals (see fig. 14.3), most of them short-term general hospitals. These nonprofit hospitals ac-

TABLE 14.3
Hospital Trends by Type of Hospital, 1980–1989

Percentage Change in	Type of Hospital			
	Nonprofit	Government	For-Profit	Total
Hospitals	−3%	−17%	+28%	−4%
Beds	−4	−28	+41	−11
Expenditures	+90	+43	+156	+80

SOURCE: American Hospital Association, *Hospital Statistics*, 1990–1991, tables 2A and 2B; *Hospital Statistics, 1981*, tables 2A and 2B.

count for 56 percent of the country's hospital beds and nearly two-thirds (65%) of all hospital expenditures.[8]

About a third of all hospitals are operated by governmental authorities, chiefly at the state and local levels. Most of these are short-term general hospitals, many of them in central cities. However, relative to the other two sectors, the government role is particularly prominent in the operation of long-term specialized hospitals, such as those for the mentally ill. Nearly 60 percent of long-term psychiatric hospitals, for example, are under government ownership and control, and they account for 77 percent of all the long-term care facility expenditures. More generally, government accounts for 32 percent of all specialty hospitals, but because these facilities tend to be large, they represent 54 percent of all specialty hospital expenditures and 70 percent of specialty hospital beds.

Historically, for-profit corporations have played a considerably smaller role in the hospital field. As of 1989, they accounted for only 17 percent of all hospitals and 11 percent of all hospital beds. However, for-profit providers have been the most rapidly growing component of the hospital sector. In fact, despite the considerable strain that the hospital sector has been under in recent years as a result of efforts to constrain the growth of both public and private health costs, for-profit hospitals have significantly increased their market share. This reflects a complex set of shifts in the basic composition of the hospital industry, as shown in table 14.3.

In the first place, there was a sharp decline in government hospitals. Between 1980 and 1989, the number of government-owned and -operated hospitals declined by 17 percent, and the number of beds in government-owned hospitals declined by 28 percent. This sharp drop resulted from two major developments: increased pressure on publicly run inner-city hospitals squeezed by rising health costs, reduced Medicaid reimbursement, and limited fee income; and a movement that began in the 1970s to "deinstitutionalize" mentally ill and other long-term ill persons. As a result, 359 of the 2,167 publicly owned, short-term general hospitals were forced to close between 1980 and 1989, and the number of government-run specialty hospitals declined by nearly 40 percent.

The sharp decline of inner-city government hospitals was itself part of a broader contraction that affected short-term hospitals more generally during the 1980s. Overall, the number of short-term general hospitals declined by 8 percent during this decade, and the number of short-term general hospital beds declined by 6 percent. Although this hit public hospitals particularly hard, nonprofit general hospitals were also affected, declining in number by 3 percent and in the number of beds by 4 percent (see table 14.3).

Notwithstanding the overall decline in the number of hospitals and the particular drop in the number of long-term government specialty hospitals, specialty hospitals as a group experienced significant growth during the 1980s. This was especially true among short-term specialty institutions—for the mentally ill, rehabilitation patients, and patients with other specialized diseases. The number of such hospitals grew by almost 80 percent between 1980 and 1989, and the number of beds they were able to offer almost doubled. What seems to have been under way, in short, is a movement away from large-scale general hospitals toward specialized hospitals, and from long-term institutionalized treatment to shorter term hospitalization coupled with in-home care.

Because for-profit businesses have been particularly active in the formation of short-term specialty hospitals, they have benefited substantially from these shifts. Reflecting this, the number of for-profit hospitals grew by 28 percent and the number of beds they control grew by 41 percent between 1980 and 1989 (see table 14.3). Of the 239 short-term specialty hospitals added in the 1980s, over three-fourths were for-profit companies, and these companies accounted for 70 percent of the net gain in short-term specialty hospital beds. For-profit businesses also gained ground in the other components of the hospital industry as well, adding short-term general and long-term facilities and beds. In the process, the for-profit component of the hospital industry grew from 13 percent of the facilities in 1980 to 17 percent in 1989.

Nonprofit organizations have also taken part in this general expansion of short-term specialty hospitals. Thus, although the number of nonprofit short-term general and long-term hospitals and beds has declined, the number of nonprofit short-term specialty institutions increased by 38 percent between 1980 and 1989—far lower than the growth in the for-profit segment but significant nevertheless. What this suggests is that while nonprofit organizations are experiencing pressures and being forced to consolidate in their traditional area of concentration—short-term general hospitals—they are also venturing out into the more rapidly growing field of short-term specialty care. In this new field, however, the for-profit institutions have established a commanding lead.

Clinics and Home Health Care

A similar set of changes has been under way in the field of home health and outpatient clinic care. The past decade or more has witnessed a striking growth of spending on this facet of the social welfare system. Between 1975 and 1988, spending on outpatient care grew by 208 percent in inflation-adjusted terms, and spending on home health care grew by 450 percent (see fig. 14.4). By comparison, overall health spending increased by 94 percent. By 1988, therefore, the home health care field accounted for 10 percent of all health expenditures, or about $52 billion.[9]

This spending growth reflected the move toward deinstitutionalization of long-term hospital patients during the 1970s and early 1980s, which increased the need for home health care and outpatient clinic care. Also at work were the pressures on hospitals resulting from a shift in the Medicare reimbursement system, which induced hospitals to release patients earlier and produced a corresponding increase in the need for outpatient care facilities. Finally, these changes were aided by the broadening during the 1980s of Medicare and Medicaid coverage of home health care services, 75 percent of the costs of which were funded by government by 1988.[10]

These changes have had a significant effect not only on the scale, but also on the structure, of the home health and clinic field. As of 1977, nonprofit organizations enjoyed a dominant position in this field, with 55 percent of the establishments and 64 percent of the employees (U.S. Census Bureau 1981). As figure 14.4 makes clear, however, the dramatic expansion of spending in this field has attracted a tremendous burst of for-profit activity. Between 1977 and 1987, the number of for-profit establishments grew by 270 percent, the number of people they employed grew by 433 percent, and the revenues they earned swelled by 493 percent—all well above the comparable rates for nonprofit organizations. For-profit institutions thus accounted for

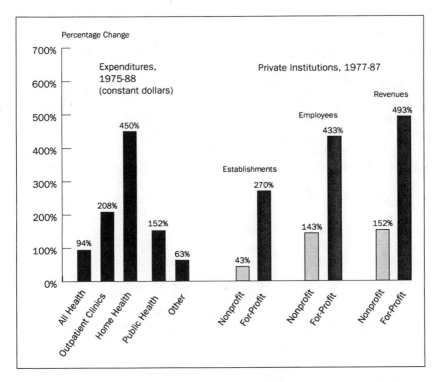

Figure 14.4. Recent trends in clinic and home health care, 1975–1988. *Source:* Office of National Cost Estimates (1990, 30); U.S. Bureau of the Census (1981), vol. 2, part 1, tables 2 and 3, pp. 9-8 and 9-9; (1989a), table 1B, p. US-13.

almost 85 percent of the new clinics and related health service providers created between 1977 and 1987, 65 percent of the new revenues, and 63 percent of the new employment. In the process, nonprofit organizations lost their once-dominant position in this field, dropping from 55 percent of the establishments and 64 percent of the employees in 1977 to 32 percent of the establishments and 45 percent of the employees 10 years later.[11]

In short, as institutionalized medical care has moved out of large, general-purpose hospitals and long-term specialized care facilities into specialized clinics and outpatient care facilities, for-profit firms have moved aggressively into the field. Although nonprofit organizations retain a considerable, and still-growing, role, the for-profit providers have clearly gained the upper hand.

Social Services

A third field of social welfare in which the structural shifts of the 1980s are evident is social services. Included in this category are day care services, adoption assistance, family counseling, residential care for individuals who cannot function on their own (e.g., the elderly or the physically or mentally handicapped), vocational rehabilitation, disaster assistance, refugee assistance, emergency food assistance, substance abuse treatment, neighborhood improvement, and many more. Such services accounted for approximately $43 billion in spending as of 1987, or about 0.4 percent of the U.S. gross national product. This is, therefore, a significant industry, though it pales in comparison to the $540 billion spent on health or even the $52 billion spent on home health and outpatient clinic care.[12]

Nonprofit organizations have long held a dominant position in the social services field. As of 1977, for example, they accounted for 64 percent of all social service agencies, 55 percent of all social service employment, and 48 percent of all social service revenues.[13] As figure 14.1 indicated, only in the day care portion of the social services field did for-profit firms outdistance nonprofit ones, and even here nonprofit organizations accounted for 43 percent of the total.

During the 1980s, however, this situation changed significantly. While government spending for outright social service programs declined markedly, the demographic and social changes outlined in chapter 13 continued to expand the need for social services (e.g., the growth of the elderly population increased the need for residential care and caretaker services, and the growing workforce participation of women increased the need for child day care). In addition to these changes, the increased funding available for home health and outpatient care created opportunities for social service agencies to "repackage" at least a portion of their services as "health care." Many home health services, such as nutrition assistance, physical therapy, and caretaker services, bear a strong resemblance, after all, to the kinds of services that individual and family service agencies have traditionally provided. What is more, the movement toward early hospital release may have aided a variety of residential care facilities.

Despite the decline in government social service spending, therefore, social service agencies registered considerable growth during the 1980s. Between 1977 and 1987, the number of private social service agencies recorded by the Census of Service Industries grew by 66 percent, the number of employees working for these agencies grew by

TABLE 14.4
Growth of For-Profit Presence in the Social Service Field, 1977–1987, by Subfield

| | For-Profit Share of | | | |
| | Establishments | | Employees | |
Subfield	1977	Growth, 1977–1987	1977	Growth, 1977–1987
Day care	57%	+80%	46%	+68%
Individual and family services	15	22	9	6
Job training, vocational rehabilitation	18	39	9	10
Residential care	45	45	27	32
Other	15	6	8	
Total	36%	+48%	21%	+29%

SOURCE: U.S. Census Bureau, *1977 Census of Service Industries; 1987 Census of Service Industries.*

72 percent, and the revenues these agencies collected expanded, after adjusting for inflation, by 111 percent.[14]

As in the case of hospital and outpatient care, however, the for-profit providers seem to have claimed a disproportionate share of this growth. Constituting only 36 percent of all social service establishments in 1977, for-profit firms accounted for 48 percent of the new establishments created between 1977 and 1987, as table 14.4 shows. This included 80 percent of the new day care centers, 45 percent of the new residential care facilities, and 39 percent of the job training and vocational rehabilitation facilities.

The picture with respect to employment is less dramatic, but equally telling. Employing 21 percent of all social service workers in 1977, for-profit firms accounted for 29 percent of the employment growth between 1977 and 1987. Except for the field of individual and family services, for-profit firms accounted for a larger proportion of the employment growth in every social service subfield than their starting share would have suggested.

Although nonprofit organizations ended the 1980s still in the dominant position in the social services field, their dominance was thus seriously challenged by for-profit organizations that managed to take better advantage of the essentially commercial opportunities that this period offered. What growth the nonprofit organizations experienced during this period, moreover, was largely fueled, as we have seen, by expanded fee income, which grew from an estimated 11 percent of all nonprofit social service agency income in 1977 to 29 percent a decade later.[15] In the social services field as well, therefore, marketization was the overwhelming trend of the decade.

TABLE 14.5

Nursing Home Growth, 1977–1987 vs. 1970–1980, by Type of Provider

	Percentage Change	
	1970–1980	1977–1987
Total expenditures, inflation adjusted	+102%	+50%[a]
Number of homes		
Nonprofit	20	76
For-profit	29	24
Government	29	N/A
Total	27%	34%
Number of employees		
Nonprofit	82	84
For-profit	97	45
Government	145	N/A
Total	+98%	+54%

SOURCES: Office of National Cost Estimates (1990), table 3; U.S. Census Bureau, *1977 Census of Service Industries*, vol. 2; *1987 Census of Service Industries;* Strahan (1984).
NOTE: N/A = not available.
[a]Expenditure figures cover the period 1980–88.

Nursing Home Care

In only one major social welfare field did for-profit firms lose ground relative to nonprofit organizations during the 1980s: nursing home care. However, this was a field in which for-profit firms had already established a clearly dominant position by 1977 and in which overall growth between 1977 and 1987 was unusually slow. The nursing home industry absorbed about 8 percent of all health spending in 1988, or about $43 billion. Unlike hospital and outpatient clinic care or the social service field, however, nonprofit organizations have for some time played a subsidiary role in the nursing home industry. Already by the late 1960s, for example, 72 percent of the nursing and related care homes identified by the National Master Facility Inventory were under for-profit control.[16] During the 1970s, a period of substantial growth in this industry, for-profit organizations widened their lead, accounting by 1977 for 82 percent of all establishments.

During the decade of the 1980s, a different dynamic seems to have been at work. In the first place, the growth of government support slowed considerably, as both the federal government and state and local governments sought to reduce the escalating costs of Medicaid, despite the fact that the need for nursing home services continued to grow. Thus, nursing home expenditures grew by only 50 percent between 1980 and 1988 compared to its 102 percent real growth between 1970 and 1980 (see table 14.5). Faced with this constraint in public support, the for-profit and nonprofit components of the nursing home industry seem to have responded somewhat differently. Whereas for-profit homes expanded more extensively during the 1970s, it was the nonprofit firms that moved to meet the demand in the constrained climate of the 1980s. Thus, the number of nonprofit homes increased by 76 percent between 1977 and 1987 compared to 24 percent for for-profit providers (see table 14.5). Similarly, the number of employees at nonprofit homes grew by 84 percent during this period, compared to a 45 percent growth among for-profit providers. As a result, the nonprofit sector boosted its share of the nursing home industry from 22 percent of all employees in 1977 to 26 percent in 1987.

Although the nonprofit sector enjoyed relatively stronger growth between 1977 and 1987, it did not in any sense outdistance the for-profit sector as a provider of nursing home care. To the contrary, for-profit organizations still accounted for 60 percent of the net new establishments created during this period and 64 percent of the added employment. And they ended the period with 77 percent of the homes and 72 percent of the employment.[17]

In short, faced with a tight market, nonprofit nursing homes managed to grow slightly more rapidly than for-profit providers during the 1980s, perhaps by drawing on religious and other affiliations. This demonstrates the value of nonprofit involvement in the social welfare field since nonprofit organizations were able to meet a growing social need despite a decline in the resources available through the regular market. At the same time it made at best a modest dent in the overall trend toward marketization of social welfare that seems to have been under way during this decade.

Conclusion

The 1980s may thus prove to have been a watershed period in the development of the American social welfare system, a period during which its basic structure changed in fundamental ways. As such, it is comparable to two other watershed periods in our history: the 1930s, when the country moved from almost sole reliance on private action and mutual aid in the social welfare field toward at least the rudiments of a national system of governmental protections; and the 1960s, when the skeletal governmental system of protections was expanded and a widespread partnership between government and the nonprofit sector put in place.

During the 1980s, this partnership between government and the nonprofit sector was substantially dismantled in many fields and significantly altered in others. The avowed goal was to return the country to an earlier "golden era" of mutual help and voluntary action. Despite some heroic effort, however, what happened in fact was something far different. Squeezed by government cuts and unable to make up the shortfall or cover increased needs from private charitable sources, nonprofit organizations turned increasingly to the only alternative available to them: the market. During the 1980s, commercial income accounted for well over half of the growth the nonprofit sector achieved and emerged not only as the largest single source of nonprofit income but as the source of over half of all nonprofit support. What is more, the growth of commercial income was not restricted just to one or two parts of the sector; rather, it was quite pervasive. Even among social service agencies, commercial income accounted for a larger share of the growth during the 1980s than did any other source. In other words, the private charitable system proved no more capable of coping with the social crises of the 1980s than it had with the economic crises of the 1920s. And in the absence of government support, the nonprofit sector moved massively, and perhaps decisively, into the commercial market.

But this was only part of the story. During the same period, private for-profit firms that had initially been enticed into the social welfare field by the availability of government support found themselves unusually well positioned and equipped to compete in the social welfare "market" that emerged during the 1980s. For-profit firms moved aggressively to benefit from the restructuring of the hospital sector by establishing a commanding lead in the newly expanding field of short-term specialty care. Similarly, for-profit firms managed to gain the upper hand in the rapidly expanding field of outpatient clinics and home health care, once an almost exclusive nonprofit preserve. In the social service field, for-profit organizations began the decade with only 36 percent of the establishments but accounted for about half of the growth. Only in the nursing home field did nonprofit growth surpass for-profit growth in relative terms, but here for-profit firms already account for 80 percent of the activity.

In short, the 1980s have witnessed a pervasive "marketization" of the American social welfare system, as nonprofit organizations have been sucked increasingly into market-type relations and for-profit firms have steadily expanded their market niche. To be sure, the fee-based relationships in which nonprofit organizations now increasingly find themselves may differ from the pure arms-length transactions of classical economic theory. Third-party reimbursements by insurance providers or employers and subsidies from Social Security or private pension plans may also be involved, adding an outside agent to the transaction between buyer and seller. In addition, although government may not be playing a direct role, it may indirectly influence the transactions by controlling the fees it is willing to pay for the similar services it does purchase from many of the same types of providers. But these features are true of transactions in many parts of our "mixed economy." While they may impose some limits on the extent to which the shifts just described can be characterized as pure "marketization," they hardly challenge the basic thrust of what is underway.

Whether these shifts in the basic structure of our social welfare system will have long-term good or bad consequences is difficult to determine at this point. Efforts to document the advantages and disadvantages of nonprofit versus for-profit provision of social welfare services have so far proved inconclusive due to the problems of measuring outcomes with sufficient precision.[18] Whatever decline in quality may result from having services provided by organizations principally concerned with profit may be more than offset, for example, by the increased productivity that profit-seeking behavior may bring. What is more, there are doubtless advantages to be gained from a greater degree of competition in the social marketplace. Like government agencies, nonprofit organizations can become insulated from their target populations and insensitive to their needs. A dose of the client-driven, customer-conscious discipline of the market can therefore produce positive results.[19]

At the same time, however, there are serious risks. As Henry Hansmann (1980, 835–901) and others have shown, the flow of information required for the effective functioning of the market may not exist in the welfare field. Consumers of services in this field are often not the same people as those who pay, severing a link that is crucial for the market's operation. As for-profit firms enter the social market, moreover, they will inevitably siphon off the more affluent "customers," leaving nonprofit firms with the most difficult, and least profitable, cases. If nonprofit firms are forced by this competition to behave similarly, the focus of attention of the nonprofit sector will also shift increasingly toward those able to pay, leaving the disadvantaged with few places to turn. Finally, as scarce management talent in the nonprofit sector is forced to focus increasingly on the management of for-profit commercial ventures, the time and attention required to oversee the central operations of the sector will suffer.

How these pressures balance out will likely be debated empirically and theoretically for the next several decades. What this chapter makes clear, however, is that the pressures, and the issues they raise, can no longer be ignored.

CHAPTER 15

The Global Associational Revolution

The Rise of the Third Sector on the World Scene

The growth of the nonprofit sector reflected in the previous chapters is not restricted to the United States. To the contrary, over the past two decades a striking upsurge has taken place in organized voluntary activity, in the formation and increased activism of private, nonprofit, or nongovernmental, organizations in virtually every part of the world.[1] In the developed countries of North America, Europe, and Asia, in the developing societies of Asia, Africa, and Latin America, and in the former Soviet bloc, people are forming associations, foundations, and other similar institutions to deliver human services, promote grassroots development, prevent environmental degradation, protect civil rights, and pursue a thousand other objectives. The situation may not yet have reached the proportions that led eighteenth-century British politician Charles Greville to complain that "We are just now overrun with philanthropy and God knows where it will stop, or wither it will lead us,"[2] but the scope and scale of the phenomenon are nevertheless immense. Indeed, a veritable "associational revolution" now seems underway at the global level that may constitute as significant a social and political development of the latter twentieth century as the rise of the nation-state was of the latter nineteenth.

This development is all the more striking, moreover, in view of the decline that is simultaneously under way in many of the more traditional forms of participation, such as voting, political party identification, and labor union membership. How can we explain this phenomenon? What lies behind the global "associational revolution" that seems to be under way at the present time? Why is it occurring now? And what implications does it hold for our social and political life and for the relative roles of government and the private sector?

My purpose in this chapter is to begin answering these questions. To do so, the discussion falls into four major sections. First, I briefly review the recent record of "third sector" growth at the global level. In the second section I look behind this record to identify the processes that have been involved, the mechanisms through which third-sector expansion has occurred. In the third section I examine the underlying causes that seem to have given rise to third-sector growth in recent years. Finally, in the fourth section I explore some of the lessons this experience holds and the challenges it poses for the future.

What emerges most clearly from this analysis is the conclusion that the rise of the third sector at the international level does not spring from a single source, as is sometimes assumed. In addition to the pressures from below commonly emphasized in what might be termed the "romantic image" of this sector are a variety of pressures from the outside and from above. These pressures in turn reflect the impact of a broader set of historical developments—including four crises and two revolutions—that have come together at roughly the same time to weaken the hold of the state and expand the potentials for voluntary citizen action. The result is a process of change that bears close resemblance to the "third wave" of democratic political revolutions recently identified by Samuel Huntington (1991), but that goes far beyond it as well, affecting democratic as well as authoritarian regimes, developed as well as developing societies. It is also a process that is redefining the role of the state and giving rise to patterns of collaboration between government and the nonprofit sector that bear marked resemblance to those examined throughout this book.

The Rise of the Third Sector on the Global Level: Scope and Contours

Establishing the existence of a significant upsurge of organized, private, voluntary activity at the global level in recent years is, of course, no simple task. Nonprofit organizations are incredibly diverse, raising questions for some observers about whether it is possible to talk about a coherent sector at all. Serious definitional problems consequently confront any analyst. Compounding this is the varied treatment of these organizations in national legal structures. Some countries make explicit provision for the incorporation of "charitable" or other non-profit organizations, while others do not, or do so only partially. Official listings of such organizations are therefore notoriously incomplete. What is more, the treatment of such organizations is grossly imperfect in national economic statistics. The U.N. System of National Accounts, which guides the collection of national economic statistics throughout the world, does identify the nonprofit sector as one of four "sectors" about which economic data are to be collected, but the definition of the sector used limits its scope severely by including only organizations that receive half or more of their income from private gifts (Salamon and Anheier 1992b; Anheier, Rudney, and Salamon 1992). Under this definition, most of the major types of American nonprofit service organizations—such as hospitals, universities, and social service agencies—would be defined away since private giving accounts for less than 20 percent of their total income (Salamon 1992, 26). Finally, clear assessment of the nonprofit sector has been impeded by a set of ideological blinders that have long obscured the sector's true scope and role. For much of the past fifty years or more, politicians on both the political Right and the political Left have tended to downplay this set of institutions, the Left to justify the expansion of state involvement in the social welfare field and the Right to justify attacks on the state as the destroyer of such "intermediary institutions." As a consequence, the rise of the welfare state brought with it the virtual disappearance of the nonprofit or voluntary sector from both public discussion and scholarly inquiry even though this sector continued to grow in both scale and role.[3]

Given these realities, how do we know that we are witnessing something new as opposed to the rediscovery of a sector that has long existed but been long ignored? The answer, of course, is that both processes are doubtless involved, but the evidence of a dramatic upsurge is still hard to deny.

In the developed countries, for example, a significant upsurge of citizen activism has been evident for the past several decades. A survey I conducted of nonprofit human service organizations in sixteen American communities in 1982, for example, showed that 65 percent of the organizations then in existence had been created since 1960 (Salamon 1985). Virtually every one of the major social movements of the past three decades in the United States—such as the civil rights movement, the environmental movement, the consumer movement, the women's movement, and the conservative movement—have had their roots in the nonprofit sector. The number of private associations has similarly skyrocketed in France. More than 54,000 such associations were formed in 1987 alone, compared to 10,000 to 12,000 per year in the 1960s (Tchernonog 1992, 217). Between 1980 and 1986, the income of British charities increased an estimated 221 percent. Recent estimates record some 275,000 charities in the United Kingdom, with income in excess of 4 percent of the gross national product (Billis 1989). In Italy recent research records a substantial surge of voluntary organization formation during the 1970s and early 1980s. Forty percent of the organizations surveyed in 1985 had been formed since 1977 (Pasquinelli 1992, 201–2). Similarly, the Green Movement has experienced unparalleled growth throughout the developed world. The German Green Party has become a major national force, and Green parties have sprung up in sixteen European countries. In October 1988, the Swedish Green Party became the first new party to enter Parliament in seventy years. In Italy environmental groups organized an election campaign that in November 1987 ended the Italian nuclear energy program. At the European level as well, the nonprofit sector has become a significant force. In 1989 and 1990, several new organizations were formed to represent the voluntary sector before the European community—a European Foundation Centre for foundations, CEDAG (Comité européen de associations d'intérêt général) for associations, and ECAS (the European Citizen Action Service) for the voluntary sector more generally.

These developments have, in turn, been accompanied by greater recognition of this sector in policy circles. The Socialist government of François Mitterand created a special Interministerial Delegation on Social Economy in 1981 and then elevated this to Secretary of State status in 1984. In England Margaret Thatcher made the promotion of the voluntary sector and of "active citizenship" a centerpiece of her campaign to scale back the size of the British welfare state. The European Commission has created a special directorate, DGXXIII, to handle this sector and a draft statute to govern nonprofit organizations operating at the European level. A new law was passed in Japan in 1990 permitting Japanese corporations to deduct charitable contributions for the first time, and the Japanese Keidandren, or Business Association, declared 1990 " the inaugural year for Japanese corporate philanthropy." In short, while the nonprofit or voluntary sector had hardly disappeared in the preceding years, the evidence of a recent dramatic expansion is quite striking.

Even more dramatic developments are under way in the developing countries of Asia, Africa, and Latin America. Some 4,600 Western voluntary organizations are now active in the developing world, and they provide support to approximately 20,000 indigenous nongovernmental organizations (Smith 1990, 3). In India the Village Awakening Movement, which grew out of the Gandhian tradition, is active in thousands of villages. In addition, organized philanthropy is on the rise, and an Indian Council on Foundations was formed in 1987. In Bangladesh the Grameen Bank has provided a mechanism for channeling credit into rural areas using an innovative cooperative collateral scheme, under which groups of farmers guarantee each other's loans. In addition, Bangladesh now boasts approximately 10,000 nongovernmental organizations (NGOs) registered with various government agencies. In Sri Lanka over 8,000 villages are involved in the Sarvodala Shramadana village awakening movement that organizes local villagers to produce small-scale community improvement projects (Durning 1989, 11–12). In the Philippines some 21,000 nonprofit organizations were formed in the 1970s and 1980s, beginning with grassroots empowerment groups and leading in the early 1980s to the rise of support groups providing training and research and, more recently, to umbrella groups and networks (Ledesma and Decena 1992). In Brazil efforts to build a "people's church" based on local action groups has led to the creation of some 80–100,000 Christian Base Communities throughout the countryside. At the same time, neighborhood associations have sprung up among the squatters in São Paolo and other Brazilian cities. One estimate puts the number of these organizations in São Paolo alone at 1,300 (Fisher 1987, 5). Some 25–27,000 nonprofit organizations are now reported to exist in Chile, and Argentina has witnessed the emergence of almost 2,000 since the early 1980s (Thompson 1992). In Kenya the Harambee movement has led to the mobilization of voluntary action at the community level to stimulate a wide variety of development projects. Recent estimates indicate that 30 percent of the capital development in the country since the 1970s has come from this source (Thomas 1987, 465).

These developments, in turn, have spawned their own policy response. A special "Enabling Environment Conference" convened by the Aga Khan Foundation in October 1986 specifically endorsed more active reliance on private voluntary organizations to promote development in Africa. By the late 1980s, even staid agencies like the World Bank were ready to acknowledge the "explosive emergence of nongovernmental organizations as a major collective actor in development activities" (Cernea 1988, 29–32).

Finally, similar developments have also been in evidence recently in Central and Eastern Europe and the former Soviet Union. Well before the dramatic political events that captured world attention in 1989, important changes were taking place beneath the surface of Eastern European society, and voluntary organizations were very much in the center of them. Indeed, a veritable "second society" had come into existence in much of Eastern Europe consisting of thousands, perhaps millions, of networks of people who provided each other mutual aid to cope with the economy of scarcity in which they lived (Binder 1989).

By the second half of the 1970s, these networks were already acquiring political significance. Ecology clubs, environmental "circles," and a variety of other groups began forming throughout the region. For example, the Polish Ecology Club took shape in Kraków in the late 1970s. A Poor Relief Fund was established in Hungary in 1979. In 1982 the Hungarian Cooperative for Human Services (LARHS) was formed. In Czechoslovakia the Charter 77 Foundation and the Civic Forum—a private nonprofit group—provided some of the early foundation for what ultimately became the "velvet revolution." Under pressure from the Catholic Church and with the encouragement of overseas foundations, Poland passed a new law on foundations in 1984 granting a degree of autonomy for Polish charitable organizations. This opened the way to the formation in 1988 of the Foundation for the Development of Polish Agriculture (FDPA), the result of a joint effort by the Rockefeller Brothers Fund, the Rockefeller Foundation, and the Ford Foundation.

This process of foundation formation then accelerated in the late 1980s following the overthrow of the Communist governments. As of 1992, several thousand foundations were registered with governmental authorities in Poland. In Hungary 6,000 foundations and 11,000 associations had been registered by mid-1992 (Kuti 1992). A Foundation Forum was established in Bulgaria in 1991, linking close to thirty newly created private foundations. This process was somewhat slower in the former Soviet Union, but has recently speeded up. A Foundation for Social Innovations was formed in 1986, in the second year of "perestroika," as a way to translate citizen initiatives into effective social action.[4] Since then dozens of other foundations and nonprofit organizations have been created—to assist gifted and talented children, to protest Chernobyl, to call attention to the disappearance of the Aral Sea, to encourage cultural heterogeneity, and for dozens of other purposes.

In short, although systematic data are sparse, it seems clear that a major expansion has taken place in the scope and scale of organized, private, voluntary activity throughout the world, and in the high-level attention that is being showered on the resulting set of organizations. Although the terminology used, and the precise purposes being served, may differ markedly from place to place, the underlying social reality involved is quite similar: a virtual associational revolution is under way throughout the world that is giving rise to a sizable global "third sector" comprised of (1) structured organizations, (2) located outside the formal apparatus of the state, (3) not intended to distribute profits from their activities to a set of shareholders or directors, (4) self-governing, and (5) involving significant private, voluntary effort.[5] Whether this global third sector will continue to prosper and grow is difficult to predict, but its reality is hard to deny.

Processes

How can we explain this phenomenon? And why is it happening at the present time? Not surprisingly, firm answers to these questions are difficult to obtain, but an examination of the forces giving rise to the third sector in different parts of the world may offer some clues. What becomes clear from such an examination is that more than one such force is involved. Rather, the pressures to expand the voluntary sector seem to be coming from at least three different directions: (1) from below, (2) from the outside, and (3) from above.

Pressures from Below

Perhaps the most basic source of momentum for the recent upsurge of nonprofit and voluntary organization throughout the world has been pressure from below, from ordinary people who decide to take matters into their own hands and organize to improve their condition or seek basic rights. This factor is most clearly at work in the emergence of organized voluntary activity in the former Soviet Union and Central Europe. Many of the dramatic changes that shook the Soviet bloc in the late 1980s and early 1990s had their origins in the emergence of dozens of semistructured voluntary groupings over the previous decade or more. Solidarity in Poland is the most obvious, and most structured, of these, but various informal groupings existed in other countries as well—such as the "Danube Circle," which fought the construction of a hydroelectric plant on the Danube in Hungary; or ARCHE, the environmental organization that protested acid rain in

East Germany by tying thousands of bed sheets to apartment roofs and then recording the pollution that accumulated.

Activists in Eastern Europe and the Soviet Union describe their efforts as the creation of a "civil society," a society in which individuals have the right not only to speak out as individuals, but also to join together in organizations. As Andras Biro, a Hungarian activist, has put it: "We are witnessing an escape from the enforced immaturity of the socialist system. For the first time in 40 years we are reclaiming responsibility for our lives."[6]

The intricate networks of mutual assistance that developed beneath the surface of Central and Eastern European societies under Communism provided the transmission belts for this new democratic fervor once conditions for its blossoming became ripe. As one account has put it: "This second society . . . created the connections that came to life in the mass demonstrations against the Honecker regime in early October [1989]. Doctors called mechanics. Mechanics called construction workers. Construction workers called nurses. Nurses called doctors. Neighbors called neighbors. This is how the demonstrations came to life in Plauen, Dresden, and above all, Leipzig"(Binder 1989, A14).

Pressure from below has also been quite important in the upsurge of voluntary nonprofit activity in the third world. Neighborhood improvement associations have thus reportedly taken root in a sizable proportion of the 20,000 or so squatter settlements of Latin America. Cooperatives, women's groups, craft associations, housing associations, and mutual aid groupings of many other types have also grown rapidly over the past two decades in other parts of the developing world. CHIPKO, an Indian environmental movement, for example, emerged from the spontaneous efforts of rural residents to save their dying forest by linking their arms around the trees (Fisher 1987, 8). The General Federation of Iraqi Women, created in 1968, sprang from the militancy of Iraqi women who took advantage of the stated ideology of the ruling party emphasizing women's equality to organize rural women in cooperative farms and train them for production and marketing activities (El-Baz 1992, 13). The so-called urban popular movement in Mexico and elsewhere in Latin America is another example of a grassroots effort to improve local living conditions (Annis 1988, 138–39). In Colombia, for example, peasants, small farmers, and student groups created a network of independent organizations in the 1970s that, between 1971 and 1980, sponsored almost 130 demonstrations and strikes affecting communities with a combined population of 4.4 million people (Smith 1990, 242–43). In Africa as well, a "new wind" of popular democratic protest has gained prominence and stimulated the formation of private, nonprofit groups.[7] Finally, such pressures have also been evident in the emergence of thousands of self-help and community development groups in much of the developed world (U.S. Department of Health and Human Services 1988).

Encouragement from the Outside

If pressures from below have been a fundamental impetus for the recent upsurge of organized private, voluntary activity around the world, these pressures have received important encouragement from a variety of outside forces, including particularly (1) the church, (2) western private voluntary organizations (PVOs), and (3) official aid agencies.

The Church. The Catholic Church has been one of the most significant outside actors contributing to the recent rise of the third sector, especially in Latin America. Historically allied with the powers-that-be, various Catholic dioceses in Latin America began in the 1950s to set up their own charitable organizations to relieve the suffering of the urban and rural poor. In response to the spread of Marxist doctrines among the lower classes and the success of the Castro revolution, this gave way in the 1960s to a more radical approach focused on the underlying structural causes of poverty, such as inequitable land tenure. With the Second Vatican Council between 1962 and 1965, this approach gained papal sanction, as the church assumed a more active role in the promotion of social justice and the alleviation of poverty. At a Catholic Bishops Conference in Medellin, Colombia, in 1968, church leaders set out to create a people's church in Latin America through the formation of thousands of *Communidades Eclesasis de Base,* or "Church Base Communities."[8] In Brazil alone, 80,000 such communities were created in the 1970s and 1980s, each representing a locus for community problem solving and organization. Though refraining from direct political activity, these "base communities" have provided useful leadership training and a critical mechanism for overcoming traditional attitudes of submissiveness (Krischke 1991, 189–92).

The role of the church in promoting the third sector has not been limited to the developing countries, however. The Catholic Church under Pope John Paul II was a powerful vehicle in fostering the growth of the protest movement in Central Europe in the late 1980s. Catholic churches in Warsaw, Gdansk, Kraków, and elsewhere provided a crucial neutral meeting ground and source of moral support for those agitating to change the system. Similarly, the Lutheran

Church played a comparable role in East Germany, providing shelter, working space, and moral authority to the protest groups that ultimately toppled the Communist regime in October 1989 (Whitney 1989).

Northern PVOs. A second crucial outside force helping to foster the growth of nonprofit organizations has been the sizable network of Northern NGOs, or private voluntary organizations (PVOs), working in the developing countries. Over 4,600 such organizations were in existence as of the early 1980s, including church-related missionary and service agencies, secular nonprofit agencies, foundations, labor and educational groups, and others (Smith 1990, 3).

Historically, northern PVOs have approached the problems of the developing world with an essentially "humanitarian relief" perspective, and this perspective still tends to dominate the U.S.-based organizations. Beginning in the 1960s and accelerating in the 1970s, however, a new "empowerment" focus came to animate the PVO community, as attention turned increasingly from relief of suffering to efforts to eliminate the social and economic conditions that made suffering so chronic. Traditional U.S. organizations such as Church World Service and Lutheran World Relief, newer organizations such as Oxfam America and Coordination in Development (CODEL), as well as some of the larger foundations such as Rockefeller, Ford, and Aga Khan, thus turned increasingly toward support for indigenous third world organizations working to organize self-help activities among the poor at the grassroots level. Canadian and European PVOs were even more deeply involved in such empowerment work, as were other private development institutions.[9] Delivering $4.7 billion of assistance to some 20,000 indigenous nonprofit organizations as of the mid-1980s, these outside PVOs have provided both the moral and financial support to help promote indigenous grassroots organization.

Western PVOs have also contributed to the development of the nonprofit sector in Eastern Europe. The Rockefeller Brothers Fund channeled important support to developing nonprofit organizations in Central Europe beginning in the early and mid-1980s, as did U.S. labor unions to the emerging Solidarity organization in Poland. In Western Europe as well, U.S. foundations and other charitable institutions have provided significant encouragement to emerging nonprofit institutions. Thus U.S. foundations have actively supported the recently created European Foundation Center; the Charles Stewart Mott Foundation has launched a project to promote the development of "community foundations" in the United Kingdom; and United Way International has established alliances with Western European nonprofit organizations to introduce the concept of workplace giving in the United Kingdom and elsewhere.

Official Aid Agencies. These private initiatives have in turn been supplemented, and to a considerable degree subsidized, by official government institutions. Changes in U.S. assistance policy pushed by congressional critics beginning in the mid-1960s placed increased emphasis on involvement of the poor in development activities and on aid to indigenous NGOs and the U.S.-based private voluntary organizations working with them (Smith 1990, 67–68; U.S. Congress 1975, 75). Other developed countries have backed this approach even more vigorously, and the Development Assistance Committee of the OECD has adopted "participatory development" as the keystone of its development strategy for the 1990s (OECD 1991, 43–44).

Multinational aid agencies such as the World Bank have also joined the effort to foster nonprofit organizations in the developing world, though somewhat more belatedly. Throughout the 1970s, Bank support for NGOs in the developing countries was sporadic at best. In 1982, however, the Bank was persuaded to form a World Bank–NGO Committee composed of senior bank managers and twenty-six NGO leaders from around the world, three-fifths of them from the developing countries. Since then, Bank involvement with NGOs has expanded, and a formal Bank policy adopted encouraging cooperation with NGOs and client government adoption of policies favorable to NGO activity.[10]

Support from Above

While pressures from below and from the outside have figured prominently in the emergence of nonprofit organizations in recent years, the surge of interest in voluntary organizations has also resulted from pressure from above. The conservative regimes of Ronald Reagan and Margaret Thatcher made support for the voluntary sector a central part of their strategy to cut back government social spending. As Mr. Reagan put it in justifying his budget cuts in 1981, "We have let government take away many of the things that were once ours to do voluntarily." Mrs. Thatcher took the argument one step further and proposed to eliminate not only government spending but also the organized voluntary sector and to leave social care wholly to volunteers, whom she called "the heart of all our social welfare provision."[11]

While this line of argument has been particularly characteristic of conservative regimes in England and the United States, however, it has also attracted attention elsewhere. Thus the government of Socialist President François Mitterand in France moved to liberalize the laws on charitable giving in the mid-1980s and recently sponsored a European conference on "social economy organizations" to put the voluntary sector on the map of the European Community. As part of a major decentralization of French government enacted in 1982, local authorities acquired an important new function of animating and orchestrating the associative life of local communities and enlisting nonprofit organizations in the implementation of social welfare policies (Tchernonog 1992). In Norway as well, a Labor government recently issued a long-term program stressing the importance of voluntary organizations as mediating institutions between the individual and the larger society and emphasizing that "[t]he government itself does not have the capacity to consider all questions related to the social welfare sector." [12]

Pressures from the top have also figured prominently in the development of organized nonprofit activity in the third world. In Thailand, for example, the Ministry of Agriculture helped form the Farmers' Association and Farmers' Cooperatives, and the Defense and Interior Ministry the Scouts Movement. The Federation of Free Farmers in the Philippines is affiliated with the government-sponsored National Congress of Farm Organizations. The Harambee movement in Kenya is a direct result of explicit governmental policy to promote community involvement in development. The First Egyptian Five-Year Plan in 1961 specifically invited NGOs to participate in implementing social policies, and government ministries now regularly provide paid staff to indigenous NGOs. Similarly, the sixth five-year plan in Pakistan put heavy stress on NGO involvement in the development process as a way to ensure popular participation in development. [13]

Interestingly, this same phenomenon is even evident in the former Communist bloc. One of the earliest, formal nonprofit organizations in the Soviet Union, the Foundation for Social Innovations, received early encouragement from Mikhail Gorbachev, who read an article about the concept in *Komsomolskaya Pravda* and decided to back it. [14] The embryonic nonprofit sector in China similarly benefited from official encouragement, beginning with the landmark Third Plenum of the Eleventh Central Committee in December 1978, which signaled the start of a process of reform to tap the initiative and creativity in Chinese society (Whiting 1989).

The support from above that has helped to promote the development of nonprofit organizations has not come exclusively from official channels, however. Equally important has been the role of middle-class professionals and intellectuals. Nonprofit organizations have often provided such educated elites an alternative source of both employment and engagement in the social and political life of their countries. This has been particularly true under authoritarian regimes, but it has been a source of support for grassroots nonprofit organizations in other settings as well (Smith 1990, 275; Huntington 1991, 64–65).

Summary

In short, no single route characterizes the path of recent third-sector development. Although pressures from below have been a significant factor, they do not suffice on their own to explain the remarkable upsurge that has occurred. Rather, support from the outside and from above have also played often-decisive roles. Under these circumstances, it is necessary to dig a little more deeply to understand why these various actors, in widely disparate settings, happened to coalesce around a set of activities supporting the expansion of nonprofit organizations in the 1970s and 1980s.

Underlying Causes: Four Crises and Two Revolutions

The result of such digging suggests that four crises and two revolutions seem to lie behind the pressures from below, outside, and above that have stimulated the rise of the global third sector over the past two decades. Let us examine each of these in turn.

The Crisis of the Welfare State

In the first place, the recent surge of interest in private, nonprofit organizations has resulted from the perceived crisis of the modern "welfare state," the growing sense over the past decade and a half that the system of governmental protections against old age and economic misfortune that had taken shape in most of the West by the 1950s, and that led sociologist Daniel Bell (1960, 402) to declare the "end of ideology in the West," was no longer working.[15] What shattered the consensus in support of the welfare state were at least four key developments: (1) the oil shock of the early 1970s, which significantly slowed economic growth and gave rise to the belief that social welfare spending, which had grown substantially in the previous decades, was crowding out private investment in plant and equipment; (2) a growing conviction that government had simply become overloaded, over-professionalized, and over-bureaucratized, and was incapable of performing the expanded tasks that were being assigned to it; (3) a growing deficit problem resulting from the fact that the politics of the welfare state continually produced pressures for expanded services that exceeded the willingness of people to pay; and (4) a growing body of rhetoric suggesting that far from improving economic performance by protecting individuals against unreasonable risk, the welfare state was stifling initiative, absolving people of personal responsibility, and encouraging dependence. In a way, the welfare state proved to be its own worst enemy. By improving standards of living, it fostered rising expectations and growing dissatisfaction with the basic level of services it was able to provide.[16] The upshot was the election in the late-1970s and early-1980s of a spate of right-of-center or conservative leaders and the inauguration of cost-cutting programs in a number of countries, including Germany, Belgium, Britain, Norway, the United States, and, after some initial resistance, even Socialist-dominated France.

With government programs discredited and public budgets restricted, attention naturally turned to other ways to address public problems. Because of their small scale, their relative flexibility, and their use of private volunteers and private philanthropic support, nonprofit organizations emerged as a potentially important alternative to state-provided services, and one that could offer the "self-determination, self-responsibility, freedom of choice, solidarity, and participation in everyday life" that were increasingly demanded (Flora 1986).

The Crisis of Development

As significant as the "crisis of the welfare state" in stimulating the recent expansion of the nonprofit sector globally has been a parallel "crisis of development." Although world economic growth was robust between 1960 and 1973 and developing countries benefited greatly, the oil shock of the 1970s and the recession of the early 1980s changed things rather dramatically. In sub-Saharan Africa and Western Asia in particular, average per capita incomes began to fall in the latter 1970s, and this accelerated in the 1980s, with declines spreading to Latin America and the Caribbean as well. By 1990, in fact, output levels per economically active person in these regions were lower than they had been in 1980. Indeed, economic growth in the least developed countries was so poor that, given their high rate of population growth, average output per person in 1990 was some 5 percent lower than it had been in 1970! Although progress has been made in some places—most notably the Pacific Rim and parts of Latin America—the problem of poverty, far from declining, has grown significantly in many parts of the developing world, leaving roughly one in five of the planet's five billion men, women, and children in absolute poverty today.[17]

These discouraging realities naturally stimulated considerable rethinking about the requirements for economic progress. One school of thought, rooted in the developing countries and articulated forcefully in the U.N. General Assembly's 1974 "principles for a new international economic order" and in the Club of Rome's Reshaping the International Order (RIO) report in 1976, stresses the need for fundamental changes in the basic international trading system to improve the bargaining position of third world nations (Smith 1990, 98–99). A second school of thought, incorporated in World Bank policies, has stressed the need for "structural adjustments" in the developing countries themselves to reduce the role of the state and increase the role of the market.

Increasingly, however, one of the consensus views emerging from this debate has encouraged support for a mode of development called "assisted self-reliance," or "participatory development," which stresses the need to engage the energies and enthusiasm of those at the grassroots in the developing countries as a key to development success. As one recent study puts it: "Anti-poverty programs that the official political-administrative hierarchy designs and implements in a heavily, almost exclusively top-down fashion tend to be ineffective. Such efforts have a hard time reaching their grassroots clienteles through all the intervening bureaucratic layering—and a still harder time engaging local people in the conduct and management of their own poverty alleviation."[18] One reason for this is the weakness of the state in many developing settings, particularly in Africa, where the modern state is an alien intrusion compared to the natural associational life that exists (Bratton 1989). Noted one World Bank official, "we overestimated what governments could do."[19] Beyond this, there is a growing recognition of the productivity gains that come from making the poor active participants in the development process (United Nations 1990, 8). Indeed, a study of twenty-five World Bank–funded agricultural development projects found that virtually every one of the projects with positive long-term results involved active beneficiary participation in project design and management, most often through grassroots organizations that the participants control (Cernea 1987). The upshot has been a growing consensus about the limitations of the state in promoting development and a growing interest in participatory development approaches and the third-sector organizations that implement them.[20]

The Crisis of the Environment

A third key development stimulating the rise of nonprofit organizations around the world is the continued and deepening crisis of the environment. Despite some improvements, the overall environmental picture at the global level has continued to deteriorate, in some respects at an accelerating rate. This is due in part to the continued poverty of the developing countries, which causes the poor to degrade their immediate environment in order to survive. In part, however, it is due to wasteful practices or inattention on the part of the wealthy. Between 1950 and 1983, for example, 38 percent of Central America's and 24 percent of Africa's forests disappeared, and the pace of decline escalated during the early 1980s. In fact, recent studies show that the loss of the tropical forests has been even more extensive than earlier thought, with serious implications for the levels of carbon dioxide in the atmosphere, and hence for global warming (Shabecoff 1990; Sewell 1987, xi). Similarly, overuse threatens to turn two-fifths of Africa's nondesert land, one-third of Asia's nondesert land, and one-fifth of Latin America's nondesert land, into desert (United Nations 1990, 87). Although emissions of nitrogen oxides, which produce acid rain, declined slightly or stabilized during the period 1970–85 in some of the developed market economies, the total amount of nitrogen released annually is still rising. And in some areas, such as Central and Eastern Europe, acid rain and related air and water pollution are endangering food supplies and significantly reducing life expectancy.

As these and other aspects of the environmental crisis have become apparent, citizens have grown increasingly frustrated with government and eager to organize their own responses. The stunning rise of Green parties in Western Europe is one sign of this. Similarly, environmental degradation was one of the prime motivations for the emergence of an embryonic nonprofit sector in Central and Eastern Europe. Ecology clubs are active in Poland, Hungary, Russia, and the Czech Republic.

In the developing countries as well, ecological activism has stimulated the rise of nonprofit organizations. As in the development field, reliance on technological fixes or government action has proved ineffective, in part because of the social organization that effective management of natural resources requires. By mobilizing those who would otherwise do the polluting or who would overuse the scarce natural resources, and equipping them with the wherewithal to alter their behavior, nonprofit organizations can significantly fill the organizational vacuum that frustrates environmental protection in these settings (Cernea 1988, 24).

The Crisis of Socialism

The fourth major development that has contributed to the rise of the third sector in recent years is the crisis of socialism, the collapse of faith in the capacity of the communist system to deliver on its promise of social justice and economic plenty. While this promise had long been suspect, the replacement of laggard economic growth with actual retrogression in the mid-1970s destroyed whatever limited legitimacy the communist system retained and ushered in a search for new ways to meet social and economic needs. One manifestation of this was the emergence of a variety of market-oriented "cooperative enterprises," first in Hungary and then elsewhere in Central Europe and even the Soviet Union. At the same time, however, efforts were made to shape other components of a "civil society" as well. Slowly at first, but increasingly as time went on, citizens began experimenting with a variety of nongovernmental organizations that could meet needs and provide vehicles for citizen expression without involvement of the increasingly discredited state. By 1988, for example, well before the collapse of the Soviet empire in 1989, there were approximately 6,000 voluntary organizations and 600 private foundations in Hungary alone, including everything from small dance groups and self-help circles to large environmental and human rights organizations. The vigor with which these new organizations were formed reflected what one analyst termed "the deep distrust of central government and its institutions. People prefer not to give the state a free hand any more. They want to control economic, political, and social processes as directly as possible. Voluntary associations and nonprofit organizations seem to be appropriate opportunities for this control" (Kuti 1990, 36–37).

The Communications Revolution

Important as they are in explaining the significant upsurge of organized voluntary activity in the world over the past two decades, the four "crises" just examined would very likely not have sufficed to produce this result in the absence of two further significant developments.

The first of these was the dramatic revolution in communications that took place during the 1970s and 1980s. The invention and widespread dissemination of the computer, the breakthroughs in fiber optic communications, the blanketing of the earth with television and communications satellites—these and other similar developments suddenly opened even the most remote areas to the image of the modern world, and with it, to the capability for organization and concerted action. This was accompanied, moreover, by a significant increase in education and literacy. Between 1970 and 1985, adult literacy rates in the developing world rose from 43 percent to 60 percent. Among males, it reached 71 percent (UNDP 1990, 17).

As a result of this combined expansion of literacy and communications, it became far easier for people to concert their actions, to organize, and to mobilize others. Communications between a capital and a rural area that once required days in a developing country could be accomplished in minutes, as computers and telephone lines penetrated the rural hinterlands. Authoritarian regimes that successfully controlled their own communications networks were powerless to stop the flow of information through satellite dishes and faxes. Isolated activists could consequently maintain links with sympathetic colleagues in their own countries and abroad, thus strengthening their resolve. What is more, communications greatly facilitated education about what other groups were doing and helped create networks of activists in different fields.

The Bourgeois Revolution

The final factor that seems to have been critical to the emergence of the third sector throughout the world in the 1970s and 1980s was the considerable economic growth that took place just prior to this—in the 1960s and early 1970s. During this earlier period, the world economy grew at the rate of 5 percent per year, with all regions sharing in the expansion. In fact, the growth rate of Eastern Europe, the USSR, and the developing countries actually exceeded that of the developed market economies.[21]

What is important about this growth is not just the material improvement it permitted or the set of expectations it engendered. Perhaps most important was the contribution it made to the creation of a sizable urban middle class in a wide assortment of countries. As we have seen, middle-class leadership was critical to the emergence of private, nonprofit organizations in much of Latin America in the 1970s and 1980s, and the same was true in Asia and Africa (Baron 1989, 2).

The unusual strength of voluntary organizations in South Africa, Kenya, and Zimbabwe, for example, seems to be due in no small part to the unusually high level of economic growth that has taken place in these countries, and the sizable urban middle classes that were consequently created (Bratton 1989, 421). If economic crisis ultimately provoked the middle class into action, in other words, prior economic growth was needed to create a middle class that could organize to respond.

Challenges and Implications

The rather dramatic expansion of organized, private, nongovernmental activity that has taken place over the past two decades in virtually every part of the world thus springs from a multitude of pressures and reflects a deep-seated series of crises and an important set of social and technological changes that have put the role of the state in question in capitalist, socialist, and developing countries alike and opened the way for alternative institutional arrangements that can respond more flexibly and effectively to human needs. By virtue of their smaller scale, their relative flexibility, their ability to engage grassroots energies, their private character, and their perceived trustworthiness, nonprofit organizations have seemed ideal candidates for this role. While the third sector may not yet be viewed as *the* solution to the interrelated crises of development, socialism, the environment, and the welfare state, it is certainly being called on to play a far more important role than ever before.

How effectively the third sector can live up to these expectations, however, is open to serious question. For all its recent dynamism, this sector remains a fragile plant, vulnerable to a variety of internal tensions and external constraints. What is more, it suffers from a number of dysfunctional myths that impede its ability to deal effectively with the real challenges it faces. How the sector evolves, therefore, will be shaped in important part by how well these myths are understood, how the sector balances the trade-offs it faces, and how other institutions respond.

Dysfunctional Myths

So far as the myths are concerned, three seem most important.

The Myth of Pure Virtue. The first of these is what I will term the "myth of pure virtue." The nonprofit sector has grown and gained prominence in recent years fundamentally as a trustworthy and flexible vehicle for elemental human yearnings for self-expression, self-help, participation, responsiveness, and mutual aid. With roots often in religious and moral teachings, the sector has acquired a saintly self-perception and persona. The upshot has been a certain romanticism about its inherent purity, about its distinctive virtues, and about its ability to produce significant change in people's lives.

Without denying the fundamental validity of this image, it is nevertheless important to recognize that this set of institutions has "other sides" as well. For one thing, for all their much-vaunted flexibility, non-profit organizations remain organizations. As such, they are prone to all the limitations that afflict bureaucratic institutions of all types, especially as they grow in scale and complexity—unresponsiveness, cumbersomeness, routinization, lack of coordination. Nonprofit organizations may be less prone to these disabilities than government agencies, but they are hardly immune to the inevitable tensions that all organizations confront between flexibility and effectiveness, between grassroots control and administrative accountability, between short-term responsiveness and long-term organizational maintenance.

Beyond this, as we have seen, a complex mixture of pressures and considerations seems to have given rise to the recent growth of the third sector in disparate parts of the world. While some of these are consistent with "the myth of pure virtue," others are more complicated indeed. In at least some settings, for example, support for the voluntary sector has provided a convenient smoke screen for the conservative assault on the modern welfare state and for a resulting set of policies designed to slash social expenditures. Indeed, rhetorical support for the nonprofit sector has at times been accompanied by tangible policies that undermine the sector's capacities, as was the case in the United States in the 1980s (Salamon 1984b, 261–86). Similarly mixed motivations have contributed to the growth of the voluntary sector in the developing world. Far from an instrument of grassroots independence, nonprofit organizations have also functioned as a vehicle for extending the influence of national political leaders. The top-down support for nonprofit organizations in Thailand, the Philippines, and Kenya, for example, seems to have been motivated at least in part by this consideration. Even where the pressure to form nonprofit organizations comes from below, these organizations nevertheless perform an essentially "system maintenance" function from the point of view of political elites. A recent study of the Harambee movement in Kenya, for example, notes that while Harambee channels some highly visible private wealth into socially useful projects, it also serves to "justify the accumulation of wealth and power and the perpetuation of inequities" (Thomas 1987, 477). More generally, as Brian Smith has argued (1990, 277), even change-oriented nonprofit organizations can bolster the position of local powers-that-be by helping to "harness the energies of regime opponents from the middle class, which might have been channelled into more radically political or even revolutionary alternatives. They help placate the working-class sectors and give them a sense of hope that the system is malleable and responsive to their needs. They are signs to foreign critics that authoritarian, one-party, or elite-controlled governments allow a certain degree of pluralism and space for private initiative in their societies." This is not to say that the rise of the third sector is simply a cynical smoke screen for other, more powerful motives. The argument, rather, is that the motivations for the recent rise of the third sector are more mixed than the widely held "myth of pure virtue" would lead us to believe, and this must be taken into account when contemplating the sector's capabilities and role.

The Myth of Voluntarism. Closely related to the myth of pure virtue is the "myth of voluntarism," the belief that true nonprofit organizations rely chiefly, or even exclusively, on private voluntary action and private philanthropic support. This myth is particularly pervasive in American thinking about the nonprofit sector, but since the American nonprofit sector is widely perceived as one of the largest and most highly developed, it has affected thinking more broadly as well. Underlying it is a view of the relationship between government and the state that springs from conservative political philosophy and that builds on a "paradigm of conflict." According to this paradigm, an inherent conflict exists between "the state" and the multitude of so-called mediating institutions such as voluntary groups that stand between it and the individual. The growth of the state thus poses a fundamental challenge to voluntary groups, robbing them of functions and ultimately leading to their demise.[22] Under these circumstances, the key to the expansion of the third sector is to reduce the role of the state and rely on private action, and private charitable support, instead.

In fact, however, as the previous chapters of this book have demonstrated, the relationship between government and the nonprofit sector has not been primarily conflictual. Rather, it has been characterized by extensive cooperation as well. Instead of a "paradigm of conflict," what has functioned in fact has been a "paradigm of partnership" in which government has turned extensively to the nonprofit sector to assist it in meeting human needs. In the United States, in fact, government reliance on the nonprofit sector is part of a broader pattern that I have termed "third-party government." In short, government does very little itself in the domestic sphere. What it does, it does through a host of "third parties"—colleges, universities, research institutes, commercial banks, private industrial firms, hospitals, and a host of others. Because of their peculiar character as semipublic institutions, nonprofit organizations have long been favorite partners in this third-party system. The result is an intricate network of relationships linking government and the nonprofit sector in a hundred different ways. Reflecting this, government has emerged as a major source of nonprofit support even in the United States, outdistancing private philanthropy by almost 2:1 (Salamon 1987a, 1992). In other advanced countries, government support is even more pronounced.

Unfortunately, this widespread partnership has escaped the notice even of otherwise well-informed observers. Given the meager local sources of philanthropic support in large parts of the developing world and in Central and Eastern Europe and the profound sense of fatalism and suspicion in which the poor are often enveloped in such settings, the result can be highly detrimental to the development of the third sector in these areas. To depend chiefly on the spontaneous upsurge of voluntary activity from below to foster and sustain voluntary organizations in these areas is almost to ensure failure. Even in developed countries, where the scope of private charitable support is far greater, such support often comes with its own strings attached. Under these circumstances, the logical consequence of the myth of voluntarism is to consign the nonprofit sector to a far more marginal role than might otherwise be the case. While voluntarism and private giving are vital to the special character of the sector, they must be seen as just one of a number of potential sources of support.

The Myth of Immaculate Conception. The third basic myth that threatens to impede further progress of the third sector at the global level is the myth of immaculate conception, the notion that nonprofit organizations are essentially emerging anew in most parts of the world and can consequently operate on a tabula rasa. While recent years have doubtless witnessed a dramatic upsurge in organized voluntary activity, the fact is that such activity has deep historical roots in virtually every part of the world. In Asia, for example, philanthropic activities long predated the arrival of Christianity. Such activity was evident in China in antiquity and was strengthened and institutionalized under Buddhism from at least the eighth century (Baron 1989, 2). In Japan as well, philanthropic activity can be traced back at least to the Buddhist period, and it continued in the form of mutual village aid during feudalism. The first modern Japanese foundation, the Society of Gratitude, was established by wealthy Japanese merchants in 1829, almost a century before the founding of the first modern American foundation (Yamamoto and Amenomori 1989). By the same token, the precursors of "modern" private development agencies can be found in the *tandas* of Mexico and the *tontines* of Zimbabwe—both traditional financial and savings groups—or in the community organizations that have been found operating in the Peruvian highlands in the late nineteenth century (Fisher 1987, 4). Efforts to establish development-oriented nongovernmental organizations in Africa and India can similarly not proceed very far without coming to terms with existing traditional institutions based on tribe and caste. In Central Europe, too, the recent emergence of nonprofit organizations builds on a rich philanthropic tradition that long predated the communist takeover. Recent developments thus represent not simply the emergence of wholly new arrangements but, in significant measure, the reemergence of earlier patterns.

Implications

What the above discussion makes clear is that the evolution of the third sector at the global level is a far more complex matter than may at first appear. Crucial trade-offs exist both for the managers of these organizations and those who would support their activities. While the resolution of these trade-offs will naturally depend on the values of the participants, certain broad directions of change seem most important if the associational revolution that is now under way is to become a permanent force for positive change.

Beyond Benign Neglect. First, there is a fundamental need to begin taking the third sector more seriously in public discussions, in policy debates, and in academic research. The nonprofit sector has arrived as a major actor on the world scene, but it has hardly arrived as a serious presence in public consciousness, in policy circles, in the media, or in the scholarly world. In much of Central and Eastern Europe and the developing world, even the legal basis of the third sector is unsettled, inhibiting the growth of organizations and their ability to attract support. Elsewhere, policies on this set of organizations are ill formed or undefined. And almost everywhere, basic information is grossly lacking, making it difficult to perceive the sector and gauge its scope or role. While there are important signs of change—such as the formation of the World Bank–NGO Committee and the recent launching of an International Society for Third-Sector Research—a tremendous amount remains to be done to make public and private leaders and the general public aware of this sector and of the tremendous potential it represents.[23]

Beyond Amateurism and "Feel-Good Philanthropy." For emerging third-sector organizations to be taken seriously by others, of course, they must take themselves seriously first. Among other things, this will require sensitivity to the trade-offs that exist between voluntarism and professionalism, between the informality that has given these organizations their special character and the institutionalization that is often necessary to translate individual victories into more permanent achievements. Evaluations of the performance of nongovernmental organizations in developing countries, for example, regularly credit these organizations with the ability to reach outlying communities, promote participation, innovate, and operate at low cost, but fault them for their limited replicability, lack of technical capacity, and isolation from broader policy considerations.[24] The failure to focus explicitly on institution-building has similarly been one of the major criticisms of the Harambee process in Kenya. Harambee projects tend to be effective, but ad hoc, leaving behind no continuing local organization capable of taking on additional tasks (Thomas 1987, 478).

To deal with this problem, managers of third-sector organizations will have to give more attention to training and technical assistance, and those providing support to these organizations will have to go beyond project grants to longer term institutional support. In the process, conceptions of these organizations as dispensers of "relief" or sponsors of occasional cultural events must give way to a recognition of their longer run development and social-change objectives. This means that the "feel-good philanthropy" that has tended to characterize particularly corporate involvement in many parts of the world, as typified by the "mesena," or cultural sponsorship, activities in parts of Europe, must give way to a philanthropy that encourages and allows nonprofit organizations to engage the central issues of their societies—like inner-city poverty, homelessness, AIDS, environmental degradation, and grinding third world poverty. The third sector has clearly come of age on the global scene, but it must find ways to strengthen its institutional capacities and contribute more meaningfully to the solution of major problems—all without losing its popular base or its flexibility and capacity for change.

Beyond the Paradigm of Conflict. One of the central determinants of the third sector's capacity to do this, paradoxically enough, will be the relationship it is able to forge with government. Despite the significant tensions that exist between the third sector and the state, and the sector's need to maintain a significant degree of independence from the state, the fact remains that the "paradigm of conflict" that has dominated the perception of government-nonprofit relations in much of the West has never accurately described the relationship that has existed in fact, and provides an increasingly unsatisfactory guide for the future. Where the "paradigm of conflict" posits an inherent conflict between the voluntary sector and the state, the reality in most of the West has been one of active cooperation instead. Even in the United States, as we have seen, government has long been a major source of support for private nonprofit organizations, outdistancing private charity by a substantial margin. This situation is even more pronounced elsewhere in the developed world. In the Netherlands, for example, 88 percent of nonprofit spending comes from government, and the figure in Sweden is almost as large. As economist Estelle James (1987, 407) has noted: "from the international perspective, reliance on nonprofit service provision and substantial government support go together . . . it appears that large nonprofit sectors cannot be long sustained without substantial government support." If anything, this situation is likely to be even more pronounced in most of the developing world. As one development theorist has put it: "It may well be that wildflowers grow by themselves. But grassroots organizations do not. They are cultivated, in large measure, by just policies and competent government agencies that do their job" (Annis 1987, 133). Advocates of "assisted self-reliance" in the developing world thus argue against *both* the fallacy of "paternalism," which involves exclusive reliance on the center to promote development, and the fallacy of "populism," which involves sole reliance on local grassroots groups. Similarly, in Eastern Europe, although the Stalinist regimes are in full retreat, it would be naive to assume that the substantial protections of the state in such fields as housing, education, and health care will be eliminated altogether. More likely is a pattern of cooperative action between the nonprofit sector and the state. What all this suggests is that government-nonprofit relations have become one of the most decisive determinants of third-sector growth and one of the central challenges of nonprofit management. The task for third-sector organizations is to find a modus vivendi with government that provides sufficient legal and financial support while preserving a meaningful degree of independence and autonomy. This can be done by mixing government support with other forms of assistance and by clarifying the ground rules under which cooperation with the state takes place.

Beyond the "Made in America" Syndrome. Finally, efforts must be made to appreciate the peculiar historical roots of the emerging third sector in different parts of the world. As we have seen, these roots are quite substantial, even in apparently underdeveloped institutional settings such as Africa, where the weakness of the national state has long obscured the existence of a vibrant associational life that predated the colonial era (Bratton 1989, 409). Unless this is recognized, serious mistakes can be made—for example, by failing to appreciate the negative connotations surrounding the term *filantropia* in much of Latin America, or overlooking the customarily close working relationships that exist between the corporate sector and the state in Japan and the likelihood that this will carry over into the philanthropic operations of Japanese corporations.[25]

For the leaders of emerging or reemerging nonprofit organizations, this extensive historical base creates a dilemma as well as an opportunity. Often tied to traditional power-wielders and traditional modes of operation, existing organizations can undermine the efforts to build new institutional arrangements geared to social and economic change. The task, therefore, is to find ways to utilize traditional ties and institutions, but mobilize them in support of new forms of action.

Conclusion

One hundred and fifty years ago, the Frenchman Alexis de Toqueville came to the United States to understand how democracy works. The most important prerequisite, he concluded, was a functioning set of private associations, what we would now term a private nonprofit sector. "Among the laws that rule human societies," de Toqueville observed, "there is one which seems to be more precise and clear than all others. If men are to remain civilized or to become so, the art of associating together must grow and improve in the same ratio in which the equality of condition is increased" (1835, 118).

A century and a half later a veritable "associational revolution" seems to be under way at the global level, as traditional institutional ties loosen and people become available for new forms of "associating together." The resulting surge of interest in nonprofit organizations opens gates to vast reservoirs of human talent and energy, even while it creates dangers of stalemate and dispute. While it is far from clear what all must be done to keep these gates open and allow the maximum number of people to pass through them, a crucial first step must certainly be to understand better the dramatic process that is under way and the immense challenges it entails. Even here, however, our work has just begun.

Notes

Introduction

1. The one major inquiry into the scope and structure of the nonprofit sector was launched in the early 1970s by John D. Rockefeller III. While usefully acknowledging the immense role of government in the financing of nonprofit activities, however, this inquiry focused chiefly on the need to expand the sector's private, philanthropic base. See Commission on Private Philanthropy and Public Needs (1975).

2. See, e.g., Rosenbaum (1981).

3. For a recent statement of some of these concerns, see Smith and Lipsky (1993).

Chapter 1: Rethinking Public Management

1. For further explication of this point see Salamon (1980).

2. U.S. Office of Management and Budget (1981, 254); U.S. Advisory Commission on Intergovernmental Relations (1977b, 25). Interestingly, the 1979 budget marks the first decline in the grant-in-aid share of the budget, and this downward trend is projected to continue. Thus the FY 1982 budget estimates that grants-in-aid will account for only 14 percent of FY 1982 outlays, compared to a high of 17.3 percent in FY 1978 (U.S. Office of Management and Budget 1981, 252).

3. U.S. Office of Management and Budget, FY 1981, Special Analyses, G, pp. 230–34; U.S. Congress, Joint Economic Committee (1974, 5). These estimates reflect orders of magnitude only because of uncertainty over the interactions that exist among various tax provisions.

4. The term "street-level bureaucrat" was used by Michael Lipsky to refer to the service providers who enjoy substantial operational autonomy in the delivery of local police, welfare, educational, and other services (see Lipsky 1971, 391–409).

5. See, e.g., U.S. Congress, Joint Economic Committee (1965).

6. One exception, which reviews the accountability problems resulting from increased public use of the private sector, is Smith (1975).

7. U.S. Interagency Council on Accident Compensation and Insurance (1979).

Chapter 2: Of Market Failure, Voluntary Failure, and Third-Party Government

1. For further details, see Salamon (1987a; chap. 7 below).

2. Nielsen (1979) criticizes conventional scholarship on the voluntary sector because of this tendency, though Nielsen himself also takes a generally critical stance toward government support to nonprofits. For one of the few early alternative views, see Pifer (1966).

3. For a more complete statement of the criteria for choosing among theories or models of different social or physical processes, see Salamon (1970).

4. Burton Weisbrod, the principal architect of this theory, does acknowledge the possibility of government subsidization of voluntary organizations, but this is treated as an exception, not as the core of our human service system (Weisbrod 1977, 66).

5. This reformulation is also more consistent with American traditions of freedom and individualism, which suggest that the creation of a sense of "social obligation" of the sort that is required to support collective action is best done on a voluntary basis and at the local or group level, where individuals can participate with their neighbors without sacrificing their freedom of choice (Schambra 1982). The more the fostering of a sense of social obligation moves away from this level, therefore, the more tenuous it becomes. Treating government, particularly the national government, as the first line of defense for the provision of needed collective goods, as is done in economic theory, is therefore to create a far less secure basis for the provision of these goods than voluntary action can provide. Only when voluntary action proves incapable, then, should government be called into action. Viewed from this perspective, government support to voluntary organizations, and government-nonprofit partnerships, emerge as the ideologically most palatable form that the government response to "voluntary failure" can take.

Chapter 3: What Is the Nonprofit Sector?

1. These organizations generally fall under two of the more than twenty sections of the Internal Revenue Code under which organizations can claim tax-exempt, or nonprofit, status: section 501(c)(3), which covers the primarily service-oriented agencies, and 501(c)(4), which covers primarily advocacy and lobbying-oriented organizations. The 501(c)(3) organizations are the only ones eligible to receive tax-deductible gifts. These two sections also cover churches, foundations, and other fund-raising organizations that are not of concern

here. Our focus, therefore, is on a subset of all 501(c)(3) and 501(c)(4) organizations—i.e., those that deliver services of a charitable, educational, or related character or are engaged in advocacy for these purposes.

2. "Service" here is defined broadly to include not just traditional services such as counseling, health care, day care, cultural events, or material assistance, but also information and referral, advocacy, and networking.

3. In the IRS data, for example, the Rockefeller Foundation is listed as a medical research institute instead of a foundation, the Carnegie Corporation is classified as an educational institution, and Loyola University of Chicago shows up as a church. Recently, this situation has been improved somewhat.

4. Chief among these was the list of organizations that had applied for exemption from payment of Social Security taxes, a privilege granted only to nonprofit firms.

5. Focusing on organizations with at least one paid employee, the Census survey identified 165,614 nonprofit service organizations as of 1977. Of these, 103,066 fall within the charitable, service-providing category of organizations of interest to us here. The remaining 62,548 organizations identified by the census survey included 23,418 labor unions, 1,123 political organizations, 16,618 business and professional associations, 7,386 other membership organizations, 446 business service organizations, 5,910 sports and recreation clubs, 3,096 organizational hotels and lodging houses, 826 sporting and recreational camps, and 3,725 other organizations. Taken together, the census identified $85.4 billion in expenditures by all nonprofit organizations as of 1977, of which $72.8 billion represented expenditures by what we have termed the public-benefit service portion of the nonprofit sector. See U.S. Bureau of the Census, *1977 Census of Service Industries: Other Service Industries* (January 1981). An update of this 1977 survey was conducted in 1982, but its coverage was far less complete.

6. The aging of the census data was done by assuming that all parts of the nonprofit sector other than the health care component grew at about the same rate as the gross domestic product, and that the health care component grew at about the same rate as overall health care expenditures. Because the large federal public sector employment program was created during this period and benefited nonprofits, a special modification was also introduced to accommodate it.

The IRS data were adjusted in three steps: First, using a tape of all 501(c)(3) and 501(c)(4) organizations provided by the IRS from its Exempt Organizations Master File, we deleted all organizations with activity codes suggesting they were not part of the charitable service component of the nonprofit sector of interest to us here. This adjustment reduced the total revenues of the sector from $215 billion on the raw IRS list to $174 billion, chiefly by deleting double counting. Second, to correct for miscoding among the remaining organizations, we examined the five hundred largest organizations individually and deleted those that should have been coded in the excluded codes and shifted those that were appropriately included but in the wrong category. As it turned out, organizations representing another $38.8 billion in revenues that should have been deleted were identified through this process; dropping them reduced the total revenues of the nonprofit sector from $174.1 billion to $135.3 billion.

Finally, a random sample of one thousand organizations was selected from the overall IRS file and the activity code listings for the entire file were adjusted in proportion to the miscoding found through an inspection of this random sample. For example, in our sample of one thousand organizations, several large hospitals were found coded as educational institutions. To correct for this, an equivalent share of the total revenue of the set of organizations found in this activity code was allocated to the health care subsector. Similarly, numerous foundations, federated funding agents, Blue Cross organizations, business associations, and other organizations that lay outside our area of interest were discovered, and proportionate adjustments made to delete these from the overall totals as well. This final adjustment reduced the total revenues reported by another $6.7 billion, to $128.6 billion, which represents our best estimate of the size of the charitable and educational nonprofit service sector as it is portrayed in the IRS 990 data.

7. These data on the share of nonprofit income coming from private giving find confirmation in a survey we have done of some 3,400 nonprofit agencies exclusive of hospitals and higher education institutions. What these data reveal is that, as of 1981, private giving accounted, on average, for only 20 percent of the income of these agencies. By contrast, these agencies received 40 percent of their income from government and 28 percent from fees. For further details see Salamon (1984a) and chapter 4.

Chapter 4: The Nonprofit Sector at the Local Level

1. One reason for this is that large numbers of nonprofit organizations simply do not show up on the national registers. A preliminary comparison of the Internal Revenue Service's Exempt Organization Master File (EOMF) for a handful of jurisdictions to listings built up from local sources revealed, for example, that there were approximately 25 percent more agencies in existence than the EOMF indicated, many of them quite massive institutions.

2. I am indebted particularly to Dr. Michael Gutowski, Dr. Carol De Vita, and Dr. Jaana Myllyluoma for assistance with this survey work.

3. In seventeen previous studies of the nonprofit sector that we reviewed, samples rarely exceeded 1,000 agencies, and survey response rates typically averaged below 30 percent. In two of the surveys most comparable to the one reported here in terms of sample size and depth of analysis, response rates of less than 15 percent were achieved.

4. For a fuller elaboration of the results of this survey, and of a follow-up survey conducted in 1990–91, see Salamon (1995).

Chapter 5: The Federal Budget and Nonprofit Revenues

1. For further elaboration of this point, see chapter 1.

2. For a statement of the consensus view, see Commission on Private Philanthropy and Public Needs (1975). For further evidence on the consequences of nonprofit federalism, see chapter 7. For a discussion of the theory of government-nonprofit relations, see chapter 2.

3. Specific provisions for state contracting out to nonprofit organizations were included in the original proposals advanced for federal social service funding by the Kennedy administration in 1962, but the provisions had to be abandoned when religious groups expressed concern about constitutional prohibitions against federal support of religiously affiliated social service agencies. These objections were dropped in 1967 and the provisions added.

4. I am indebted to Dr. Alan Abramson for assistance with this work. For a more detailed discussion of the estimating procedure, see Salamon and Abramson (1981). Included in the figures on federal support to nonprofits is the federal subsidy to nonprofits through reduced mail rates. The total federal mail rate subsidy has been apportioned among the various types of nonprofit organizations according to estimates based in part on U.S. Postal Service studies.

5. This finding is consistent with the estimates developed by the Commission on Private Philanthropy and Public Needs (the Filer Commission) in 1974. According to these estimates, all public support to the nonprofit sector (including state and local as well as federal government support) totaled $23.1 billion in 1974, compared with a total of $13.6 billion in private giving to nonprofits excluding churches and other religious organizations. See Rudney (1977).

6. Private giving appears to outdistance federal support only for educational and cultural organizations, but in both these cases the private giving figure is swelled by the inclusion of the full value of bequests and appreciated assets in the year in which they are given even though they are not available for use.

Chapter 6: The Government-Nonprofit Partnership in Local Welfare Regimes

1. For a detailed discussion of the methodology used, see Musselwhite, Katz, and Salamon (1985). I am indebted to Dr. James Musselwhite for his invaluable assistance in supervising the collection and assembly of the data reported here.

2. For a more general argument along these lines, see Salamon (1989).

Chapter 7: The Scope of Government-Nonprofit Relations

1. For further details on this work, see chapters 4 and 6.

2. The data reported here cover only the central city/county of each site,

not the entire standard metropolitan statistical area. In the case of the Twin Cities area of Minnesota, data are reported separately on Hennepin and Ramsey counties.

3. Using the medians, nonprofits account for 36 percent of all spending, government for 41 percent, and for-profits for 20 percent.

4. The estimate of the share of the tax expenditures attributable to religious organizations is based on the assumption that 46 percent of all private giving flows to religious congregations, but that itemizers (who alone receive the tax deduction) give a smaller proportion of their total charitable contributions to religious congregations than do nonitemizers.

5. The distribution of funds shown in table 7.3 differs from that in table 7.1 because table 7.3 reports estimated receipts by type of organization and some programs distribute funds to several different types of organizations. This is particularly true of the employment and training program, which channeled funds to employment and training, social service, community development, and arts organizations.

6. For further details on the derivation of these estimates, see chapter 3, n. 6.

7. Using a different approach, Rudney (1982) estimates total government support for nonreligious nonprofits in 1980 at 35 percent.

Chapter 8: The Government-Nonprofit Partnership in Practice

1. Until recently, for example, little private support was available for inner-city minority organizations, particularly those with an advocacy mission. In recent years, many local United Way and corporate donors have insisted that agencies raise more of their funds from fees and charges and make other management changes, such as merging with other organizations. In addition, many foundations have standing policies against ongoing institutional support, which makes it necessary for nonprofit organizations to generate successive "novel" or "experimental" programs to attract foundation support.

2. This changed somewhat in 1982 with the adoption of the diagnostic-related group (DRG) system of reimbursement, under which the federal government has fixed the amount it will pay under Medicare for treatment of certain ailments and thus created incentives for hospitals to reduce costs.

Chapter 9: The Charitable Behavior of the Charitable Sector

I would like to express my appreciation to Dr. Jaana Myllyluoma for invaluable assistance in developing the data reported here.

1. This usage is close to the concept of "social services" originally embodied in the Federal Title XX program (now renamed the Social Service Block Grant Program). Under this program social services were defined as any activities that helped to support five broad goals: (1) economic self-support; (2) self-sufficiency; (3) protective care for children or adults; (4) prevention of institu-

tionalization; or (5) provision of services to help people in institutions (Wickenden 1976, 572). In the first year of implementation of this program, states specified 1,313 different services that fell within these five broad goals. These were subsequently grouped into no fewer than forty-one different Title XX service categories, including adoption assistance, case management, chore services, counseling, day care, education and training services, family planning, foster care, information and referral, legal services, protective services, provision of meals, recreational services, residential care, special services for the handicapped or disadvantaged, sheltered workshops, and vocational rehabilitation (Gilbert and Specht 1981, 4). This concept is considerably narrower than what the Social Security Administration covers in its "social welfare services" data series. In addition to the human service programs covered here, the Social Security definition also includes social security, unemployment insurance, Medicare, Medicaid, welfare assistance, education, veterans' programs, and related assistance (Bixby 1990, 11).

2. The term "charitable nonprofit service sector" is used here to refer to organizations exempt from taxation under section 501(c)(3) of the Internal Revenue Code that are engaged in the provision of other-than-religious services. These organizations are not only themselves exempt from taxation but are also eligible to receive tax-exempt gifts from individuals and corporations to pursue "charitable, educational, scientific" and related purposes. Not included are business and professional associations or membership associations. Also excluded are non–service-providing 501(c)(3) organizations such as foundations (which provide financial support to other nonprofits) and sacramental religious congregations and churches.

3. Data on nonprofit expenditures here are computed from Hodgkinson and Weitzman (1987, 183). Data on government spending are computed from Bixby (1990, 18–19). Data on primary metals and aviation are from U.S. Bureau of the Census (1989b, 422). The picture of the nonprofit human service sector presented here is somewhat incomplete because social services are delivered by many other types of organizations as well. Thus, counseling is often provided directly by hospitals, which have also recently moved into the field of home health. Employment and training, considered a form of social service, is also provided by training institutes and community colleges. Similarly, numerous churches operate day care centers that do not show up as separately incorporated nonprofits. The $37 billion in estimated human service agency expenditures thus probably understates the size of the nonprofit human service industry.

4. United Way of America, for example, regularly solicits information on the clientele served by the agencies to which its local chapters provide support, but information is collected on only three client characteristics—age, sex, and race. Data on client income are not solicited. What is more, the data collected apply to "programs," not to actual recipients of services. In other words, United Way asks what the primary client focus is of the various programs its local affiliates are funding in terms of these three client characteristics, but it

does not ask who is actually served. Since many programs do not have a primary client focus, however, the results turn out to be fairly ambiguous even in these limited terms. Thus, in the 1988 *Funds Distribution Profile* (United Way 1990, 66, 69, 72), we learn that 10 percent of United Way service dollars went to support programs specially targeted on the aged, but 57 percent went for programs open to all age groups. What we do not learn is how many aged people were actually served by these latter programs. Similarly, we learn that 11 percent of all dollars went for programs targeted to blacks, but 53 percent went for programs open to persons of all races with no indication of how many blacks are served by these latter programs.

Similar problems exist with the client surveys regularly conducted by Catholic Charities USA, another large federation of human service agencies. For example, the *1989 Annual Survey Report* (Catholic Charities USA 1990) reports that Catholic Charities agencies throughout the United States provided eleven different types of services that touched 9,123,337 persons in 1989, including 2.4 million children, 5.4 million adults, and 1.3 million elderly. While it is possible to infer from the services they received what income level at least some of these individuals were in, income data were not collected on the clients. Nor is any attempt made to assess the different service efforts represented by the different agency activities—for example, the provision of food to 3,895,340 persons compared to the provision of counseling to 599,374 persons. While it is possible to assess the number of people touched by the Catholic Charities network, therefore, it is extremely difficult to work out the distributional consequences of the network's activities.

5. For more detail on this survey and its results, see Salamon (1995).

6. The actual question read as follows: "Please estimate the percentage of your clients who fall into the following major target groups:

_____% working class	_____% single parents
_____% income below poverty	_____% disabled
_____% women	_____% unemployed
	_____% ex-offenders"

The "% income below poverty" is the variable used here. Throughout this chapter, I use the terms "poor" and "low income" to refer to the clients with "income below poverty."

7. For the purposes of this chapter, we focus on a subset of the agencies covered by this survey. In particular, we exclude from the analysis the agencies primarily engaged in arts, culture, and recreation since these agencies typically provide services that lie outside the human service field of prinicpal concern to us here. In addition, we focus here only on those respondents to both rounds of our survey that actually responded to the question about the percentage of their clientele who are poor. These two exclusions leave us with a sample of 1,474 agencies. Excluding agencies that failed to indicate what proportion of their clients are poor probably overstates somewhat the extent

of poverty focus within the nonprofit human service sector since the agencies that failed to respond to this question are most likely to have few poor clients. Had these agencies been included in the analysis, therefore, it would have reduced considerably the percentage of agencies with significant proportions of low-income clients.

8. This general conclusion is consistent with the results of a series of surveys conducted by Family Services of America, a network of some two hundred family service agencies throughout the United States. Although the most recent FSA client data that are available cover only 1970, they are quite revealing. In particular, FSA reported that in 1970 only 10 percent of the white clients and 35 percent of the nonwhite clients of FSA's local affiliates had incomes below the official poverty line (Beck and Jones 1973, 29). This was somewhat higher than for the population at large (7 percent and 25 percent, respectively), but not overwhelmingly so. More generally, after combining measures of income, education, and occupational status, FSA found that only 20 percent of the clients of its member agencies fell in the bottom third of the socioeconomic status index. Similarly a study of the service offerings of over a thousand private social welfare agencies conducted by Michael Sosin in twelve communities in the early 1980s reached a similar conclusion. Sosin (1986), too, found that relatively few human service nonprofits focused on the most pressing needs of the poor. In particular, only 13.5 percent of the agencies offered material assistance, compared to 34 percent that offered individual or family counseling, 22 percent that offered recreation, and 20 percent that offered information and referral.

9. This is similar to the so-called ecological fallacy in social or political research, in which characteristics of individuals are erroneously attributed to the social units (neighborhoods, voting districts, counties, etc.) of which they are a part.

10. Median income levels in the four rural counties averaged some 16 percent below those in the urban areas, and the share of the population eligible for public assistance in the rural counties averaged 35 percent higher.

11. These data utilize an approach similar to that used in compiling the data in table 9.5. In particular, lacking any basis for allocating different sources of income differently among agency clientele, we assumed that agencies allocated all of their sources of income equally among the clients served by the agency. Because agencies differ in size and have different revenue structures as well as different client focuses, however, important differences emerge in the extent to which different income sources support services for the poor once the results for all the agencies are aggregated. These aggregated results are reported in table 9.8.

12. This observation applies principally to the federal tax structure, rather than state or local taxes. Since about 70 percent of government human service spending comes from the federal government, this caveat probably alters the overall point only slightly.

13. See n. 9.

Chapter 10: The Reagan Revolution and Nonprofit Organizations

1. These included provisions to soften the "payout" requirements facing foundations, to liberalize the treatment of charitable contributions of appreciated property, and to permit taxpayers who take the standard deduction to claim "above the line" deductions for charitable contributions. The payout requirement in the 1969 tax act stipulated that private foundations must pay out in grants either the full value of their earnings or 5 percent of their assets, whichever was higher.

2. I am indebted to Dr. Alan J. Abramson for assistance in developing these data.

3. "Programs in fields where nonprofits are active" includes all programs for which changes in the funding levels are judged to have direct implications either for the demand for nonprofit services or for the revenues of nonprofit organizations. For a fuller discussion, see Salamon and Abramson (1982a, 22–25).

4. Because agencies frequently do not know which level of government is the actual source of the government funds they receive, the figures reported here are for all levels of government.

5. The survey results also compare 1982 agency receipts to 1981 levels rather than the 1980 levels used as a baseline for the earlier budget discussion.

6. This conclusion finds support as well in the data on national patterns of private giving as of 1983. According to these data, nonreligious private giving increased from $26 billion to $33.9 billion between 1980 and 1983. After adjusting for inflation, this represents a real increase of $2.05 billion, or 8 percent. Of this total, almost half represents contributions to hospitals and other health providers, leaving an increase of $1.07 billion for all other nonreligious organizations. By comparison, between FY 1980 and FY 1983 we estimate that federal government support for these same types of nonprofits declined by $4.2 billion. In other words, with these data, it appears that private giving made up for about one-fourth of the projected government cuts experienced by nonprofit service organizations outside of hospitals. Although some portion of the increased religious giving that occurred during this period may also have found its way to these organizations, the overall picture from the national giving estimates still seems highly consistent with our more detailed survey results. See AAFRC (1984).

Chapter 11: The Impact of the 1981 Tax Act on Individual Charitable Giving

This chapter is a revised version of "The Federal Government and the Nonprofit Sector: The Impact of the 1981 Tax Act on Individual Charitable Giving," August 1981, coauthored with Charles T. Clotfelter, Duke University. The study benefited greatly from the programming assistance of Melodie Feather and Keith Fontenot, the helpful comments of Michael Moorman and

Randall Weiss, and the production skills of Harriett Page, Janet Haynes, and Ellen McLamb. Research support was provided by Independent Sector and the Institute for Research in Social Science, University of North Carolina at Chapel Hill.

1. Data on the expenditures of the nonprofit sector in 1977 are from U.S. Census Bureau (1981, 53-1-3). Data on nonreligious private giving from AAFRC (1981).

2. Under previous law, foundations were required to pay out each year 5 percent of their assets or all of their earnings, whichever is larger. The 1981 law removed the "whichever is larger" clause, permitting a maximum 5 percent pay-out even when revenues exceed 5 percent.

3. Under the 1981 law, in 1982 and 1983, 25 percent of the first $100 of gifts was made deductible for nonitemizers. The amount was to increase to 25 percent of the first $300 in 1984, 50 percent without limit in 1985, and all contributions in 1986.

4. See, e.g., Taussig (1967), Schwartz (1970), Feldstein (1975), Morgan, Dye, and Hybels (1977), and Clotfelter and Steurle (1981).

5. In fact, the above-the-line charitable deduction was canceled in the 1986 tax act.

6. The deduction for nonitemizers in 1982 and 1983 was limited to $100 of gifts, which is below the mean projected giving for nonitemizers at every income level. In 1984, however, the limit was raised to $300 and most nonitemizers were projected to give less than $300 without additional incentive. For a discussion of simulating nonlinear rules, see Feldstein and Lindsey (1981).

7. In 1975 dollars of net income, Clotfelter and Steurle (1981, 428) present elasticities of $4,000–$10,000: −9.45 and 0.393; $10,000–$20,000: −1.346 and 0.621; $20,000–$50,000: −1.657 and 0.364; $50,000–$100,000: −1.360 and 0.668; and $100,000 and over: −1.779 and 1.089.

8. Where R is the odds of itemizing, the proportion of itemizers is $R/(1 + R)$.

9. For a more complete treatment of the maximum tax, see Lindsey (1981).

10. Earned income may include more or less than 30 percent of business-related income, depending on whether the income is professional and the extent of capital used. The 30 percent figure is used as a baseline in the tax code for dividing business-related income in many cases. The proportion of earned income for the top six income brackets in 1978 was 0.86, 0.71, 0.63, 0.51, 0.36, and 0.23.

11. For a comparison of estimates from different studies, see Clotfelter and Steurle (1981).

12. Although more recent data on giving by individuals have been collected, no other survey interviewed such a large number of households (about 1,900 in all), particularly high-income households, as did the 1973 University of Michigan survey. The Michigan study found that average contribution levels for nonitemizers generally rose with income. Averages for nonitemizers

with incomes over $30,000 are less precise, however, because of the small number of nonitemizers with high incomes. In order to account for the high variability at the upper end, the figures were smoothed by extending the $20,000–$30,000 average up one bracket and simply averaging the figures for the $50,000–$200,000 and above classes together.

These income brackets were then inflated by the growth in the GNP price deflator between 1973 and 1978 (141%), the average giving estimates were inflated by the rate of growth of per capita itemized charitable contributions between 1973 and 1978 (154%), and the resulting averages were interpolated to yield averages for the 1978 income brackets used in the statistics of income.

13. In the IRS tabulations, "other charitable organizations" included such organizations as community chests, American Red Cross, American Cancer Association; while "other organizations" include "literary educational, and scientific foundations, libraries, museums, and zoos" (U.S. IRS 1962, 8).

Chapter 12: Government and the Voluntary Sector in an Era of Retrenchment

1. For further details on the scope and structure of the nonprofit sector at the local level in the United States, see Grønbjerg, Kimmich, and Salamon (1984); Gutowski, Salamon, and Pittman (1984); Harder, Kimmich, and Salamon (1985); Lukermann, Kimmich, and Salamon (1984); and other reports of the Urban Institute Nonprofit Sector Project.

2. By the early 1980s, almost three-fourths of all taxpayers were using the standard deduction rather than itemizing deductions for tax purposes.

Chapter 13: The Voluntary Sector and the Future of the Welfare State

1. This shift is consistent with the "drift toward universalism" discussed by Gilbert (1983).

Chapter 14: The Marketization of Welfare

1. In this chapter I draw on material developed in greater length in Salamon (1992).

2. Compiled from data in Bixby (1988, 22, 29).

3. Computed from data in Hodgkinson and Weitzman (1989, 164–77).

4. Data on day care and social service agencies from U.S. Census Bureau (1981, vol. 2, pt. 1, tables 2 and 3); data on hospitals from American Hospital Association (1978, 6–9).

5. Computed from data in Bixby (1988, 23–26), and Bixby (1983, 10–12). Adjusted for inflation using implicit price deflators for personal consumption expenditures.

6. Based on data in Bixby (1991, 10–19).

7. Author's computations based on data in Hodgkinson et al. (1992, 147–48). For further details, see Salamon (1992).

8. Nonprofit organizations generally play a smaller role among specialty hospitals, e.g., psychiatric, tuberculosis, chronic disease, and rehabilitation hospitals. Among this last group, nonprofit firms account for only 28 percent of the institutions and 14 percent of the beds. American Hospital Association (1991, tables 2A and 2B).

9. Of this total, about one-third represented government public health activities, which include local public health screening and the federal government's Public Health Service and Centers for Disease Control. An even larger share (43%) went for outpatient clinics (e.g., kidney dialysis centers, drug treatment centers, and rehabilitation centers). This component bears strong resemblance to the short-term specialty institutions that are gaining ground within the hospital industry, except that these facilities are tailored to "outpatient" care. Another 8 percent of this portion of health care spending was allocated for the relatively new field of home health care (i.e., skilled nursing or medical care provided in the home), a field that has some resemblance to traditional social services. Finally, the remaining 20 percent went for other personal health services such as drug abuse treatment and school health. Computed from data in Office of National Cost Estimates (1990). For further details, see Salamon (1992).

10. Based on data in Office of National Cost Estimates (1990, 30).

11. Computed from data in U.S. Census Bureau (1981), and U.S. Census Bureau (1989a, table 1B, US-13).

12. Data on health spending from Office of National Cost Estimates (1990, table 15, 30). No data series comparable to that for education or health spending is available on social services spending. The estimate of social services spending reported hence was constructed by adding data on revenues of nonprofit and for-profit social service organizations provided in the *1987 Census of Service Industries* (see n. 11) to an estimate of the revenues of direct government social service providers. The latter was developed by subtracting from total government social services expenditures the amount of government support to nonprofit social services agencies reported in Hodgkinson and Weitzman (1989, 177), and an estimate of government support to for-profit social service providers. The latter was calculated assuming that for-profit providers received proportionally half as much government support as their size in relationship to nonprofit providers might suggest. For further detail, see Salamon (1992).

13. For-profit providers accounted for 36 percent of the agencies, 14 percent of the employees, and 12 percent of the revenues. The balance represented government agencies. Data on government agencies are from Bixby (1983, 10);and Bixby (1990, 18–20). Data on government employment in public welfare are from U.S. Census Bureau (1990, 300), and (1979, 313). Data on private establishments, employment, and revenues are from U.S. Census Bureau (1981 and 1989a). Estimates of revenue growth are probably over-

stated because 1977 data refer to expenditures only and 1987 data include all revenues. For further details, see Salamon (1992).

14. Based on data in n. 13.

15. Author's estimates based on data in Hodgkinson et al. (1992).

16. Only facilities with twenty-five or more beds are included here. See Strahan (1984).

17. These data are from the U.S. Census Bureau (1981 and 1989a). The Census definition of nursing homes differs slightly from that in the Inventory of Long-Term Care Places (ILTCP) carried out for the National Center for Health Statistics, and that used in the National Master Facility Inventory (NMFI). Despite these technical differences, the broad trends and differences identified here are still valid. For further elaboration, see (Salamon 1992).

18. These efforts are analyzed in Gilbert (1984, 66–67); and Weisbrod (1989).

19. These arguments are outlined forcefully in Kotler (1982); and Drucker (1990).

Chapter 15: The Global Associational Revolution

1. See, e.g., U.S. Agency for International Development (1990, 3).

2. Quoted in Owen (1964, 89).

3. For an example of the conservative tendency to downplay the continued role of the nonprofit sector, see Nisbet (1962). On the continued strength of the nonprofit sector despite the rise of the modern welfare state, see Salamon (1987a, 99–117); Anheier (1992, 31–56); Stein Kuhnle and Per Selle (1992, 75–99).

4. Interview with Valery Nikolaev, Executive Director, Foundation for Social Innovations, Baltimore, Maryland, May 5, 1990.

5. For further elaboration on these defining features, see Salamon and Anheier (1992b).

6. Statement to the Interphil Conference on Nonprofit Organizations in Central Europe, Budapest, Hungary, June, 1989.

7. "A New Wind in Africa," *New York Times*, 1990.

8. Durning (1989, 11); Huntington (1991, 75–79); Smith (1990, 82–83 and 232–33).

9. Smith (1990, 59–68, 112–19, 159–61); Drabek (1987, x); Brodhead (1987, 2–5); Fox (1987, 11–12).

10. Cernea (1988, 29–32, 44–45); Williams (1990, 33); Qureshi (1988).

11. Quoted in Brenton (1985, 143).

12. Quoted in Grindheim and Selle (1989, 5).

13. Yanagitsubo and Agustin (1989); Thomas (1987, 464); El-Baz (1992, 13); Personal Interview, Dr. M. A. A. El-Banna, Ministry of Social Affairs, Cairo, Egypt, January 20, 1992.

14. Personal Interview, Genady Alferenko, Moscow, September 30, 1989.

15. On the varied pattern of welfare state development, see Flora (1986, x–xxix).

16. Johnson (1987, 38–40); Heclo (1981, 383–406); OECD (1981).

17. United Nations (1990, 14–15); United Nations Development Programme (UNDP) (1990, 5).

18. Lewis (1987a, 9). See also Uphoff (1987, 47–60).

19. Qureshi (1988, 2).

20. See, e.g., Aga Khan Foundation (1987, 13); OECD (1989, 77).

21. Between 1961 and 1973, the average annual rate of gross domestic product (GDP) growth, after adjusting for inflation, was 5.0 percent for the developed market economies, 7.0 percent for Eastern Europe and the USSR, and 6.1 percent for the developing countries. U.N. (1990, 32).

22. Nisbet (1962).

23. Three other recent examples of efforts to increase awareness of the nonprofit sector at the global level are the Aga Khan Foundation's "Enabling Environment" conference in 1986, the European Foundation Center's New Europe Conference in 1992, and the Johns Hopkins Comparative Nonprofit Sector Project described in Salamon and Anheier (1992a).

24. See, e.g., Cernea (1988, 18–20).

25. Council on Foundations, "Symposium on the Status of Philanthropy in Latin America and the Caribbean," San Juan, Puerto Rico, February 24–26, 1988; Baron (1989, 4–5).

References

Abramson, Alan, and Salamon, Lester M. 1986. *The Nonprofit Sector and the New Federal Budget*. Washington, D.C.: Urban Institute Press.

Aga Khan Foundation. 1987. "The Nairobi Statement." Report of the Enabling Environment Conference: Effective Private Sector Contribution to Development in Sub-Saharan Africa, Nairobi, Kenya. Geneva: Aga Khan Foundation.

American Association of Fund-Raising Counsel (AAFRC). 1981. *Giving U.S.A. 1982 Annual Report*. New York: American Association of Fund-Raising Counsel.

———. 1984, 1985, 1990. *Giving USA*. New York: American Association of Fund-Raising Counsel.

American Hospital Association. *Hospital Statistics*. Various years. Chicago: American Hospital Association.

Anheier, Helmut. 1992. "An Elaborate Network: Profiling the Third Sector in Germany." In *Government and the Third Sector: Emerging Relationships in Welfare States*, ed. Benjamin Gidron, Ralph M. Kramer, and Lester M. Salamon. San Francisco: Jossey-Bass, pp. 31–56.

Anheier, Helmut, Rudney, Gabriel, and Salamon, Lester M. 1992. "The Nonprofit Sector in the U.N. System of National Accounts." *Working Papers of the Johns Hopkins Comparative Nonprofit Sector Project*. Baltimore: Johns Hopkins Institute for Policy Studies.

Annis, Sheldon. 1987. "Can Small-Scale Development Be a Large-Scale Policy? The Case of Latin America." In *Development Alternatives: The Challenge For NGOs. World Development*, vol. 15, supplement, ed. Anne Gordon Drabek, pp. 129–34.

———. 1988. "What Is Not the Same about the Urban Poor: The Case of Mexico City." In Lewis 1987b, pp. 133–48.

Baron, Barnett. 1989. "An Overview of Organized Private Philanthropy in East and Southeast Asia." Paper prepared for Delivery at the John D. Rockefeller 150th Anniversary Conference, Pocantico Hills, N.Y.

Beck, Bertram M. 1971. "Government Contracts with Nonprofit Social Welfare Corporations." In *The Dilemma of Accountability in Modern Government*, ed. Bruce L. R. Smith and D. C. Hague. New York: St. Martin's Press, pp. 213–38.

Beck, Dorothy Fahs, and Jones, Mary Ann. 1973. *Progress on Family Problems: A Nationwide Study of Clients' and Counselor's Views on Family Agency Services*. New York: Family Service Association of America.

Bell, Daniel. 1988 [1960]. *The End of Ideology: On the Exhaustion of Political Ideas in the Fifties*. Cambridge: Harvard University Press.

Benton, Bill, Field, Tracey, and Millar, Rhonda. 1978. *Social Services: Federal Legislation vs. State Implementation*. Washington, D.C.: Urban Institute Press.

Berger, Peter L., and Neuhaus, Richard J. 1977. *To Empower People: The Role of Mediating Structures in Public Policy*. Washington, D.C.: American Enterprise Institute for Public Policy Research.

Berger, Renee. 1984. "Private Sector Initiatives in the Reagan Era: New Actors Rework an Old Theme." In *Reagan Presidency and the Governing of America*, ed. Lester M. Salamon and Michael Lund. Washington, D.C.: Urban Institute Press, pp. 181–211.

Berman, P. 1978. "The Study of Macro and Micro Implementation of Social Policy." *Public Policy* 26, no. 2, pp. 157–84.

Billis, David. 1989. "Unravelling the Metaphors." Paper prepared for delivery at the International Conference on Voluntarism, Nongovernmental Organizations, and Public Policy, Jerusalem.

Binder, Advid. 1989. "At Confessional East Berlin Congress: An Absolute Break with Stalinism." *New York Times*, December 18.

Bixby, Ann Kallman. 1983. "Social Welfare Expenditures, Fiscal Year 1980." *Social Security Bulletin* 46, no. 8, pp. 9–18.

———. 1988. "Public Social Welfare Expenditures, Fiscal Year 1985." *Social Security Bulletin* 51, no. 4, pp. 21–31.

———. 1990. "Public Social Welfare Expenditures, Fiscal Years 1965–1987," *Social Security Bulletin* 53, no. 2 (February), pp. 10–26.

———. 1991. "Public Social Welfare Expenditures, Fiscal Year 1990." *Social Security Bulletin*, 54, no. 10, pp. 10–19.

Bolling, Landrum R. 1982. *Private Foreign Aid: U.S. Philanthropy for Relief and Development*. Boulder: Westview Press.

Boulding, K. E., and Pfaff, M. 1972. *Redistribution to the Rich and the Poor: The Grants Economics of Income Distribution*. Belmont, Calif.: Wadsworth Publishing.

Brandt, Lillian. 1907. *The Charity Organization Society of the City of New York: 1882–1907*. 25th Annual Report. New York: Charity Organization Society.

Bratton, Michael. 1989. "Beyond the State: Civil Society and Associational Life in Africa." *World Politics* 41 (April), pp. 407–30.

Brenton, Maria. 1985. *The Voluntary Sector in British Social Services*. London: Longman.

Brodhead, Tim. 1987. "NGOs: In One Year, Out the Other?" *World Development* 15, supplement (August), pp. 2–5.

Butler, Stuart. 1980. *Philanthropy in America: The Need for Action*. Washington, D.C.: Heritage Foundation and Institute for Research on the Economics of Taxation.

———. 1985. *Privatizing Federal Spending: A Strategy to Eliminate the Deficit*. New York: Universe Books.

Catholic Charities USA. 1990. *1989 Annual Survey Report*. Washington, D.C.: Catholic Charities USA.

Cernea, Michael. 1987. "Farmer Organizations and Institution Building for Sustainable Development." *Regional Development Dialogue* 8, no. 2 (Summer), pp. 1–19.

———. 1988. "Nongovernmental Organizations and Local Development." *World Bank Discussion Papers, No. 40*. Washington, D.C.: World Bank.

Chase, G. 1979. "Implementing a Human Services Program: How Hard Will It Be?" *Public Policy* 27, no. 4 (Fall), pp. 385–435.

Clotfelter, Charles T. 1990. "The Impact of Tax Reform on Charitable Giving: A 1989 Perspective." In *Do Taxes Matter?* ed. Joel Slemrod. Cambridge: MIT Press, pp. 203–35.

Clotfelter, Charles T., and Salamon, Lester M. 1982. "The Impact of the 1981 Tax Act on Individual Charitable Giving." *National Tax Journal* 35 (June), pp. 171–87.

Clotfelter, Charles T., and Steurle, C. Eugene. 1981. "Charitable Contributions." In *How Taxes Affect Economic Behavior*, ed. Henry Aaron and Joseph Pechman. Washington, D.C.: Brookings Institution, pp. 403–66.

Cloward, Richard A., and Epstein, I. 1965. "Private Social Welfare's Disengagement from the Poor: The Case of Family Adjustment Agencies." In Zald 1965, pp. 623–43.

Commission on Private Philanthropy and Public Needs. 1975. *Giving in America: Toward a Stronger Voluntary Sector*. Washington, D.C.: Commission on Private Philanthropy and Public Needs.

Crimmins, Lawrence. 1985. *Enterprise in the Nonprofit Sector*. Washington, D.C.: Partners for Livable Places.

Dahl, R., and Lindblom, C. E. 1953. *Politics, Economics, and Welfare*. New York: Harper and Row.

DeHoog, Ruth Hoogland. 1985. "Human Services Contracting: Environmental, Behavioral and Organizational Conditions." *Administration and Society* 16, pp. 427–54.

Dess, Gregory C., and Beard, Donald W. 1984. "Dimensions of Organizational Task Environment." *Administrative Science Quarterly* 29 (March), pp. 52–73.

de Toqueville, Alexis. [1835] 1945. *Democracy in America*. The Henry Reeves Text. Vol. 2. New York: Vintage Books.

Deutsch, Karl. 1963. *The Nerves of Government: Models of Political Communication and Control*. New York: Free Press.

De Vita, Carol, and Salamon, Lester M. 1987. "Commercial Activities in Nonprofit Human Service Organizations." Paper presented at the Independent Sector Spring Research Forum, New York City (March 19–20).

Drabek, Anne Gordon. 1987. "Development Alternatives: The Challenge for NGOs—An Overview of Issues." *World Development* 15, Supplement (August), pp. ix–xv.

Dripps, Robert D. 1915. "The Policy of State Aid to Private Charities." In *Proceedings of the 42nd National Conference of Charities and Corrections.* Chicago: Hildman Printing, pp. 458–73.

Drucker, Peter. 1969. "The Sickness of Government." *The Public Interest* (Winter), no. 14, pp. 3–23.

———. 1990. *Managing the Nonprofit Organization.* New York: Harper-Collins.

Durning, Alan. 1989. "Action at the Grass Roots: Fighting Poverty and Environmental Decline." *Worldwatch Paper 88.* Washington, D.C.: Worldwatch Institute.

Egan, John, Carr, John, Mott, Andrew, and Roos, John. 1981. *Housing and Public Policy: A Role for Mediating Structures.* Cambridge, Mass.: Ballinger Publishing Company.

Elazar, Daniel J. 1962. *American Partnership: Intergovernmental Cooperation in Nineteenth Century United States.* Chicago: University of Chicago Press.

———. 1972. *American Federalism: The View from the States,* 2nd edition. New York: Thomas Y. Crowell.

El-Baz, Shahida A. 1992. "Historical and Institutional Development of Arab NGOs." Paper prepared for delivery at the Third International Conference on Research on Voluntary and Nonprofit Organizations, Indianapolis (March 15).

Etzioni, A. 1964. *Modern Organization.* Englewood Cliffs, N.J.: Prentice-Hall.

Feldstein, Martin. 1975. "The Income and Charitable Contributions: Part I— Aggregate and Distribution Effects." *National Tax Journal* 28, no. 1, pp. 81–100.

Feldstein, Martin, and Lindsey, Lawrence. 1981. "Simulating Nonlinear Tax Rules and Nonstandard Behavior: An Application to the Tax Treatment of Charitable Contributions." Working Paper No. 682. Washington, D.C.: National Bureau of Economic Research.

Fetter, Frank. 1901–2. "The Subsidizing of Private Charities." *American Journal of Sociology,* pp. 359–85.

Fisher, Julie. 1987. "Micropolitics: Third World Development Organizations and the Evolution of Pluralism." Paper prepared for the International Symposium on the Nonprofit Sector and the Welfare State, Bad Honef, Germany (June 10–13).

Fitch, L. D. 1974. "Increasing the Role of the Private Sector in Providing Public Services." In *Improving the Quality of Urban Management,* ed. W. D. Hawley and D. Rogers. Beverly Hills: Sage Publications, pp. 264–306.

Fleisher, A. 1914. "State Money and Privately Managed Charities." *Survey* 33, pp. 110–12.

Flora, Peter. 1986. "Introduction." In *Growth to Limits: The Western European Welfare States since World War II.* Vol. 1, ed. Peter Flora. Berlin: Walter de-Gruyter, pp. x–xxix.

Fox, Thomas H. 1987. "NGOs from the United States." *World Development* 15 (August), supplement, pp. 11–20.

Gidron, Benjamin, Kramer, Ralph, and Salamon, Lester M. 1992. *Government and the Third Sector: Emerging Relationships in Welfare States.* San Francisco: Jossey-Bass.

Gilbert, Neil. 1983. *Capitalism and the Welfare State: Dilemmas of Social Benevolence.* New Haven: Yale University Press.

———. 1984. "Welfare for Profit: Moral, Empirical and Theoretical Perspectives," *Journal of Social Policy* 13, no. 1, pp. 6–67.

Gilbert, Neil, and Sprecht, Harry, eds. 1981. *Handbook of the Social Services.* Englewood Cliffs, N.J.: Prentice-Hall.

Gould, Stephen J. 1977. *Ever Since Darwin: Reflections in Natural History.* New York: Norton.

Grindheim, Jan Erik, and Selle, Per. 1989. "The Role of Voluntary Social Welfare Organizations in Norway: A Democratic Alternative to a Bureaucratic Welfare State." *LOS-senter Notat* 89/5.

Grodzins, Morton. 1966. *The American System: A New View of Government in the United States,* ed. Daniel Elazar. Chicago: Rand-McNally.

Grønbjerg, Kirsten A., Kimmich, Madeleine, and Salamon, Lester M. 1984. *The Chicago Nonprofit Sector in a Time of Government Retrenchment.* Washington, D.C.: Urban Institute Press.

Grønbjerg, Kirsten A., Musselwhite, James C., Jr., and Salamon, Lester M. 1984. *Government Spending and the Nonprofit Sector in Cook County/Chicago.* Washington, D.C.: Urban Institute Press.

Gutowski, Michael, Salamon, Lester M., and Pittman, Karen. 1984. *The Pittsburgh Nonprofit Sector in a Time of Government Retrenchment.* Washington, D.C.: Urban Institute Press.

Hansmann, Henry. 1980. "The Role of Nonprofit Enterprise." *Yale Law Journal,* 89, no. 5, pp. 835–901.

———. 1981. "Why are Nonprofit Organizations Exempted from Corporate Income Taxation?" In *Nonprofit Firms in a Three-Sector Economy,* ed. Michelle J. White. COUPE Papers. Washington, D.C.: Urban Institute Press, pp. 115–34.

Harder, Paul, Kimmich, Madeleine, and Salamon, Lester M. 1985. *The San Francisco Nonprofit Sector in a Time of Government Retrenchment.* Washington, D.C.: Urban Institute Press.

Harder, Paul, Musselwhite, James C., Jr., and Salamon, Lester M. 1984. *Government Spending and the Nonprofit Sector in San Francisco.* Washington, D.C.: Urban Institute Press.

Hargrove, Erwin. 1975. *The Missing Link: The Study of the Implementation of Social Policy.* Washington, D.C.: Urban Institute Press.

Hartogs, Nelly, and Weber, Joseph. 1978. *Impact of Government Funding on the Management of Voluntary Agencies.* New York: Greater New York Fund.

Hartz, Louis. 1948. *Economic Policy and Democratic Thought: Pennsylvania, 1776–1860.* Cambridge: Harvard University Press.

Hasenfeld, Yeheskel and English, Richard A., eds. 1974. *Human Service Organizations: A Book of Readings*. Ann Arbor: University of Michigan Press.

Heclo, Hugh. 1981. "Toward a New Welfare State," In *Development of Welfare States*, ed. Peter Flora and Arnold J. Heidenheimer. New Brunswick, N.J.: Transaction Books, pp. 383–406.

Hodgkinson, Virginia, and Weitzman, Murray. 1989. *Dimensions of the Independent Sector: A Statistical Profile*, 3rd edition. Washington, D.C.: Independent Sector.

Hodgkinson, Virginia, Weitzman, Murray S., and the Gallup Organization. 1990. *Giving and Volunteering in the United States*. Washington, D.C.: Independent Sector.

Hodgkinson, Virginia, Weitzman, Murray, Toppe, Christopher M., and Noga, Stephen N. 1992. *Nonprofit Almanac, 1992–93: Dimensions of the Independent Sector*. San Francisco: Jossey-Bass.

Hollingshead, August B., and Redlich, Frederick C. 1965. "Social Class and the Treatment of Neurotics." In Zald, 1965, pp. 609–22.

Hornbeck, David. 1988. Speech to Private Industry Councils, Annapolis, Md. (March 1).

Huntington, Samuel. 1991. *The Third Wave: Democratization in the Late Twentieth Century*. Norman, Okla.: Oklahoma University Press.

Ingram, H. 1977. "Policy Implementation through Bargaining: The Case of Federal Grants-in-Aid." *Public Policy* 25, no. 4, pp. 498–526.

James, Estelle. 1987. "The Nonprofit Sector in Comparative Perspective." In Powell 1987, pp. 397–415.

Johnson, Norman. 1987. *The Welfare State in Transition: The Theory and Practice of Welfare Pluralism*. Amherst: University of Massachusetts Press.

Kamerman, Sheila B., and Kahn, Alfred J. 1976. *Social Services in the United States: Policies and Programs*. Philadelphia: Temple University Press.

Kerrine, Theodore M., and Neuhaus, Richard John. 1979. "Mediating Structures: A Paradigm for Democratic Pluralism." In *The Annals of the American Academy of Political and Social Sciences*, No. 446 (November), pp. 10–18.

Kotler, Philip. 1982. *Marketing for Nonprofit Organizations*, 2nd edition. Englewood Cliffs, N.J.: Prentice-Hall.

Kramer, Ralph. 1980. *Voluntary Agencies in the Welfare State*. Berkeley: University of California Press.

Krischke, Paulo J. 1991. "Church Base Communities and Democratic Change in Brazilian Society." *Comparative Political Studies* 24, no. 2 (July), pp. 189–92.

Kuhn, Thomas S. 1962. *The Structure of Scientific Revolutions*. Chicago: University of Chicago Press.

Kuhnle, Stein, and Selle, Per. 1992. "The Historical Precedent for Government-Nonprofit Cooperation in Norway." In Gidron, Kramer, and Salamon 1992, pp. 75–99.

Kuti, Eva. 1990. "The Possible Role of the Nonprofit Sector in Hungary." *Voluntas* 1, no. 1, pp. 26–40.

———. 1992. "The Nonprofit Sector in Hungary." Paper delivered at the

Third International Research Conference on Nonprofit Organizations, Indianapolis (March 15).

Ledesma, Cesar R., and Decena, Cesar. 1992. "Political Science Activism among NGOs in the Philippines." Paper delivered at the Third International Research Conference on the Nonprofit Sector, Indianapolis (March 15).

Lewis, John P. 1987a. "Strengthening the Poor: Some Lessons for the International Community." In Lewis 1987b, pp. 3–44.

―――. ed. 1987b. *Strengthening the Poor: What Have We Learned?* New Brunswick: Transaction Books.

Lilly, W., III, and Miller, J. C., III. 1977. "The New Social Regulation." *The Public Interest,* no. 47 (Spring), pp. 49–61.

Lindsey, Lawrence B. 1981. "Alternatives to the Current Maximum Tax on Earned Income." Paper presented at the Conference on Simulation Methods in Tax Policy Analysis, National Bureau of Economic Research (January).

Lipsky, M. 1971. "Street-Level Bureaucracy and the Analysis of Urban Reform." *Urban Affairs Quarterly* 6, no. 4, pp. 391–409.

Lukermann, Barbara, Kimmich, Madeleine, and Salamon, Lester M. 1984. *The Twin Cities Nonprofit Sector in a Time of Government Retrenchment.* Washington, D.C.: Urban Institute Press.

Monypenny, P. 1960. "Federal Grants-in-Aid to State Governments: A Political Analysis." *National Tax Journal* 13, no. 1, pp. 1–16.

Morgan, James N., Dye, Richard F., and Hybels, Judith H. 1977. "Results from Two National Surveys of Philanthropic Activity." In Commission on Private Philanthropy and Public Needs, *Research Papers.* Washington, D.C.: Department of the Treasury, Vol. 1, pp. 157–323.

Musselwhite, James C., Jr., Katz, Rosalyn B., and Salamon, Lester M. 1985. *Government Spending and the Nonprofit Sector in Pittsburgh/Allegheny County.* Washington, D.C.: Urban Institute Press.

Musselwhite, James C., Jr., Hawkins, Winsome, and Salamon, Lester M. 1985. *Government Spending and the Nonprofit Sector in Atlanta/Fulton County.* Washington, D.C.: Urban Institute Press.

Musselwhite, James C., Jr., and Salamon, Lester M. 1986. "Social Welfare Policy and Privatization: Theory and Reality in Policymaking." In *Urban Policy Choices: Theory and Prescription in an Era of Uncertain Resources,* ed. Mark S. Rosentraub. New York: Praeger, pp. 65–87.

Nathan, Richard P., Manrel, Allen D., and Calkins, Susannah E., and Associates. 1975. *Monitoring Revenue Sharing.* Washington, D.C.: Brookings Institution.

Nathan, R. P., and Doolittle, Frederick C., and Associates. 1987. *Reagan and the States,* Princeton: Princeton University Press.

National Performance Review. 1993. *From Red Tape to Results: Creating A Government That Works Better and Costs Less. Report of the National Performance Review.* Washington, D.C.: U.S. Government Printing Office.

Newsweek. 1982. "The Hard-Luck Christmas of '82: With 12 Million Unemployed and 2 Million Homeless, Private Charity Cannot Make Up for Federal Cutbacks," December 27.

New York Times. 1990. "A New Wind in Africa," June 6.

Nielsen, Waldemar. 1979. *The Endangered Sector.* New York: Columbia University Press.

Nisbet, Robert. 1953. *The Quest for Community: A Study in the Ethics of Order and Freedom.* New York: Oxford University Press.

———. 1962. *Community and Power,* 2d edition. New York: Oxford University Press.

O'Connell, Brian, ed. 1983a. *America's Voluntary Spirit: A Book of Readings.* New York: Foundation Center.

———. 1983b. Testimony Before the Subcommittee on Legislation and National Security of the Government Operations Committee of the U.S. House of Representatives, March 1, 1983. Mimeo.

OECD (Organization for Economic Cooperation and Development). 1981. *The Welfare State in Crisis.* Paris: OECD.

———. Development Assistance Committee. 1989. *Development and Cooperation.* Paris: OECD.

———. Development Assistance Committee. 1991. *1991 Report.* Paris: OECD.

———. 1992. "Social Welfare Services Delivered by the Private Sectors." *Innovation and Employment,* no. 10 (November).

Office of National Cost Estimates. 1990. "National Health Expenditures, 1988." *Health Care Financing Review* 11, no. 4, pp. 1–4.

Osborne, David, and Graebler, Ted. 1992. *Reinventing Government: How the Entrepreneurial Spirit Is Transforming the Public Sector.* Reading, Mass.: Addison-Wesley.

Owen, David. 1964. *English Philanthropy, 1660–1960.* Cambridge: Harvard University Press.

Pasquinelli, Sergio. 1992. "Voluntary and Public Social Services in Italy." In Gidron, Kramer, and Salamon 1992, pp. 196–214.

Pear, Robert. 1988. "Expanded Right to Medicaid Shatters the Link to Welfare." *New York Times,* pp. 1, 32, March 6.

Peat, Marwick, Mitchell and Co. 1978. "Loan Insurance and Loan Guarantee Programs: A Comparison of Current Practices and Procedures." In Congressional Budget Office, *Loan Guarantees: Current Concerns and Alternatives for Control.* Washington, D.C.: U.S. Government Printing Office, pp. 145–314.

Pechman, Joseph, and Okner, Benjamin A. 1974. *Who Bears the Tax Burden?* Washington, D.C.: Brookings Institution.

Pifer, Alan. 1966. "The Nongovernmental Organization at Bay." In *Annual Report Essays 1966–1982* (New York: Carnegie Corporation of New York), pp. 1–13.

Powell, Walter, ed. 1987. *The Nonprofit Sector: A Research Handbook.* New Haven: Yale University Press.

Pressman, J. L., and Wildavsky, A. 1973. *Implementation: How Great Expectations*

in Washington Are Dashed in Oakland. Berkeley: University of California Press.
Public Papers of the President of the United States: Ronald Reagan, 1981. 1982. Washington, D.C.: U.S. Government Printing Office.
Qureshi, Moeen A. 1988. "The World Bank and NGOs: New Approaches." Paper delivered at the Washington Chapter of the Society for International Development Conference on "Learning from the Grassroots" (April 23).
Random House Dictionary. 1978. New York: Ballantine Books.
Riley, Patrick. 1981. "Family Services." In Gilbert and Sprecht 1981, pp. 82–401.
Rose-Ackerman, Susan. 1985. "Nonprofit Firms: Are Government Grants Desirable?" Mimeo.
Rosenbaum, N. 1981. "Government Funding and the Voluntary Sector: Impacts and Options." *Journal of Voluntary Action Research* 10, pp. 82–89.
Rosner, David. 1980. "Gaining Control: Reform, Reimbursement and Politics in New York's Community Hospitals, 1890–1915." In *American Journal of Public Health* 790, pp. 533–42.
———. 1982. *A Once Charitable Enterprise: Hospitals and Health Care in Brooklyn and New York, 1885–1915.* New York: Cambridge University Press.
Rudney, Gabriel. 1977. "The Scope of the Private Voluntary Charitable Sector." In Commission on Private Philanthropy and Public Needs, *Research Papers.* Washington, D.C.: U.S. Department of the Treasury, Vol. 1, pp. 135–41.
———. 1982. "A Quantitative Profile of the Nonprofit Sector." Yale University, Program on Non-Profit Organizations Working Paper no. 40.
Salamon, Lester M. 1970. "Comparative History and the Theory of Modernization." *World Politics* 23, no. 1, pp. 88–103.
———. 1980. "The Rise of Third-Party Government." *Washington Post,* June 29.
———. 1981. "Rethinking Public Management: Third-Party Government and the Changing Forms of Government Action." *Public Policy* 29, no. 3 (Summer), pp. 255–57.
———. 1984a. "Nonprofits: The Results Are Coming In." *Foundation News* 26, pp. 116–23.
———. 1984b. "Nonprofit Organizations: The Lost Opportunity." In *The Reagan Record,* ed. John Palmer and Isabel Sawhill. Cambridge, Mass.: Ballinger, pp. 31–68.
———. 1985. "Government and the Voluntary Sector in an Era of Retrenchment: The American Experience." *Journal of Public Policy* 6, pp. 1–20.
———. 1987a. "Partners in Public Service: The Scope and Theory of Government Nonprofit Relations." In *The Nonprofit Sector: A Research Handbook,* ed. Walter Powell. New Haven: Yale University Press, pp. 99–117.
———. 1987b. "Of Market Failure, Voluntary Failure, and Third-Party Government: The Theory of Government-Nonprofit Relations in the Modern Welfare State." *Journal of Voluntary Action Research* 16, nos. 1–2 (January–June), pp. 29–49.

———. ed. 1989. *Beyond Privatization: The Tools of Government Action.* Washington, D.C.: Urban Institute Press.

———. 1989. "The Voluntary Sector and the Future of the Welfare State." *Nonprofit and Voluntary Sector Quarterly* 18, no. 1 (Spring), pp. 11–24.

———. 1992. *America's Nonprofit Sector: A Primer.* New York: Foundation Center.

———. 1993. "The Marketization of Welfare: Changing Nonprofit and For-Profit Roles in the American Welfare State." *Social Service Review* 67, no. 1 (March), pp. 16–39.

———. 1994. "The Rise of the Nonprofit Sector." *Foreign Affairs* 73, no. 4 (July/August), pp. 111–24.

———. 1995. *The Invisible Sector: Nonprofit Agencies in an Era of Retrenchment.* Chicago: University of Chicago Press.

Salamon, Lester M., and Abramson, Alan J. 1981. *The Federal Government and the Nonprofit Sector: Implications of the Reagan Budget Proposals.* Washington, D.C.: Urban Institute.

———. 1982a. *The Federal Budget and the Nonprofit Sector.* Washington, D.C.: Urban Institute Press.

———. 1982b. "The Nonprofit Sector." In *The Reagan Experiment,* ed. J. Palmer and I. Sawhill. Washington, D.C.: Urban Institute Press, pp. 219–43.

———. 1985. "Nonprofits and the Federal Budget: Deeper Cuts Ahead." *Foundation News* 26, pp. 45–52.

———. 1986. *The Nonprofit Sector and the New Federal Budget.* Washington, D.C.: Urban Institute Press.

———. 1992. *The Federal Budget and the Nonprofit Sector: FY 1993.* Baltimore: Institute for Policy Studies, Johns Hopkins University.

Salamon, Lester M., and Anheier, Helmut K. 1992a. "Toward an Understanding of the International Nonprofit Sector: The Johns Hopkins Comparative Nonprofit Sector Project." *Nonprofit Management & Leadership* 2, no. 3, pp. 311–24.

———. 1992b. "In Search of the Nonprofit Sector I: The Question of Definitions." *Voluntas* 3, no. 2, pp. 125–51.

Salamon, Lester M., Musselwhite, James C., Jr., and De Vita, Carol J. 1986. "Partners in Public Service: Government and the Nonprofit Sector in the American Welfare State." Paper delivered at the Independent Sector Spring Research Forum, New York City.

Sanford, T. 1967. *Storm over the States.* New York: McGraw-Hill.

Savas, E. S. 1984. *Privatizing the Public Sector: How to Shrink Government.* Chatham, N.J.: Chatham House.

———. 1987. *Privatization: The Key to Better Government.* Chatham, N.J.: Chatham House.

Schambra, William. 1982. "From Self-Interest to Social Obligation: Local Communities vs. the National Community." In *Meeting Human Needs: Toward a New Public Philosophy,* ed. Jack Meyer. Washington, D.C.: American Enterprise Institute, pp. 33–50.

Schultze, C. 1977. *The Public Use of Private Interest.* Washington, D.C.: Brookings Institution.

Schwartz, Robert A. 1970. "Personal Philanthropic Contributions." *Journal of Political Economy* 78, no. 6 (November–December), pp. 1264–91.

Scott, Robert A. 1974. "The Selection of Clients by Social Welfare Agencies: The Case of the Blind." In Hasenfeld and English 1974, pp. 485–98.

Sewell, John W. 1987. "Foreword." In Lewis 1987b, pp. ix–xiii.

Shabecoff, Philip. 1990. "Loss of Tropical Rain Forest is Found Much Worse Than Was Thought. " *New York Times,* June 8, p. A1.

Smith, Brian H. 1990. *More Than Altruism: The Politics of Private Foreign Aid.* Princeton: Princeton University Press.

Smith, Bruce. 1975a. "The Public Use of the Private Sector." In Smith 1975b, pp. 1–45.

———. ed. 1975b. *The New Political Economy: The Public Use of the Private Sector.* New York: John Wiley.

Smith, Bruce, and Rosenbaum, Nelson. 1981. "A Quantitative Profile of the Voluntary Sector." Unpublished manuscript.

Smith, Stephen R., and Lipsky, Michael. 1993. *Nonprofits for Hire: The Welfare State in the Age of Contracting.* Cambridge: Harvard University Press.

Sosin, Michael. 1986. *Private Benefits: Material Assistance in the Private Sector.* Orlando: Academic Press.

Spann, B. M. 1977. "Public vs. Private Provision of Government Services." In *Budgets and Bureaucrats,* ed. T. E. Borcharding. Durham, N.C.: Duke University Press.

Staats, Elmer. 1975. "New Problems of Accountability for Federal Programs." In Smith 1975b, pp. 46–67.

Stevens, Rosemary. 1982. "A Poor Sort of Memory: Voluntary Hospitals and Government before the Depression." *Milbank Fund Quarterly/Health and Society* 60, no. 4, pp. 551–84.

Strahan, Genevieve W. 1984. *Trends in Nursing and Related Care Homes and Hospitals.* Series 14, no. 30. Washington, D.C.: U.S. Department of Health and Human Services.

Taussig, Michael K. 1967. "Economic Aspects of the Personal Income Tax Treatment of Charitable Contributions." *National Tax Journal* 20, no. 1, pp. 1–19.

Taylor, Marilyn. 1992. "The Changing Role of the Nonprofit Sector in Britain: Moving Toward the Market." In Gidron, Kramer, and Salamon 1992, pp. 147–75.

Tchernonog, Vivianne. 1992. "Building Welfare Systems Through Local Associations in France." In Gidron, Kramer, and Salamon 1992, pp. 215–37.

Thomas, Barbara. 1987. "Development Through Harambee: Who Wins and Who Loses? Rural Self-Help Projects in Kenya." *World Development* 15, no. 4, pp. 463–87.

Thompson, Andres. 1992. "The Nonprofit Sector in Latin America." Paper delivered at the Third International Research Conference on the Nonprofit Sector, Indianapolis (March 15).

United Nations. 1990. *Global Outlook 2000: An Economic, Social, and Environmental Perspective*. New York: United Nations.

United Nations Development Programme (UNDP). 1990. *Human Development Report, 1990*. New York: Oxford University Press.

United Way of America. 1981. *United Way Allocations, 1981*. Alexandria, Va.: United Way of America.

————. 1990. *Fund Distribution Results, by Agency, by Program, 1988 Metros I-VIII*. Alexandria, Va.: United Way of America.

Uphoff, N. 1987. "Assisted Self-Reliance: Working With, Rather than For, the Poor." In Lewis 1987b, pp. 47–60.

U.S. Advisory Commission on Intergovernmental Relations. 1977a. *Block Grants: A Comparative Analysis (A-62)*. Washington, D.C.: U.S. Government Printing Office.

————. 1977b. *The Intergovernmental Grant System as Seen by Local, State, and Federal Officials*. Washington, D.C.: U.S. Government Printing Office.

————. 1978. *Categorical Grants: Their Role and Design*. Washington, D.C.: U.S. Government Printing Office.

————. 1979. *A Catalog of Federal Grant-in-Aid Programs to State and Local Governments: Grants Funded Feb. 78*. Washington, D.C.: U.S. Government Printing Office.

U.S. Agency for International Development, Advisory Committee on Voluntary Foreign Aid. 1990. *Responding to Change*. Washington, D.C.: U.S. Government Printing Office.

U.S. Census Bureau. 1981. *1977 Census of Service Industries*. Washington, D.C.: U.S. Government Printing Office.

————. 1985. *1982 Census of Service Industries*. Geographic Area Series: United States. SC82-A-52. Washington, D.C.: U.S. Government Printing Office.

————. 1986. *Statistical Abstract of the United States: 1986*. Washington, D.C.: U.S. Government Printing Office.

————. 1989a. *1987 Census of Service Industries*. Geographic Area Series, Washington, D.C.: U.S. Government Printing Office.

————. 1989b, 1990. *Statistical Abstract of the United States: 1989, 1990*. 109th and 110th editions, Washington, D.C.: U.S. Government Printing Office.

U.S. Commission on Government Procurement. 1972. *Report*. Washington, D.C.: U.S. Government Printing Office.

U.S. Congress. 1975. House Committee on International Relations, *Implementation of "New Directions" in Development Assistance*. 94th Congress, 1st Session, Washington, D.C.: U.S. Government Printing Office.

U.S. Congress, Joint Economic Committee. 1965. *Subsidy and Subsidy-Effect Programs of the U.S. Government*, 89th Congress, 1st Session (March). Washington, D.C.: U.S. Government Printing Office.

U.S. Congress, Joint Economic Committee. 1974. *Federal Subsidy Programs*.

U.S. Department of Education. 1985–86. *Digest of Education Statistics*.

————. 1991. *Digest of Education Statistics*.

U.S. Department of Health and Human Services. 1981. *Social Services U.S.A.* Washington, D.C.: U.S. Government Printing Office.

————. 1988. *Surgeon General's Workshop on Self-Help and Public Health.* Washington, D.C.: U.S. Government Printing Office.

U.S. Department of Labor. 1988. *Workforce 2000.* Washington, D.C.: Government Printing Office.

U.S. General Accounting Office. 1978. *Federal Regulatory Programs and Activities.* Washington, D.C.: General Accounting Office.

————.1980. *Economic Analysis of Alternative Program Approaches: Program Plan.* Washington, D.C.: General Accounting Office.

U.S. Interagency Council on Accident Compensation and Insurance. 1979. "Partial Inventory of Current Federal Accident and Insurance Initiatives and Programs." Mimeo (January 31).

U.S. Internal Revenue Service. Various Years. *Statistics of Income—Individual Income Tax Returns.* Washington, D.C.: U.S. Government Printing Office.

U.S. National Commission on Urban Problems. 1968. *Building the American City.* Washington, D.C.: U.S. Government Printing Office.

U.S. National Performance Review. 1993. *From Red Tape to Results: Creating a Government That Works Better and Costs Less.* Report of the National Performance Review. Washington, D.C.: U.S. Government Printing Office.

U.S. Office of Management and Budget. 1980a. *Managing Federal Assistance in the 1980s.* Washington, D.C.: U.S. Government Printing Office.

————.1980b. *Budget of the United States Government for FY 1980, Special Analyses.* Washington, D.C.: U.S. Government Printing Office.

————. 1981. *Budget of the Untied States Government for FY 1982, Special Analyses.* Washington, D.C.: U.S. Government Printing Ofifce.

————. 1982. *Budget of the United States Government, FY 1983, Special Analyses.* Washington, D.C.: U.S. Government Printing Office.

————. 1986. *Budget of the United States Government, FY 1987, Special Analyses.* Washington, D.C.: U.S. Government Printing Office.

————. 1988. *Special Analyses, Budget of the United States Government, Fiscal Year 1989.* Washington, D.C.: U.S. Government Printing Office.

————. 1991. *Budget of the United States Government, FY 1992.* Washington, D.C.: U.S. Government Printing Office.

U.S. Office of Personnel Management. *Manager's Handbook.* Washington, D.C.: U.S. Government Printing Office.

U.S. Senate, Committee on Government Affairs. 1980. *Nonprofit Organizations Participation in the Federal Aid System,* Hearings, 96th Congress, 2nd Session.

Warner, Amos G. 1894. *American Charities: A Study in Philanthropy and Economics.* New York: Thomas Y. Crowell.

Wedel, Kenneth R. 1976. "Government Contracting for Purchase of Service." *Social Work* 21.

Weisbrod, Burton A. 1977. *The Voluntary Nonprofit Sector: An Economic Analysis.* Lexington, Mass.: D.C. Heath.

————. 1989. *The Nonprofit Economy.* Cambridge: Harvard University Press.

Whitehead, John S. 1973. *The Separation of College and State: Columbia, Dartmouth, Harvard, and Yale, 1776–1876.* New Haven: Yale University Press.

Whiting, Susan. 1989. "The Non-governmental Sector in China: A Preliminary Report." Mimeo. Beijing: Ford Foundation.

Whitney, Craig. 1989. "Lutheran Church Gets a Bigger Role." *New York Times*, December 7.

Wickenden, Elizabeth. 1976. "A Perspective on Social Services: An Essay Review." *Social Service Review* 50 (December), pp. 570–85.

Williams, Aubrey. 1990. "A Growing Role for NGOs in Development." *Finance and Development* 27 (December), pp. 31–33.

Wilson, William Julius. 1987. *The Truly Disadvantaged: The Inner City, the Underclass, and Public Policy*. Chicago: University of Chicago Press.

Woodson, Robert. 1981. *A Summons to Life*. Washington, D.C.: American Enterprise Institute for Public Policy Research.

Wuthnow, Robert. 1990. "Religion and the Voluntary Spirit in the United States: Mapping the Terrain." In *Faith and Philanthropy in America*, ed. Robert Wuthnow and Virginia A. Hodgkinson. San Francisco: Jossey-Bass.

Yamamoto, Tadashi, and Amenomori, Takayoshi. 1989. "Japanese Private Philanthropy in an Interdependent World." Paper delivered at the International Symposium on Organized Private Philanthropy in East and Southeast Asia, Bangkok, August 1989.

Yanagitsubo, Hiroyuki, and Agustin, Anthony. 1989. "Overview of the Non-Profit Sector in Asia: Its Features, Role, and Prospects." Paper delivered at the Salzburg Seminar on the Role of Nonprofit Organizations (April 29–May 11).

Zald, Mayer N., ed. 1965. *Social Welfare Institutions: A Sociological Reader.* New York: John Wiley and Sons.

Index

public administration, 2, 6, 16, 84; traditional concerns of, 22. *See also* public
management
public-benefit service organizations, 7,
54–56, 185–86
public management, 17–18, 23, 43; new
focus for research on, 23–32; traditional techniques of, 22. *See also* public administration
public management paradox, 31
public sector. *See* government
purchase-of-service contracts, 108,
222–23

quality-control standards, 49, 107
Qureshi, Moeen A., 284n. 10

Ramsey County, Minn., 61, 77–78, 80–
81, 96
Reagan administration: administrative
changes of, 153, 156–58; budget cuts
of, 3, 9, 63, 81, 145, 153–55, 194–99,
205–6, 240, 253; and commercialization of nonprofit sector, 10; executive
order of, 157; goals of, 149, 152,
227; and government-nonprofit partnership, 9–10, 149; impact of, on
nonprofit organizations, 146–47,
153, 158–66, 197; lost opportunity
of, 149–66; and nonprofit postal subsidy, 157; and nonprofit sector, 3–4,
9–10, 63, 81, 145–99, 201; and political advocacy, 157–58; and private
charity, 9, 152, 163; private sector initiatives of, 9, 149, 152, 155–56, 166,
168; and privatization of human services, 75–76, 141; program reforms
of, 3, 81, 146, 152, 166; tax policies of,
9, 145, 152–55, 167–83, 194–95, 198–
99. *See also* Economic Recovery Tax
Act of 1981, effects of; retrenchment
Red Cross, 161
Redlich, Frederick C., 122, 127
regulation, 5, 16, 20, 24, 28, 30, 32, 47,
64; of nonprofits, 68, 105, 108. *See
also* social regulation
religion/religious organizations, 54, 57,
68, 86–87, 90, 99, 126, 132–33, 140–
42, 144, 163, 165, 175, 185, 189
research/research institutes, 54, 56, 58,

62–64, 70, 72–73, 87–90, 92, 117,
121, 160–62, 165, 195–96, 223
residential and institutional care/resi-
dential and institutional care organi-
zations, 62, 64, 69, 92, 117–19, 122–
23, 143, 162, 165, 196, 236–37
retrenchment, 5, 9, 67, 144–99, 206,
225–27
revenue sharing, general, 20
Riley, Patrick, 127
Rockefeller Brothers Fund, 248
Rockefeller Foundation, 248, 252
Rockefeller, John D., III, 193, 271n. 1
Rose-Ackerman, Susan, 40
Rosenbaum, Nelson, 107, 271n. 2
Rosner, David, 85, 214
Rudney, Gabriel, 86–87
Russia, 258

Salamon, Lester M., 41, 43, 61–62, 65,
87, 89–92, 121–23, 125, 129–32,
134, 137, 139, 154–55, 161, 186,
188, 189, 193, 195–97, 205–7, 214,
219, 222, 245, 262, 264, 271n. 1,
274nn. 7 and 4, 275n. 4, 275nn. 1, 2,
and 4, 280n. 3, 282n. 1, 283nn. 7
and 13, 284nn. 3 and 5, 285n. 23
Salvation Army, 94
Sanford, Terry, 23
São Paolo, 247
Sarvodala Shramadana village awaken-
ing movement, 247
San Francisco, 60, 65, 77–78, 80–81,
96–97
Savas, E. S., 42, 208
Schambra, William, 272n. 5
Schwartz, Robert A., 154, 281n. 4
Scott, Robert A., 127
sectarian agencies, 46–47
Selle, Per, 284nn. 3 and 12
Sewell, John W., 258
Shaw, George Bernard, 47
Smith, Brian H., 247, 250, 252–53, 255,
257, 263, 284nn. 8 and 9
Smith, Bruce, 43, 272n. 6
Smith, Stephen R., 101, 271n. 3
social clubs, 185
social economy organizations, 254
social regulation, 24, 30, 192
Social Security, 206–7, 225, 227, 241